Starting to Teach Latin
(Second Edition)

Starting to Teach Latin
(Second Edition)

Steven Hunt

BLOOMSBURY ACADEMIC
LONDON • NEW YORK • OXFORD • NEW DELHI • SYDNEY

BLOOMSBURY ACADEMIC
Bloomsbury Publishing Plc
50 Bedford Square, London, WC1B 3DP, UK
1385 Broadway, New York, NY 10018, USA
29 Earlsfort Terrace, Dublin 2, Ireland

BLOOMSBURY, BLOOMSBURY ACADEMIC and the Diana logo are trademarks of
Bloomsbury Publishing Plc

First published in Great Britain 2016
This revised and updated edition published 2023

Cover images © Roman/Getty (top),
David Vincent, www.images4education.co.uk (bottom)

A catalogue record for this book is available from the British Library.

Library of Congress Control Number: 202946912

ISBN: PB: 978-1-3503-6813-2
        ePDF: 978-1-3503-6815-6
        eBook: 978-1-3503-6814-9

Typeset by RefineCatch Limited, Bungay, Suffolk
Printed and bound in Great Britain

To find out more about our authors and books visit www.bloomsbury.com
and sign up for our newsletters.

Contents

Acknowledgements

This book has taken rather longer to write than I had expected. I rapidly found that the scope was enormous and the timescale I originally set myself laughably short. Inevitably, therefore, there are areas for which I have not been able for reasons of time or space or personal expertise to give the fullest possible treatment. For this I apologize. I owe a debt of thanks to numerous people who either gave me or inspired in me material to use in this book. From the Cambridge School Classics Project, I wish to thank Will Griffiths and Ben Harris, who have both been ideal sounding-boards and critical friends for many of my ideas. Pat Story and Bob Lister – towering figures in the development of the *Cambridge Latin Course* – have always been a source of inspiration, along with Richard Woff and John Muir who taught me to be a teacher at the Centre for Educational Studies at King's College London back in the 1980s. It was Richard who convinced me to finish the PGCE and become a teacher and Bob Lister who gave me my first job at The Campion School, Hornchurch, in 1987 – and who then promptly resigned to go on to better things, including taking over running the PGCE at the University of Cambridge – a position I acceded to myself on his retirement in 2008. Images from the *Cambridge Latin Course* in Figures 1, 2 and 5, and quotations from the same course (*passim*) are by kind permission of the Director of the Cambridge School Classics Project. The cartoon *Boris Nukes* is by kind permission of Steve Bell. All other illustrations are the author's own. The names of the schools and students in the case studies have been anonymized.

I also owe a debt of thanks to the many teachers and trainee teachers it has been my pleasure to meet. In particular I would like to pick out the following teachers and teacher mentors: Sara Aguilar, Barbara Bell, John Chappell, Frances Childs, Alan Clague, Rowlie Darby, Sara Easton, Eileen Emmett, Frances Foster, Mair Lloyd, Jane Maguire, Gill Mead, Anna Karsten, Nicola Neto and Bar Roden. Each has contributed something to the way I teach and the way I have thought about teaching others to teach. Members of the Association for Latin Teaching, the Joint Association of Classical Teachers, the Classical Association, Peter Jones and Jeannie Cohen from Friends of Classics, Mai Musié, Arlene Holmes-Henderson and Lorna Robinson from Classics in Communities, the charities Classics for All and the Roman Society have also been kind enough to share ideas and provide inspiration. From America, I am obliged to Ronnie Ancona, Ginny Blasi, Joe Davenport, Donna Gerard, Melody Hannegan, Peter Howard, Ken Kitchell, Terry Klein, William Lee, Bartolo Natoli, Teresa Ramsby and many other teachers whom I met and worked with during the

American Classical League Institutes 2013, 2014, 2015, 2017 and 2019. Their hospitality, kindness and willingness to put up with my incessant questions are much appreciated. I have been lucky enough to hold the position of Subject Lecturer on the Postgraduate Certificate in Education course at the Faculty of Education, University of Cambridge since 2008, which has brought me into contact with more schools, teachers and students than I might ever have thought possible. It is through my almost daily interactions with trainee teachers and students themselves that perhaps I have gained most insight from how students learn. Of all of these I am perhaps most indebted to the kindly advice, sharing of ideas and occasional corrections to some of my wilder flights of fancy of Aisha Khan-Evans, the Subject Lecturer for the PGCE in Latin/Classics at King's College London. Any mistakes are my own.

I'd like to thank Emma Stafford, Francis Rupp and their daughter Gabriella for putting up with me hunkering down over the manuscript while we were on holiday together for two summers in glorious Greece. I can't have been much fun. I must, of course, thank my publishers from Bloomsbury Academic: Charlotte Loveridge who first asked me to write and Alice Wright who persisted with me during the writing. There are, of course, many others – students and teachers I have taught over the years – who have all made contributions in some way. I cannot name them all.

Finally, Jane and Olivia have stuck with me through the tasks of writing and completion. Thank you.

Addendum, to the 2nd edition

In the light of further developments in Latin teaching practices, Alice Wright kindly asked me to revise Starting to Teach Latin for its second edition. I am grateful for the opportunity to update the information and, hopefully, improve the text. I would especially like to thank Ronnie Ancona, who gave me extensive feedback, particularly on the US references, and recommendations for the new sections on gender, on race, and on equity, diversity and inclusion. I would also like to thank the two anonymous reviewers for their helpful comments. I have also updated the sections which pertain to present education policy in the UK and how it affects Latin teaching in schools – despite the first edition being published only six years ago, an awful lot has changed (mostly for the good!). I have authored / co-authored 4 books for Bloomsbury since 2016 on the subject of teaching classical subjects in schools and colleges: I have tried not to repeat what is written there; nor have I 'palmed off' the reader by merely referring them to those books as the situation arises. Such is the pace of change that already there are already new things to say since their publication.

A book like this can never be future-proofed; but I hope that it is as up to date as it can be in the rapidly changing world that is Classics Education.

Cambridge, August 2022.

Glossary

A Level the *Advanced Level* is a subject-based qualification conferred as part of the General Certificate of Education at a higher level than the GCSE and the O Level. It is an examination taken by students aged 17–18 in secondary education in England, Wales and Northern Ireland. A Levels are usually treated as a measure of attainment suitable for university entry.

AQA the *Assessment and Qualifications Alliance* examinations board.

DEI Diversity, Equity and Inclusion.

Department for Education (2010 – present) the *Department for Education* is a department of the UK government responsible for issues affecting people in England up to the age of 19, including child protection and education. It has previously been known as the Department of Education and Science (1964–92), the Department for Education (1992–5), the Department for Education and Employment (1995–2001), the Department for Education and Skills (2001–7) and the Department for Children, Schools and Families (2007–10).

EDI Equality, Diversity and Inclusion.

EDUQAS is the brand from WJEC, offering Ofqual reformed qualifications to all schools and colleges in England.

English Baccalaureate the *English Baccalaureate* (EBacc) is a school performance indicator linked to the *General Certificate of Secondary Education* (GCSE). It measures the percentage of students in a school who achieve 5+ A*–C grades in traditionally academic GCSE subjects.

Entry Level a preliminary qualification set at a standard below GCSE.

GCSE the *General Certificate of Secondary Education* is an academic qualification awarded in a specified subject to students aged 14–16 in secondary education in England, Wales and Northern Ireland.

Key Stages the *Key Stages* are the legal terms for the periods of schooling in maintained schools in England and Wales. *Key Stage 2* refers to the period of four years comprising Years 3–6, when students are aged 7–11; *Key Stage 3* refers to the period of three years comprising Years 7–9, when students are aged 12–14; *Key Stage 4* refers to the period of two years comprising Years 10–11, when students are aged 15–16. *Key Stage 5*, referring to the period of two years comprising Years 12–13, is colloquially referred to as the *Sixth Form*.

ICT information and communication technology.

OCR the *Oxford and Cambridge and RSA* examinations board.

Ofqual the *Office of Qualifications and Examinations Regulation* is a non-ministerial government department that regulates qualifications, exams and tests in England and vocational qualifications in Northern Ireland.

Ofsted The *Office for Standards in Education, Children's Services and Skills* is a non-ministerial department of the UK government. The services Ofsted inspects or regulates include: state schools, independent schools and teacher training providers, colleges, and learning and skills providers in England.

O Level the *Ordinary Level* was a subject-based qualification conferred as part of the General Certificate of Education. It was an examination awarded in a specific subject by students aged 14–16 in secondary education in England, Wales and Northern Ireland.

WJEC the *Welsh Joint Education Committee* examinations board, known as EDUQAS in England.

1

Starting to Teach Latin

Starting to teach Latin

Classics concerns whole cultures, and the whole range of our responses to those cultures. And so it concerns what is salacious, or funny, no less than what is informative or improving. Indeed [...] the same material from the ancient world may be both funny and improving, salacious and informative – the difference depending largely on the different questions we choose to ask of it, and on the different ways we frame our responses.

Beard and Henderson, 2000, p. 111

Beard and Henderson's comments remind us teachers, I am sure, why we wanted to teach Latin originally, what it was that inspired us to study it for ourselves and why we wanted to share our hobby, our scholarship and our passion with others. Teaching Latin has not always been so. In 1963, Bolgar, commenting on the pedagogical practices common at that time in UK Latin teaching, openly expressed his worries in the pages of the UK Classics teachers' journal *Didaskalos*, when he said:

The teaching we give at present does not aim merely at giving the pupil a good knowledge of Latin. The course is an educational instrument forged in the nineteenth century as a preparation for tests aimed to select the intellectually competent and emotionally reliable. This becomes immediately obvious the minute we start comparing it with methods used in the modern field. It is to be presumed that language-schools know their business. Do any of them spend weeks and months training their pupils to be accurate translators? It is worth observing that the level of accuracy demanded from a classical student in a university scholarship is far higher than the level required in UNO examinations from men who make translating their life's work. Or is anyone learning Spanish or Russian ever forced, when translating into the language, to mould his style in imitation of particular authors? Learning Latin will never be an easy task. But if we are honest with ourselves, we shall have to admit that we make it a great deal more difficult than it needs to be. [...] We have turned the simple business of instruction into a sort of puberty rite where the intelligent boy is driven to prove himself.

Bolgar, 1963, p. 24

Modern readers might shudder at the seemingly casually sexist way in which Bolgar assumes only 'the intelligent boy' as being a suitable candidate for Latin examination. Of course, in 1960s Britain, Latin was much stronger in boys' exclusive 'Public' boarding schools than in girls' day schools, A University education in Classics was less well-marked out for girls than for boys. The increase in the number of girls studying Latin in the intervening since (as well as students from a much wider range of backgrounds) has rightly necessitated many changes in the types of resource and pedagogy employed in the teaching of Latin. Latin teachers are still asking the same questions about the processes of teaching and learning it – something that is probably not necessarily unhealthy in itself and is perhaps evidence of the sort of sensible and informed discourse teachers should always be having about the nature and aims of the subject in school. But the recent interest shown by UK politicians towards the study of Latin has thrown Bolgar's points back into high relief once again. Issues such as what Latin is for, what it might consist of and who might learn it – and, for that matter, who might teach it – have risen to the surface in rapid response to government encouragement of a subject that has been ignored by mainstream educational policy for nearly thirty-five years. This book is written to help teachers of Latin and would-be teachers of Latin negotiate the current landscape and become better informed to ask some of those same questions.

The book is presented in three sections. Section 1 provides a description and occasional commentary upon the development of Latin teaching over the last fifty years or so and the main issues, which, as I see it, affect it today. Section 2 primarily concerns subject pedagogy and is written for the neophyte and practising teacher in mind. Section 3 lists resources for teachers of Latin.

What is the study of Latin all about?

Latin is the language originally spoken and written by the ancient Romans. The language became the chief conduit of thought, information and ideas after the fall of the Western Roman Empire in 476 CE. In the UK, the language studied in schools is usually that of the first century CE, the literature of the Classical period first century BCE and first century CE. In the USA, course books sometimes use material from the Classical period through to the Renaissance and sometimes even further. A very small number of UK and a larger number of US teachers advocate the teaching of spoken Latin, using modern-day situations. Examinations in Latin tend to focus on the literature of the first century BCE to the first century CE, when the great writers such as Caesar, Virgil and Cicero flourished, as well as many others. However, there is an increase in the study of writers much later than this period, right up into the modern era, where there is greater diversity in the genres of Latin texts available, and many more written by female writers – important considerations for teachers who wish to draw in students from a wider and more mixed background than those traditionally associated with the subject (as we have seen with Bolgar, above). The study of Latin in schools today does not just include the language and literature of the Romans. It often also includes the study of the civilization of the Romans and, to some extent, the civilization of those other ancient peoples with whom the Romans came into contact, such as the Greeks. The image of the Victorian Latin teacher, obsessed solely by grammar and linguistic discipline, vividly encapsulated by Stray (1998b) in the portrait of Edmund Morshead, the benevolently idiosyncratic Classicist at Winchester in 1898, seems still to be reinforced by often-repeated cinematic and televisual images (Sellers, 2012) and, as we shall see, persists in contemporary media representations (Goddard, 2013). I suspect that the media image is far from reality: in practice, Latin course books and teaching approaches have embraced more progressive ideas and begged, borrowed and stolen pedagogies from such diverse fields as modern languages teaching, the teaching of English literature, and the teaching of the humanities in general. This book reflects *modern* practice rather than the somewhat Victorian one beloved by media commentators.

Who is this book for?

There are many books of this kind to help teachers in other subject areas. Outside individual teachers' handbooks for particular Latin course books, there are none so far in the UK that describe, evaluate and guide practice in the sorts of circumstances in which Latin is often taught in schools today. There have been two books to support the teaching of Latin in the USA: Distler's *Teach The Latin, I Pray You* (1962) and Davis' *Latin in American Schools* (1991). While some of the guidance they offer is still valuable, they reflect circumstances that have changed considerably.

The book is focused on the teaching of Latin to students of secondary school age (11–18). There is an emphasis on the earlier stages of learning Latin   that is to the examination of the General Certificate of Secondary Education (GCSE) taken at age 16, details of which are given in Section 3. The teaching of Latin to students in primary schools (ages 4–11) will also be touched upon. The case studies and examples referred to nearly all originate in observations, conversations and discussion workshops with novice and other teachers with whom I have come into contact in the course of carrying out initial teacher training at the Faculty of Education, University of Cambridge, in schools of every type and at training events throughout the UK, parts of continental Europe and the USA. I also draw on some 28 years' experience of teaching students in four non-selective state-maintained secondary schools and one selective independent secondary school in the UK.

Although the book takes primarily a UK (and, I have to say, rather an English) perspective, much of the practical guidance is applicable to practice in other countries, particularly the USA where some similar teaching approaches are adopted. Periodically I also make reference to issues that affect the teaching of Latin in the USA, where interesting, and I hope useful, comparisons can be made. Sometimes the different ways in which teachers approach Latin teaching in the two countries helps to make us question our assumptions about practice and leads to perhaps a better understanding of why we carry it out in the way that we do. In other cases, lessons can be learned from each other's experiences, as Kitchell (2006, p. 10) noted: 'Cornwall can be adapted to work in San Antonio and what worked against one set of politicians can be tweaked to work against another'. Nowhere else does this stand more fully revealed than in the case of teacher training – which is why this book was written. In the USA, specialist teacher training is heavily dependent on the state in which the teacher wishes to take up a post (Ancona, 2014). The lack of centralized teacher training – particularly as it affects Latin teaching – creates great disparities of provision and quality across the country. Little, of the American Classical League, points out that demand for Latin teachers 'doubled' between 2000 and 2010, which led to a shortage of qualified staff (Bookwalter, 2015). Such a situation stands as a warning to the developing situation of specialist teacher training in the UK. I hope that the occasional comparison of the teaching of Latin in the UK with that in the USA will shed interesting light on both approaches and lead to greater understanding and maybe even cooperation and sharing of ideas across the water.

The number of training positions allocated by the Department for Education in the UK is insufficient to fill the 150–240 advertised vacancies for Classics teaching posts each year (Hunt, 2022d). Anecdotal evidence collected from my previous trainee teachers and requests received directly from schools suggests that this overall number conceals the existence of many other part-time posts: in North Norfolk, for example, several schools have taken to training their own existing modern languages staff to take lessons (Maguire and Hunt, 2014). This book is thus written for all types of Latin teachers, specialist or non-specialist alike:

- teacher trainees on one of the initial teacher training (ITT) courses in Latin or Classics;
- graduate students who have become teachers of Latin without undergoing training;
- non-specialist teachers of Latin, who have qualified as a teacher through another subject area but who do not have training specific to Latin;
- mentors of teacher trainees;
- teachers or head teachers who wish to understand more about the teaching of Latin.

Challenges in teacher training

The shortage of trained Latin teachers in the UK has been of concern for very many years (Affleck, 2003), and the same can be said of the USA (Ancona and Durkin, 2015). In the UK, the traditional Higher Education Institution (HEI) postgraduate teacher training routes historically have been unable to keep pace with providing replacements for teachers leaving Latin teaching due to inadequate planning and support from the Department for Education (Hunt, 2011). New teacher training routes, such as School Direct and Teach First, were put in place by the Coalition Government in 2013 and it was their intention that such routes ought not only complement the traditional HEI-led PGCE courses but eventually supplant them. There have been some fiery discussions about the deleterious effect of the policy on HEI-led teacher training recently (Bell, D., 2015), but both of the major political parties seem to want school-centred teacher training to remain in some form or another, whether for ideological reasons or because they provide alternative routes into teaching for mature applicants and for those who have changed career. This is not the place, however, to enter the debate about the relative efficacy of different sorts of teacher training. For the present, provision of teacher training in Latin/Classics continues to be heavily dependent on the HEI-led PGCE courses, as Table 1 shows.

The book is also aimed at those teachers who have undergone training in a subject area other than Classics. In the UK, the Department for Education has been encouraging these so-called non-specialist teachers to start Latin in the schools where they already are teaching. The term 'non-specialist' is perhaps a misnomer. It has been noted that these teachers – trained as teachers of Modern Foreign Languages

Table 1 Number of placements allocated for teacher training in Latin/Classics in the UK, 2013 to 2022.

Type of Training Programme	2013	2014	2015	2016	2017	2018	2019	2020	2021	2022
HEI-led	29	33	46	51	58	50	51	46	42	54
School-based	2	2	6	7	13	10	25	27	22	21
Teach First	0	0	0	0	0	0	0	0	0	0
Troops to Teachers	0	0	0	0	0	0	0	0	0	0
Teach Now	0	0	0	0	0	0	0	0	0	3
Total	31	35	52	58	71	60	76	73	64	78

Note: Figures for HEI-led in 2013 include the University of Cambridge and King's College London; those for 2014 onwards include the University of Cambridge, King's College London and the University of Sussex. The following HEIs have also been involved with Initial Teacher Education for Classics: Liverpool Hope University (2017), Bishop Grosseteste University (2017–19), and the University of Durham (2022).

Sources: University of Cambridge, King's College London, University of Sussex, National College for Teaching and Learning.

or English – have often studied Latin at school themselves, to GCSE or A Level; some of them even have university degrees in Classics or have studied significant amounts of Latin as part of another degree or for a Masters (Griffiths, 2010). Indeed, there has been something of a tradition of teachers of Latin who have trained as teachers of History, English or Modern Foreign Languages because they have not been able to join the traditional Classics PGCEs at Cambridge or London. These non-specialist Latin teachers have recently received some attention from the Department for Education and charitable organizations such as the Classical Association and Classics for All, and resources have been pumped into short one-off courses for developing and improving their subject knowledge – in crude parlance, 'upskilling' them. For example, the Department for Education has recently funded a Key Stage 4 Latin Initiative held in various locations around the UK for non-specialist Latin teachers in state-maintained schools (Kilby, 2014); the charity Classics for All has supported its own teacher training programmes across the country, with great success, working with some 1,116 educational organizations since 2010, including 564 primary schools and 483 secondary schools introduce Latin or classical studies (Classics for All, 2021); and the charity Capital Classics, working with Classics for All and the local government-funded London Schools Excellence Fund, was awarded a grant to help state schools in London develop their Latin provision in 2014 with the aim of training seventy teachers in both state secondary and primary schools (Capital Classics, 2014; Olive & Murray-Pollock, 2018). Meanwhile, the subject associations themselves – the Joint Association of Classical Teachers, the Association for Latin Teaching, and the Classical Association – continue to provide a number of in-service training events throughout the year for both specialist and non-specialist teachers alike. In the USA, there have been similar activities. The retraining of already in-post teachers as Latin teachers was initiated nearly fifty years ago (Rexine, 1966). To meet the needs of the future, college professors were told to be proactive in supporting school Latin by encouraging the development of high school Latin programmes where none existed and by suggesting to their brightest students that they consider Latin teaching as a career (Lawall, 1978). In the 1980s, the Classical Association of the Middle West and South set up the Committee for the Promotion of Latin, led by Richard LaFleur of the University of Georgia. The Committee worked tirelessly to promote Latin in school districts throughout the USA (LaFleur, 1980). As a result of its success, it soon became apparent that the Classical Association of the Middle West and South and other subject associations, such as the American Classical League, which drew their membership mostly from among school teachers of Latin, would achieve yet more if they were to work together with the American Philological Association (now the Society for Classical Studies), which drew most of its membership from among the college professors. Kitchell (2008) described the story of how these organizations united to promote Latin in schools and try to improve teacher training throughout the USA to the present day. As the UK education system becomes more fragmented and teacher training opportunities become less secure, the US model of close cooperation between teachers and college professors becomes increasingly attractive and mutually beneficial.

There is a clear need, therefore, for a handbook to help teachers in all forms of training. This book is not meant to be perfect – the 'only book you will ever need'. Nor is it meant to be highly academic. For the sorts of books where theory is expounded, I direct the reader to Section 3 where I have included suggestions for further reading. Instead, this book is meant to be readable and practical and useful. There have been a pitifully small number of proper research projects on the subject of teaching and learning ancient – as opposed to modern – languages. There seems to have been almost no money to support such research. Instead, any money has been (perhaps quite rightly) spent on developing textbook resources and more recently digital resources to adapt to the changes in schooling over the last fifty years. The resources have been in place now for a long time. There are plenty of students eager to take Latin. Wherever it is offered there is usually no shortage of takers. What holds head teachers and principals from offering it is a lack of appropriately informed and qualified teachers (Hunt, 2011).

Latin in the curriculum today: opportunities and challenges

The different political cultures of the UK and the USA engender different approaches to how Latin can be taught. In the UK, the pamphlet *Classics from 5–16: Curriculum Matters* (1988) published by the then Department of Education and Science (now the Department for Education) was intended as a discussion document for the development of the Classics curriculum in state-maintained schools. Overtaken by the events set in train by the introduction of the National Curriculum the same year, the pamphlet was not able to meet its aims. Today, however, even with detailed instructions provided by the Department for Education about the content of what should be taught in Latin at Key Stages 2 and 4, it is still worthwhile going back to the document to frame ideas about the nature and purpose of what could become a proper, fully accessible classics curriculum for the UK. Section 5 of the pamphlet suggests that a main aim of learning Latin should be

> [. . .] to equip pupils to read some classical literature in the original language and hence to gain a deeper insight into the Greeks and Romans – their ways of thought and expression, their attitudes and values – than they might otherwise achieve.
>
> Department of Education and Science, 1988, p. 2

It continues:

> Because it is concerned by this means to give pupils a richer appreciation of their own society and culture, a Latin or Greek course is not just a 'language' study. Like any other

classical course, it can be seen as a significant contributor to the school's work in the human and social area of experience.

Department of Education and Science, 1988, p. 2

The pamphlet goes on to advise:

> A language is part of the culture in which it exists; it would be hard to defend a study of the [...] Latin language which took no account of the ideas, values, culture and achievements of the people who spoke it. It should [...] foster the development of a number of logical and linguistic skills. But if it is divorced from its wider context it is likely to become arid and mechanical. If due attention is paid to the broader cultural dimension, then not only is the appeal of the subject widened but it offers richer and more relevant benefits to those who study it.
>
> Department of Education and Science, 1988, p. 20

Such recommendations are clearly reflected in the types of Latin course that are typically followed in the UK, where the reading approach is widely used, embedding language and, later, literature in its socio-cultural context. Indeed, this is rather the direction in which teaching of Latin has been moving over the last forty years – promoting accessibility and inclusivity – partly out of a sense of survival in schools of all types, but mostly, I suspect, out of the genuine interests of a generation of Latin teachers who themselves have been brought up on the reading approach. It is also very attractive to students.

However, although renewed government attention to the study of Latin in schools has been generally welcomed by teachers, the Department for Education, both in its refusal to consult teachers before making decisions about curriculum requirements (something not peculiar to Latin) and in its limited consultation after it has made them, seems to have created tensions between the ideals set out in *Classics from 5–16: Curriculum Matters* and its own configuration of curriculum and examination criteria. This tension can be seen in the criteria for history and language teaching in the primary phase at Key Stage 2, and in those for the teaching of ancient languages at Key Stage 4. A further difficulty can be discerned in the absence of guidelines for the study of Latin or any other classical subjects at Key Stage 3 – the 'missing link' between the end of the primary phase and the beginning of GCSE programmes of study in the secondary school (Hunt, 2022b). At the time of writing, the Department for Education has just started to fund a Latin Excellence Programme which aims to start Latin in forty non-selective state-maintained schools across England over the next four years.

 The study of Latin and the Romans occurs at two places in the 2013 National Curriculum guidelines at Key Stage 2: in the National Curriculum for History and for Ancient and Modern Languages. According to the National Curriculum, the aim of historical study should be:

[...] to develop a chronologically secure knowledge and understanding of British, local and world history, establishing clear narratives within and across the periods they study. They should note connections, contrasts and trends over time and develop the appropriate use of historical terms. They should regularly address and sometimes devise historically valid questions about change, cause, similarity and difference, and significance. They should construct informed responses that involve thoughtful selection and organisation of relevant historical information. They should understand how our knowledge of the past is constructed from a range of sources.

Department for Education, 2013, p. 190

And the aims of learning ancient and modern foreign languages:

Learning a foreign language is a liberation from insularity and provides an opening to other cultures. A high-quality languages education should foster pupils' curiosity and deepen their understanding of the world. The teaching should enable pupils to express their ideas and thoughts in another language and to understand and respond to its speakers, both in speech and in writing. It should also provide opportunities for them to communicate for practical purposes, learn new ways of thinking and read great literature in the original language. Language teaching should provide the foundation for learning further languages, equipping pupils to study and work in other countries.

Department for Education, 2013, p. 193

No explicit comment is made in the National Curriculum document that the study of Latin and the study of the Romans might be connected, or that they ought to be. Teachers might find ways of their own of linking the two subject areas together: the huge historical content that has to be covered in strict chronological order (the Stone Age to 1066) might preclude much time being spent on the Romans themselves. Suggestions for the study of these topics might (but do not have to) include:

GCSE Syllabus?

- Julius Caesar's attempted invasion in 55–54 BC;
- the Roman Empire by AD 42 and the power of its army;
- successful invasion by Claudius and conquest, including Hadrian's Wall;
- British resistance, for example, Boudica;
- 'Romanisation' of Britain: sites such as Caerwent and the impact of technology, culture and beliefs, including early Christianity; and
- Roman withdrawal from Britain in *c.* AD 410 and the fall of the western Roman Empire.

Department for Education, 2013

Enterprising teachers might find that the *Minimus* Latin course (Bell, 1999) might link language and historical elements of the National Curriculum well, with its Latin stories set on Hadrian's Wall at the time of the Roman occupation. The stories themselves are based on evidence found on the wall, which are visible at the Roman site of Vindolanda and in the British Museum (thereby covering the issue of the interpretation of evidence from original sources). The fiction series *The Roman*

Mysteries by Caroline Lawrence (2015) also provides some links between the Roman world described above, together with reinforcement of English literacy and reading, as I have seen operating in some primary schools in Cambridge.

The guidelines for ancient or modern languages at Key Stage 2 state that:

> Teaching may be of any modern or ancient foreign language and should focus on enabling pupils to make substantial progress in one language. The teaching should provide an appropriate balance of spoken and written language and should lay the foundations for further foreign language teaching at key stage 3. [...].
>
> [...] If an ancient language is chosen the focus will be to provide a linguistic foundation for reading comprehension and an appreciation of classical civilisation. Pupils studying ancient languages may take part in simple oral exchanges, while discussion of what they read will be conducted in English. A linguistic foundation in ancient languages may support the study of modern languages at key stage 3.
>
> Department for Education, 2013, p. 194

Teachers who choose an ancient language as their focus of study must therefore consider it as a foundation for the study of other languages. It is difficult to anticipate what 'substantial progress' might mean in the context of learning one language over a period of four years in Key Stage 2 because the Department for Education has not issued any guidelines for what a programme of study in ancient languages should comprise in Key Stage 3. Furthermore, while there is plenty of training for primary school teachers in modern foreign languages on initial teacher training courses, there is none provided as a matter of course for ancient languages. Instead, it has been left to individuals to provide support where they can, such as Bell's innovative one-day courses at the University of Bristol for secondary school teacher trainees in Modern Foreign Languages and English (Bell, B., 2015). In Solihull, a suburban district of Birmingham where no Latin outside the independent sector has been offered for many years, a number of schools have chosen to offer Latin to some or all of their students, mostly in addition to and as a support for the modern foreign languages on offer (Classics for All, 2014). Since then, Classics for All and the Primary Latin Project together have delivered training for teachers in primary schools, mostly for Latin, reaching 564 schools from 2010–21 (Classics for All, 2021). While this is a drop in the ocean nationally, for Latin it is a significant success story. It remains to be seen how much of an effect students who have studied Latin at Key Stage 2 will have on persuading the secondary schools to which they later transfer to allow them to continue with the study of Latin at Key Stage 3 and beyond.

At Key Stage 4, Ofqual has issued a set of criteria for the assessment of ancient languages at GCSE that examination boards need to follow for accreditation. The criteria start with general aims and learning outcomes, as follows:

> 2. GCSE specifications in ancient languages should provide a strong foundation in linguistic and cultural competence, enabling students to break the boundaries of time and space and access knowledge and understanding of the ancient world directly through reading and responding to its language and literature. They should prepare

students to make informed decisions about further learning opportunities in school and higher education and career choices.

Ofqual, 2015b, p. 3

Although we may smile at some of the initial flamboyant language, we may deem the aim of asking the student to read Latin literature in the original language to be entirely appropriate. Digging a little more deeply into the criteria we may be able to discern whether the specific requirements are going to achieve these ambitions. Section 3 of the document develops the point in more detail. The specifications will:

> [...] enable the student to:
>
> - develop and deploy their knowledge of vocabulary, morphology and syntax in order to read, understand and interpret the ancient language
> - develop their knowledge and understanding of ancient literature, values and society through the study of original texts [...]
> - select, analyse and evaluate evidence to draw informed conclusions from the literature studied [...]
> - develop and apply their critical, analytical and reflective skills to evaluate evidence from a range of sources.

Ofqual, 2015b, p. 3

Of these four aims of the GCSE, the first could be applied to the study of confected or made-up or original Latin literature, the second two seem both to specify the study of original literature, and the fourth may refer to the study of original literature, although it may also refer to the study of literature in translation or non-literary materials. When we read further in Sections 7 and 8, under 'Scope of Study', we reach what the specifications will *require* students to do. Students will be able to:

> 7.
>
> - translate accurately into English an unseen passage of the ancient language [...]
> - demonstrate their understanding of a narrative passage or passages of unseen [...] ancient language by answering a variety of comprehension questions in English
>
> EITHER
>
> - recognize, analyse and explain syntax and accidence as prescribed within the specification [...]
>
> OR
>
> - translate short sentences from English into the ancient language
>
> 8. [...]
>
> - Read a range of ancient literature, including at least one selection of prose and/or verse texts in the original language [...], along with either a further selection of

prose and/or verse texts in the original language or at least two different kinds of ancient sources (these sources can be in translation and can include non-literary sources)

- read original [...] literature and answer questions in English on aspects of content, culture, social practices and values, translating and explaining key words and phrases
- understand and evaluate verse and/or prose literature, deploying knowledge of the ancient language to focus on explaining their literary style and impact on the reader
- identify, explain and respond to the use of common literary effects appropriate to the text
- demonstrate understanding of the cultural, historical and literary context in which the literature was composed [...]
- select, analyse and evaluate evidence from ancient literature and/or other ancient sources, drawing informed conclusions to make a reasoned evidence-based response to the material studied [...]

Ofqual, 2015b, p. 4

In essence, then, there seems to be something of a mismatch between the *aims* of the specifications and the *means* by which they are to be assessed: the assessment criteria are angled as much towards the translation of confected or made-up Latin into English, the answering of English comprehension questions in English on a confected or made-up Latin passage, and the identification of grammatical features or composition of simple sentences into Latin as they are towards a student's ability to read, comprehend and respond to original Latin literature. It could also be argued that the assessment of a student's knowledge and understanding of non-literary sources and Latin literature in English translation do not accord with the fundamental aims of this GCSE. There is probably little disagreement that the development of the skills of translation, comprehension and even composition are essential stepping-stones for students to transfer to works of original Latin literature. But it seems to me that, by assessing these components separately from the components of reading, commenting upon and making a personal response to original literature, the examination may, perhaps inadvertently, achieve undesired outcomes. First, it runs the risk of engraining in the student and teacher a distinction between (a) the learning of grammatical features of the Latin language and (b) the purpose for which they are being learnt. Second, by assessing translation of English into Latin, it seems to be trying to define or endorse a particular pedagogical process that has no research basis for achieving the aims that the criteria have set out. Moreover, it seems to me to be trying to define and then assess the pedagogical activities that take place in the classroom as well as the student's ability to perform in the examination hall. If the aim of the study of Latin is to be able to comprehend, translate and comment upon confected or made-up Latin and original Latin literature, what does it matter to Ofqual or the examiners *how* the student gained the means by which they achieved it, *as long as they can do it*? There is a further contradiction: on the one hand, the option of assessment of texts in translation seems to have been designed to provide a more accessible qualification, while on the other hand, the introduction of translation from English into Latin (at the personal request of the former Minister for Education Michael Gove (Jones, 2014)) has been designed to make the qualification, as with all other GCSEs, more 'challenging' (Ofqual, 2015a). The underlying sense of contradiction contained within these criteria may therefore be just as challenging for examination boards to design a coherent examination as for the students to succeed in it. For further information about the introduction of prose composition into the GCSE, and some possible alternatives, see Hunt, (2022a).

The existence of a national assessment system in which the grades achieved by students are used for school accountability purposes means that prescriptive guidelines to the examination boards need to be laid down. Perhaps few teachers would object to the aims and learning outcomes suggested: they seem reasonable, open to a little interpretation and allow a certain degree of flexibility for the examination boards. The examination boards themselves have been at pains to include as many teachers from the different sectors as possible in consultations of their own, as well as through those brokered by the Department for Education and the A Level Content Advisory Board. But there still remains the problem of fitting everything in – time is at a premium, resources are restricted and teachers' preferred pedagogical practice might be comprised: Is it part of the specifications? Is it necessary? Do the students really *need* to do this? The freedom to choose what is best – to personalize the curriculum and to allow the teacher to teach to their own strengths and own interests – seems to be being lost in a national culture of compliance with a very narrow set of assessment criteria. While Latin is not perhaps quite as over-prescribed as some other areas of the curriculum (for example, the English curriculum names specific words that students must know how to spell at particular Key Stages and recommends specific works of literature), the high level of prescriptive detail that is described creates a challenge to the teacher to be responsive to the particular needs and interests of the students in the classroom and the community.

What is also interesting is how much the Latin criteria relate to the idea of the learner on a programme of study, which rarely looks out beyond itself. Latin, as defined here, seems to be a subject that prepares the student much more solely as scholar and much less as a participant in society. According to the criteria, the student has to compare the ancient and modern worlds and has to make a personal response to what they have learnt. In practice, when the focus on language is so resolute, questions on the comparison between the ancient and modern world (in the present qualifications at least) may merely result in a single question on Latin/English word derivations. For how else might an examination board devise a question that is able to capture the personal experiences and reflections of students across an entire nation that would be fair to everyone – unless it prescribed the specific experiences? And to what extent is the student able to make a real personal response – one that has not been checked by teacher to be 'appropriate'? Not only is the teacher forced to comply with the demands of the specifications, but also the student feels restricted in what they ought to say.

There are, of course, no easy answers to how to address these problems, and they are not peculiar to the study of Latin. Nevertheless, the teacher must always be open to new ideas and to keep seeking out inspiration from their colleagues and co-workers. Latin teachers have been adept at using all the means they can to keep their subject alive against the odds. Open-mindedness and a mind-set that seizes the opportunity to go beyond the examination specifications are essential qualities. The separation of the processes of teaching and learning from that of revision or review and preparation for examinations is vital if the dreaded activity *teaching to the test* is to be avoided. And what resources the Latin teacher has at their disposal! All the resources that are so readily available through multi-media and the internet can be deployed; and teaching and learning activities themselves should be participatory and dynamic if they are not to become sterile and mechanical. Section 2 of this book is designed to provide some examples on how this might be achieved.

In the UK, the pamphlet *Classics from 5–16: Curriculum Matters* (Department for Education and Science, 1988) provided a set of arguments about what the study of Latin (and other Classical subjects) *could* be. Because the document had no particular legal strength, the then government, in the throes of creating the National Curriculum, simply ignored it. In the vacuum of national educational policies towards Latin after 1988 and the lack of consultation of the subject communities by governments of all types, definitional consensus about the nature and aims of the study of Latin has still not been achieved. By the time, therefore, that the Coalition Government was showing interest in 2010, Latin was ill-placed to have its case already prepared and it has become subject to the whims and vagaries of individual lobbyists and government ministers.

In the USA, by contrast, the Standards for Classical Languages Learning (American Classical League, 2017) continues to provide a set of principles about what the study of Latin (and other Classical languages) *should* be. In response to the publication the previous year of the American Standards for Foreign Language Learning, teachers and university professors worked together to publish the American Standards for Classical Languages Learning (known as the '5 Cs'; see Table 2) to act as a guiding framework for teachers, teacher-trainers and administrators. The guiding principle of both sets of standards is:

> The Standards for Classical Language Learning are informed by the World-Readiness Standards for Learning Languages and reflect the continuing refinement of how contemporary students learn, and what they expect to do with their developing language skills. Additionally, the Standards reflect the growing societal expectation that students develop 21st century skills of communication, collaboration, critical thinking, creativity, and intercultural awareness, and that they are ready to use those

Table 2 The Standards for Classical Language Learning (the '5 Cs').

Goal Areas	Standards		
Communication Communicate effectively in more than one language in order to function in a variety of situations and for multiple purposes	**Interpersonal Communication** Learners interact and negotiate meaning in spoken, signed, or written conversation to share information, reactions, feelings, and opinions.	**Interpretive Communication** Learners understand, interpret, and analyze what is heard, read, or viewed on a variety of topics.	**Presentational Communication** Learners present information, concepts, and ideas to inform, explain, persuade, and narrate on a variety of topics using appropriate media and adapting to various audiences, or viewers.
Cultures Interact with cultural competence and understanding	**Relating Cultural Practices to Perspectives** Learners use Greek or Latin to investigate, explain, and reflect on the relationship between the practices and perspectives of the cultures studied.	**Relating Cultural Products to Perspectives** Learners use Latin or Greek to investigate, explain, and reflect on the relationship between the products and perspectives of the cultures studied.	
Connections Connect with other disciplines and acquire information and diverse perspectives in order to use the language to function in academic and career-related situations	**Making Connections** Learners build, reinforce, and expand their knowledge of other disciplines while using Latin and Greek to develop critical thinking and to solve problems creatively.	**Acquiring Information and Diverse Perspectives** Learners access and evaluate information and diverse perspectives that are available through Classical languages and cultures.	
Comparisons Develop insight into the nature of language and culture in order to interact with cultural competence	**Language Comparisons** Learners use Classical languages to investigate, explain, and reflect on the nature of language through comparison of the language studied and their own.	**Cultural Comparisons** Learners use Classical languages to investigate, explain, and reflect on the concept of culture through comparison of the cultures studied and their own.	
Communities Communicate and interact with cultural competence in order to participate in multilingual communities at home and around the world	**School and Global Communities** Learners use Classical languages both within and beyond the classroom to interact and collaborate in their community and the globalized world.	**Lifelong Learning** Learners set goals and reflect on their progress in using Classical languages for enjoyment, enrichment, and advancement.	

skills to problem-solve at work, enrich their lives at home, or engage in their communities as conscientious citizens.

American Classical League, 2017.

The differences between the approaches of the two countries are striking. The UK model was developed without significant teacher input. At Key Stage 2 primary level, Latin is seen as a support for language learning in general, as a foundation for the study of ancient civilization and as an end in itself. The study of the Romans is compartmentalized into a different curriculum strand altogether. At Key Stage 3 intermediate level, Latin disappears. At Key Stage 4 higher level, the focus is on assessment: specific things to know and generic skills to develop and master. Latin is inward looking – a subject for and of itself – but although it is useful for a student learning the generic and transferable skills of analysis, evaluation and critical reflection, such wider utility is not formalized in the examinations themselves through, for example, the impact of the ancient world on the modern, in language, literature and the arts.

In the USA, in contrast, the emphasis tends towards how a student's knowledge and understanding of Latin helps them to become a citizen participating in a diverse society. The specific details of what a student needs to know are not a part of the remit of the state: the teacher uses their professional judgement as to what is the most appropriate way to achieve this. Of course, with no official national assessment scheme in place, US Latin teachers have long been able to decide for themselves what is appropriate for their own students, guided only (if they wish) by the requirements of such institutions as the National Latin Examination, which is itself the creation of teachers for their own students. The American *Standards for Classical Languages* grew out of the American *Standards for Foreign Languages*, which have a clear outward looking purpose: what can learners of Latin do with their knowledge that is of benefit to them and others in contemporary society?

The different amounts of autonomy teachers have in the USA and the UK in helping to define their curriculum aims is striking. British government talk about the formation of a Royal College of Teaching – a body run by teachers for teachers – might be the way forward for teachers in the UK, by taking the micro-management of curricula out of the hands of politicians who frequently last no more than a year or two before they move on. In the meantime, the subject associations should be mobilizing support for a view of Latin that more fully accords with what they and their students want rather than that which politicians and political think-tanks tell them.

Latin for the few or for everyone?

One reason why head teachers and principals sometimes hold back from offering Latin is because of their own hostility – often based simply on ignorance. No worse a place can be found of this happening as Scotland, where accusations of elitism about the teaching of Latin has almost resulted in its death in state-maintained schools there (Williams, 2004). Despite the best efforts of campaigners, training opportunities for teachers of Classics in Scottish universities were slowly whittled away and finally withdrawn in 2004, thereby making a self-fulfilling prophecy: no teacher can teach Classics in the state-maintained sector because they are unable to achieve Scottish accreditation, and therefore no state-maintained school tries to recruit a teacher when a post-holder retires (Baker, 2013). Accordingly, Latin is likely only to be able to survive in selective independent schools in Scotland because such schools do not need to employ teachers who have Scottish teaching qualifications. Latin is not elitist in itself. It is that it risks being *made* elitist.

In England, the tale is fortunately rather different for the moment. There continue to be accusations against the study of Latin as a pointless and elitist activity. The US writer Pearcy rehearses the familiar arguments: the governing classes 'whose tastes, values, and attitudes classical education was intended to form' (Pearcy, 2005, p. 87) no longer exist: thus the purpose of teaching Latin no longer exists. A consequence, according to Pearcy, is that:

> Latin has ceased to be a subject for an elite and has become a subject merely elitist. The sheer difficulty of learning classical languages along with the traditions of pedagogy by which they are usually taught, impose a barrier that excludes all but a few students who have the leisure and mental qualities necessary to learn them.
>
> Pearcy, 2005, p. 91

Such easy and unthinking arguments continue to be prevalent today, despite all the evidence to the contrary and despite, as Affleck (2003, p. 163) reminds us, some 'fifty years of rear-guard action challenging the attack on classical learning within the curriculum'. Politicians and media commentators often regard Latin as a synonym for a traditional, even backward-looking education. For the left wing, Latin is a convenient shorthand criticism of government educational policy: the opposition Labour Party has frequently ridiculed former Conservative Education Minister Michael Gove's enthusiasm for Latin. For example, in 2013, the then Labour Shadow Education Minister Stephen Twigg castigated Gove for wanting to privilege academic over vocational qualifications in his school-accountability proposals. Comparing Gove to the Japanese soldier who had continued fighting the Second World War long after it had ended, Twigg made a coruscating attack in the *Times Educational Supplement*, with Latin as the weapon of choice:

> Similarly, in many ways, the education secretary is still fighting the battles of 30 years ago. Nearly three decades ago, in 1984, O levels were abolished for being out of date, but Gove would love to bring them back. [...] Thirty years ago, about 20,000 pupils a year learned Latin but few studied engineering at school. Today, thousands study engineering, despite the fact that Gove tried to downgrade the engineering diploma that had been designed by Rolls-Royce. [...] Imagine Gove's surprise when he finally emerges from the jungle, clutching his Latin textbooks and his abacus, and learns that

we need thousands more aerospace engineers, biotechnicians and 3D animators. If we are going to win the global race in education, we can't fight yesterday's battles.

Twigg, 2013

Twigg's condemnation of Latin as the bogeyman of irrelevant school subjects and as a pet favourite of a supposedly out-of-touch Minister of Education is part of a long line of similar casual misrepresentations mostly by the left wing: journalist Melissa Benn accused Gove's friend Toby Young of using compulsory Latin lessons in his newly founded West London Free School as a covert deterrent to applications for places from the students of 'certain kinds of parents' (Benn, 2011, p. 92) – a charge he vehemently denied in his turn (Young, T., 2012); left-wing journalist Peter Wilby snidely referred in a *Guardian* newspaper article to the new compulsory subject of computer coding as it being 'the new Latin, training the mind for the digital world as Latin supposedly trained it for an analogue world' (Wilby, 2015); and non-selective state-school activist Fiona Millar derided 'pushy' middle-class parents 'handwringing about Latin and Oxbridge' (Millar, 2015) in a *Guardian Education* article.

Even supposedly positive spins on Latin in the media draw on images of its supposedly traditional, unpleasant teaching approach and elitist nature. In 2011, *The One Show*, a BBC production, brought news of the revival of Latin in state schools, with one of its presenters Giles Brandreth posing in academic gown and clutching an enormous, antiquated Latin dictionary (BBC, 2011). Goddard noted how, in an otherwise positive 2013 BBC Breakfast News report about initiatives to teach Latin in primary schools, the presenters strongly implied by their comments that 'Latin, however beneficial a discipline, is somehow unpalatable at the point of delivery' (Goddard, 2013, p. 55). In my own reflections on a 2014 Sky News report about an initiative in Norfolk to encourage students to learn Latin, I reported on the very mixed messages presented: images of happy students and teachers in primary and secondary schools enjoying their Latin lessons, closely followed by a journalist suggesting that somehow teaching Latin was 'difficult to present in an energetic and enthusiastic way', and ending with supercilious comments from the newsroom anchor about the utility of Latin ('something which might be really *useful* for today's world. How about Mandarin?'), and the supposed elitism of the subject as being 'all very well for the corridors around Cambridge' (Hunt, S., 2014a, p. 19). Boris Johnson himself, the Eton- and Oxford-educated former

Conservative Prime Minister, receives as much censure as praise for his knowledge and enthusiasm for Classical history and his propensity for referring to Latin tags and mottoes in his speeches. There are, perhaps, too many of these to repeat here – a whole article is perhaps needed to give full flavour to their profusion – but Steve Bell in his *Guardian* comic strip frequently lampooned his Classical learning derived from his so-called elitist Etonian education and right-wingery, as seen here (Bell, 2008).

Bell's depiction of Johnson, with forehead victoriously wreathed in classical laurel, standing on a dais before the London Town Hall, fascistically salutes warplanes and looks forward to the revival of Rome in London. Meanwhile, he receives the adulation of reprieved Routemaster buses (part of his election pledge was to save the fabled and much-loved vehicles), which conjugate the diesel-rumbling 'Latin' verb 'to boggle' and which sounds suspiciously close to the 'Buller-Buller-Buller' chant of members of the Bullingdon Club, an elite Oxford drinking society to which he belonged in his student days (Wikipedia, 2015) and for which he has received much censure and ridicule, complete with an apparently drawling upper-class pronunciation of the third person plural.

At the same time, the media occasionally do unearth information that Latin actually is being taught in ordinary schools to ordinary students. In 2013, *Times* journalist Safiraz Manzoor reported on events in Kelmscott School, an inner-London state-maintained secondary in Walthamstow, which had started to offer Latin to its students:

> I am introduced to seven students who are learning Latin. The group is as multicultural as the school: Huzaifa, Humza, Zara and Hamid are all of Pakistani heritage; Kira and Gemma are white British; Charli is mixed-race white British and Jamaican, and Sefora is from Romania. I begin by asking who they assumed usually studied Latin. 'The only people you associate with studying it is posh white people,' says Charli, the daughter of a single mum who works as a bank cashier. Hamid is more blunt. 'Posh Christians,' he says. It is this impression that [their teachers] are attempting to challenge.
>
> Manzoor, 2013

Such a news report powerfully crushes the persistent view elsewhere that Latin is not for the majority of students. There is plenty of other evidence, too, that Latin ought not to be restricted to those privileged by wealth or birth. Christopher Pelling (2014) announced in *The Sunday Times* Oxford University's receipt of a Department for Education grant to upskill non-specialist teachers already serving in state-maintained schools. This was part of Gove's initiative to enable 'state school students [to] compete on equal terms with privately educated students for university classics places' (Gove, 2014), and represents something of a turn-around for the study of Latin after so many years of having been almost completely ignored by governments of all types. But it is more than about competition for university places. It is about interest in the ancient world and a feeling that students are missing out. This exchange between the author and Sean McEvoy, Deputy Head of a Sixth Form College, is revealing about why he thinks some students want to take up Latin:

McEvoy: First of all there is definitely student interest. We were really surprised how many students were desperately interested in joining in with the Classics for All project which was happening here, that's started in the local schools and is carrying on with us. I think, I think it is two things. Some of it is actually . . . because they missed out, because they haven't been able to do it, they feel they missed out on something they regard as a worthwhile and precious and useful academic subject.

Interviewer: Where do you think they get that idea from?

McEvoy: Some of it comes from their own reading. Some of it comes from Harry Potter, to be honest, and that kind of stuff as well. But some of it is their own . . . their own reading and knowledge of people and they read about other people's educations, they study history and when they study English they realise that in the past people knew Latin, they understood Latin – there's a whole world out there, of something that's worthwhile knowledge, that the present school curriculum is denying them. And they're really interested.

Interviewer: Do you think the presentation of Latin as a subject, as a discipline, as an area of study is a very positive one in the experiences that they have through English and history? When they read about Latin? They hear about it positively?

McEvoy: Yes, I think it is and it's something which is denied to them and I think the state school students in Brighton – the kind of students I am talking about – they have a strong sense that people in private schools have access to this and they are not being allowed to.

Interviewer: You think they feel that?

McEvoy: Yes I do, I do . . . and they should at least have a chance to do it.

McEvoy, 2012

This conversation, typical of many I have heard, describes state school students daily bombarded with images of and ideas about the classical world and wanting to have the same access to learning and understanding about them as they perceive students in independent schools have. The desire is not just top-down from the Department for Education; it is bottom up from the students and teachers themselves. And much of the students' desire to find out more about the classical world derives from information about it reaching them through informal channels beyond the school gate. The trouble is that many potential students do not recognize the sort of information that *does* reach them as *Classics*, as Mary Beard (2013b) commented on the Leonard Lopate Show:

Well, I think they think they don't know much about the classics, but they always say, 'Well, I don't know anything about Greece and Rome, I don't know anything.' But then you say, 'Did you see *Gladiator*? Did you watch *Rome*?' And I think it's one of those kind of myths that people have that there's boffins like kind of me, who really know about it; and then there's people – the rest of the world. And they know huge amounts about the ancient world. They can read Roman numbers. They watch the telly . . .

Beard, 2013b

The classical world is seemingly endlessly interesting and inspirational. A continuous fascination with the trinity of Roman gladiators, sexual excess and Pompeii seems to have suffused the popular imagination and spawned films like *Gladiator* (Scott, 2000), *Pompeii* (Anderson, 2014), *Agora* (Amenabar, 2009) and *Centurion* (Marshall, 2010), complemented by glossy and accessible television series such as *Rome* (Heller et al., 2005), *Atlantis* (Capps et al., 2013) and *Spartacus* (DeKnight and Tapert, 2010). The BBC television science fiction series *Doctor Who* even had an episode featuring the 79 CE eruption of Vesuvius and had the *Cambridge Latin Course* character Caecilius surviving the cataclysm as a result of the Doctor's hasty intervention (BBC, 2008). More serious but accessible television programmes abound: documentaries from Adam Hart Davis, Bettany Hughes, Andrew Wallace-Hadrill, Michael Scott, Mary Beard and others ensure the classical world is well-served by a continuing presence on the screen, DVD and the internet. Museums also play an enormous part in our appreciation and understanding of the classical world. In 2013, the British Museum's very successful exhibition *Life and Death in Pompeii and Herculaneum*, some of whose artefacts later went on tour to other museums around the UK, was of intense national media interest, which fed into the public's imaginative conception of the ancient world. As Joanna Paul (2009) said:

The mass media's seizure upon Pompeii's destruction as analogy for modern catastrophe, and its diffusion into other cultural forms, not only offers another example of the continued resonance of the ancient city in modern contexts, but also reveals to us the importance of antiquity as a vehicle through which we might address some of the most controversial and challenging issues facing our world in the 21st century.

Paul, 2009, p. 108

The film of the British Museum exhibition – shown in cinemas throughout the UK – broke new ground in bringing the exhibition to a much wider audience than those who could travel to London. The indie rock band *Bastille* played its latest single *Pompeii* in situ inside the exhibition (Bastille, 2013) – providing a further opportunity to popularize the ancient world – and travel companies reported that the exhibition seemed to be responsible for stimulating an unusual demand for holidays in the Bay of Naples that year (Urquhart, 2013). Smaller exhibitions continue to provide interest around the UK, often teaming up with re-enactment days and activity days for families during the school holidays. Books are everywhere – from the children's *Roman Mysteries* series by Caroline Lawrence and the *Percy Jackson* series by Rick Riordan through to the more serious adult works of Steven Saylor, Robert Harris and Tom Holland. And, of course, there is J. K. Rowling's *Harry Potter* cast of classically inspired characters and their pseudo-Latinate spells (DuPree, 2011). Classical references, of course, abound in everyday speech. If you want lists, Reedy (1988) has extracted 271 everyday classically inspired words from Hirsch's comprehensive list of 5,000 'essential' names, dates, phrases and concepts that 'every American needs to know' (Hirsch, 1988), ranging from *Achilles* to *Zeus*. Whether the reader needs to have full acquaintance with the backstory of the Aeneid to make sense of newspaper references to the Birmingham 'Trojan Horse' schools scandal is perhaps a moot point, but many classical references are embedded in the nation's collective conscience. They seem to serve as shorthand for something that needs no further explanation. To cap it all, any number of references to the classical world are dropped into everyday media reports – a pop-culture demonstration of an occasional modern preoccupation with the ancients. Celebrity singer-songwriter Lady Gaga, salaciously decorated in scallop shells and little else, channelling the goddess Venus via Botticelli (Gaga, 2013); or Katie Price in sugar-pink fluff centaur-couture – a bizarre wink and a nod towards the fairy-tale features of the classical world via Disney's *Fantasia* (Hyde, 2013). The essence of this casual classics (it's a highly allusive form of classical reception of no deep or lasting significance) is a playful, half-remembered, almost childlike view of the classical world – but a view that can remain powerful as the child turns into a student.

In this rich cultural mix, it should be relatively easy to make a case for the study of Classics and Latin. And it has recently become more so in both the UK and USA.

Crisis? What crisis?

This section takes its name from Culham and Edmunds' (1989) book, *Classics: A Discipline and Profession in Crisis?*, published in response to the difficulties teachers of Classics in the American education system perceived themselves to be in, as support for the subject seemed to be in permanent decline. The reason I am writing this book, of course, is to draw attention to some of the successes whereby Classics teachers, and Latin teachers in particular, have been able to address some of those difficulties. Most have been drawn from the situation in the UK, which has, over the years, become more conducive towards Classics teaching, at least in schools – although it starts from a position of semi-moribundity. Practice in the UK may reflect experiences in the USA. A little history will help explain where we stand.

I began teaching Classics in 1987, the year before the National Curriculum had its devastating effect on the teaching of Latin in UK state-maintained schools. I was well aware, through my teacher training under Richard Woff and John Muir at King's College London Centre for Educational Studies, of the history of the decline of Classics teaching in UK schools since the 1960s. I felt perhaps the same anxiety as was felt by Classics teachers twenty-five years before when I read the Classical Association's *Re-Appraisal* (Melluish, 1962b), as it dolefully contemplated the tenuous position of Latin in schools in the face of Oxford and Cambridge Universities' removal of it as an entry requirement at O Level. I direct readers to the works of Forrest (1996) and Stray (2003a) who describe these events far more effectively than there is space for in a book this size. Suffice to say, the total number of students taking Latin dropped considerably, from around 46,000 in 1968 to 33,000 in 1979, according to Jones, quoted by Tristram (2003, p. 8). Again, in 1988, school Classics departments throughout the country were under threat. Latin, excluded from the long list of compulsory subjects that every student in state-maintained schools was required to study, had to fight hard for its very survival there. The then Conservative Education Minister Kenneth Baker insisted that schools would still be able to offer Latin if they so wanted. However, his observation that schools would find it almost impossible to provide the time necessary for teaching the National Curriculum subjects in the less than 30% of the timetable available, and the realization that this remaining time would have to be shared between Drama, Business Studies, Economics, a second modern foreign language and others was not encouraging (Baker, 1989). Unlike members of the other subject associations who were welcomed in through the doors of the Department of Education to sit down with the civil service and devise schemes of work, levels of attainment and all the other paraphernalia of the national system, Latin specialists never had the chance to meet in any formal capacity with government. There was no time for introspection and development, merely survival. This situation was especially ironic since all teachers of Classics were well aware of two reports commissioned by the government some fifty years apart that had advocated that Classical studies and even Latin *could* be made accessible to a wider range of students. As far back as 1938, the first of these, the Spens Report, had recommended a major rethink of what a Latin curriculum might look like:

> Interest in Rome should first be awakened through some knowledge of Roman life and achievement, and through the large Latin element in our non-technical vocabulary; the first Latin passages read should include many which illustrate Roman life; the grammar should be simplified and the rules of syntax dealt with as they occur in the matter read; while for very many pupils the time given to the writing of Latin should be very greatly reduced. We believe that in this way it is possible to give Latin a value and an interest that the pupil can appreciate even if he leaves school at 16.
>
> The Spens Report, 1938

Note that the report's suggestion that Latin prose composition (by which it meant translation of continuous English passages into Latin) should be considered to be suitable only for the very able, whereas, by implication, much of the rest could be achieved by a broader range of students than was thitherto being accommodated. However, vested interests in schools in maintaining the grammar school system and controlling entry to the universities through matriculation in Latin militated against such recommendations. The Spens Report was ignored. With hindsight, I wonder whether Baker's reforms would have still found a place for Classical studies in his National Curriculum if the advice of this report had been taken at the time of its publication. Another game worth playing would be to wonder if the landscape of school curricula would have accommodated Latin more easily if the National Curriculum had been conceived on a less ambitious scale. Baker's enthusiasm for a ten-subject curriculum was not matched by that of his leader Prime Minister Margaret Thatcher, who, when she had instructed him to develop it, had been more inclined towards a more minimalist national curriculum consisting of only Mathematics, English and Science (Young, 1990). It had only been the threat of Baker's resignation over the matter that Thatcher conceded the development and institution of the enormous structure that he was promoting and with which we all live with the consequences to this day in the UK.

Thatcher's initial thinking about the relatively small size of the National Curriculum explains, perhaps, why in the same year as its implementation the Department of Education and Science had also busied itself with the publication of another discussion document, *Classics from 5–16* (1988). This document had made a strong case for the inclusion of Classical Civilization and also Latin in the curriculum of every type of school:

> The Greek and Latin languages are demanding subjects capable of challenging and stimulating the ablest pupils. Traditionally they were regarded as suitable only for a limited group of pupils at the upper end of the ability-range. Fresh priorities within the subject and new teaching approaches have now brought a classical language within the competence of many more pupils – at any rate in the early stages . . .
>
> Department of Education and Science, 1988, pp. 20–21

If Baker had read this document at all, he took no notice. Instead, he took as *his* starting point that no-one could have possibly thought that students of all attainments would be capable of the study of Latin. He thus opined:

> The National Curriculum core and foundation subjects are those which all pupils will be required to study throughout the relevant stages of compulsory learning. Few would argue that Latin and Greek are subjects which every pupil should learn even just at secondary level – and it is quite obvious that not every pupil has the aptitude, inclination or intellectual stamina to tackle Latin or Greek, though they may have great abilities in other directions. Most, however, would argue that Classics, and particularly Latin, should be available as an option for more able pupils [. . .] There are no time allocations specified for the National Curriculum and it will therefore be up to individual schools and teachers to decide how much time their pupils need to complete the specified attainment targets. The more able should be able to do so in less time than others and thus have more time for other subjects. I am therefore confident that there is sufficient flexibility in my proposals to enable those who wish to do so to continue to offer Latin and Greek to some of their pupils.
>
> Baker, 1989

Baker's confidence in the ability of schools to provide the sort of 'top-up' Latin lessons to those students who had already met the 'specified learning targets' betrayed a worrying lack of familiarity with what his own civil servants were busy arranging: a complex, overarching set of National Curriculum targets, each mapped against the other in complex detail, numbered from one to ten and designed to show progression from the moment a student entered the education system to when they left it: simply put, a student never had time to move onto another subject such as Latin because the number of specific targets never came to end. And even if they had done so, it would have been extraordinary for a head teacher to employ a Latin specialist on their staff to bring in at a moment's notice to provide the extra experience that such an arrangement might bring about. In practice, only schools with head teachers who were determined to keep Classics found space on the timetable (and that often only with difficulty). These schools tended to be the grammar schools, which had a long-held tradition of teaching Classics, and the independent/private schools, which, exempt from the rules of the National Curriculum (and thereby, in some senses, above the law of the land), perhaps saw it as an opportunity to set themselves further apart from the state-maintained sector. In whichever of these cases, Baker's decision had the effect of making Latin elitist just at the moment that all the arguments of the previous twenty years had been tending in the opposite direction. With one ministerial pen-stroke he consigned Latin to near oblivion in most state schools. From 1988 to 2005, the numbers of entries for Latin at GCSE (which had, by now, replaced the O Level examination) dropped by 60% from 8,493 to 3,388 in state schools of all types. During the same period, entries in independent/private schools fell by only 15% from 7,460 to 6,340 (Lister, 2007b). Further changes to the National Curriculum occurred in 2000 and 2002, when even more subjects – such as Information and Communication Technology (ICT) and Citizenship – were added. These subjects squeezed out that little bit of space that had been suggested be kept for the study of Latin by 'more able pupils'.

A further twenty years of introspection followed. No involvement in government planning meant that teachers in those schools where Latin survived were forced to carry on as best they could: no-one knew or cared what they were up to, as long as the senior management team did not try to close them down. A siege mentality developed, even within Classics departments within the private sector. These schools had perhaps been more cushioned from the effects of the National Curriculum, but they now also began to feel the pinch as the government started to measure school effectiveness by comparing examination results of one with the other – the effect being to force independent/private schools to adopt the same subjects as state-maintained schools. The fact that Latin was not part of the national entitlement for all state school students meant that its survival was highly dependent on the personal choices made by the head teacher of the school where it was taught. Latin teachers developed stronger arguments to support Latin: the supposed ability to develop intellectual rigour; to help students with understanding the foundations of other Romance languages; to help students improve their English writing through improved knowledge of Latin derivatives in English, and an increased awareness of grammar; to provide access into the high culture of Roman literature; and the opportunity it allowed students to reflect upon and make comparisons between the ancient and modern worlds. Such arguments are still common today, although there is little empirical evidence of course to suggest that Latin is unique in being able to achieve these things – apart from access to Roman literature, which tends to be the case only for the few who go on to study Latin at examination level. I would like to suggest that the study of Latin in schools – if it does indeed consist of the tripartite structure of language, literature and culture in more or less equal measures – is the perfect way to bring together a set of school disciplines that are otherwise kept zealously apart by the demands of a crude government-dictated curriculum which compartmentalizes subject areas for the practical convenience of timetabling, teacher supply and the production of examination grades by which the schools themselves are marshalled into league tables. Latin is, perhaps, the original cross-curricular, interdisciplinary subject, which refuses to fit in with the National Curriculum. It is difficult to pin down: a slippery subject – now language, now literature, now civilization – and the better for the students who study it and the school to have it because it is so. The study of Latin does have to contribute the same learning outcomes as all the other subjects if it is going to be awarded a place on the school curriculum. But it also has its own quality: it must be the same, but it must also be different. The difference lies in the sorts of materials it draws together, the way in which it examines them, the details it chooses to focus on, the conclusions it comes to and the use it makes of them.

A reawakening of interest in the teaching of Latin in schools

The number of schools offering Latin as a subject to be studied on their curricula has grown in the last ten years. A survey carried out by the Cambridge School Classics Project suggested that around one in five secondary schools offered Latin to at least some of their students, and that, of the state-maintained secondary schools, 514 or 12.9% offered Latin (Cambridge School Classics Project, 2008). This number seems to have shot up, however, more recently. According to a 2014 *Sunday Times* newspaper article, the number of state-maintained schools offering Latin had reportedly reached 1,228 (Pelling, 2014). According to figures in the *Times* newspaper, more than 600 non-selective state schools offered Latin – up from just 100 ten years before (Woolcock, 2015). This growth was echoed by a survey carried out by myself of grant applications to the Roman Society to introduce Latin: it showed that 64 of them had introduced Latin to their curricula in just the single academic year 2012–13 (Hunt, 2013d). Since the first edition of this book, although the number of students studying Latin at GCSE level has remained broadly the same, at around 10,000 per year, the number of schools which have put Latin onto the timetable has steadily increased. In the first ten years, the charity Classics for All, for example, has worked with 483 state-maintained secondary schools, for example (2022). A small number of these, according to my own unpublished research, are now showing up in the GCSE tables provided by the Department for Education.

For the first time since the National Curriculum, the landscape seems to have changed. It seems to have become easier for schools in recent years to bring Latin back onto the timetable. In the UK, there has been a slow accumulation of policy changes from governments that have made the provision of Latin more possible than it has been for thirty years. Recent interest from national politicians and media outlets in rhetorical if not always practical forms has led to an increasing awareness of what Latin can offer school-age students. Some schools have been alert to the opportunities that such changes have allowed and Latin is making something of a comeback in state schools.

The development of the *Cambridge Latin Course* e-learning resources

The educational policies of the first Labour government of Tony Blair (1997–2001) had perhaps the biggest impact on the ability of schools to offer the teaching of Latin. Blair's avowed intent to make education the centrepiece of his government's first term meant (among other things) investment in technology in education. A huge award of £5,000,000 to develop online resources for students of Latin, won by the Cambridge School Classics Project, produced the stunning array of resources that are every teacher of the *Cambridge Latin Course*'s stock in trade today (and that of teachers of Latin everywhere). Lister (2007b) and Griffiths (2008) are better narrators of the story of the development of those resources: their impact on encouraging uptake has been huge. Students who have not had access to a teacher have been able to learn online; non-specialist and specialist teachers alike use them to support their own learning as well deliver lessons to the students; and schools report increased motivation and enjoyment in learning Latin interactively. There is strong evidence that the e-learning resources are themselves improving pedagogical practices among teachers and enhancing students' learning (Hunt, 2014b; 2020).

The personalized learning agenda

The idea of the personalized learning agenda, introduced by the Labour government of 2001, helped support the introduction of classical subjects, including Latin. Schools had to show that they were ensuring the curriculum matched more closely the needs and interests of students. This seems to have had an effect in sixth-form colleges, where it provided enrichment activities for those studying other subjects. For example, at Varndean Sixth-Form College in Sussex, students studying Classical Civilization at A Level asked to be taught Latin GCSE when they realized that it was on offer, as it might bring into better focus some of the topics that they were learning, and they believed it complemented the study of English and other subject areas. They also felt that the study of Latin enhanced their *curricula vitae* and thus their prospects of becoming accepted onto university degree courses in Classics.

The Gifted and Talented scheme

Blair's educational legacy also included the Gifted and Talented scheme (originally the Young, Gifted and Talented Programme) (2002–10). Originally conceived as a way of supporting students identified as having special talents and abilities and presented as part of the personalized learning agenda in all state-maintained schools, the scheme provided funding to develop new courses, programmes and experiences delivered within schools to the highest-achieving 10% of students in a school. Gifted and Talented scheme coordinators were appointed in each school to make sure that this new law was adhered to and to provide the courses deemed necessary. Sometimes they chose Latin as a subject to be studied by a small cohort of students, often taking the classes themselves or enlisting a local retired or part-time teacher. When the Coalition government withdrew money for the scheme in 2010, many of the Latin classes seem to have persisted due to parental and student demand.

Independent/state school partnerships

Another of Blair's educational policies was the encouragement of independent/state school partnerships. The original idea was that independent schools could be encouraged to share their facilities or their teaching expertise with small groups of state-maintained schools. That this might be felt insulting to state-maintained schools was mitigated by the funds handed out to make the links happen and to pay for resources. While most such partnerships revolved around state-maintained schools being allowed to use sports, drama and music facilities, a few did offer joint Classics clubs or encouraged teachers or sixth-form students from one school to go into and teach Latin in other schools (Khan-Evans and Hunt, 2010). Long after funding for the independent/state school partnerships has been withdrawn, some schools continue to work in partnership with each other: the York Independent–State School Partnership has around twelve state-maintained and independent schools working together to teach Latin.

Innovations in examinations

Blair's governments also encouraged new examinations to flourish, seeing them as part of the personalized learning agenda where qualifications matched the needs and interests of all students, not just a few. For Latin this meant opportunities for already-existing examinations boards to provide different types of Latin qualification and for new ones to join in. The quasi-market of examination boards competing with one another for customers perhaps led to the over-hasty creation of numerous overlapping qualifications, some of dubious value. The Wolf Review (2011) recommended the withdrawal of many of these qualifications as they represented duplication of other qualifications and were considered by the government committee as being insufficiently rigorous. All national Latin exams have so far met the criteria set by Ofqual to possess sufficient academic content to survive – but the choices of different Latin examinations and pathways within them, which reflect both the interests of students and teachers and, perhaps more importantly, the learning experiences governed by the amount of time in which they have to study it, have become very limited because they have to meet the same stringent criteria set down by it. We might usefully compare the present situation with that reported in a 1984 survey of Latin in independent schools by Her Majesty's Inspectorate (Department of Education and Science, 1984). In the thirty-three independent/private schools visited in 1984, inspectors counted seven different boards offering O Level examinations in Latin (equivalent, more or less, to Level 2) and one Latin plus Classical Civilization course; reference was made in the report to the existence of a CSE examination in Latin, although this was not taken by any of the schools inspected. Interestingly, three of the schools chose to offer two different examinations in Latin to different groups of students within the same year cohort. After the debacle of the National Curriculum of 1988, the position of Latin in schools looked distinctly shaky. Between 1988 and 1997, the number of students taking Latin to GCSE virtually halved from 8,493 to 4,400 in the state-maintained sector (JCQA, 1988, 1997). This was almost entirely due to the amount of time taken up by the legally required core subjects to be taught in schools (as has been described above). Little space was left for Latin. In the independent sector, however, the number of entries was almost unscathed, with 7,460 entries in 1988 and 7,409 in 1997. By 2000, however, the overall decline seemed to have 'bottomed out', or possibly one could have said that Latin was flat-lining, just about kept afloat by the life-support system of the major independents and a small number of selective state-maintained schools. In the following decade, the total number of students in the UK who took Latin at GCSE and A Level held fairly steady at around 9,500 and 1,500 respectively, of whom around 75% were studying it in the independent sector. In the four years to 2014, however, there was an increase in the number of students taking GCSE or equivalent qualifications, with nearly 3,000 more entries. This seems to have coincided with the introduction of a new national qualification in Latin – the WJEC Level 2 qualifications. Stephenson (2014) suggested that the WJEC Level 2 examination was more attractive than traditional GCSE because it decoupled the assessment of language from that of literature, and was therefore more accessible to students who were studying in schools where little time had been allocated. Thus it might have been the case that more students felt confident enough to attempt the WJEC examination than had been able to attempt the GCSE, and that is what was reflected in the increased numbers of pupils taking examinations in Latin overall (Cambridge School Classics Project, 2015c). The WJEC Level 2s have since been discontinued, due to Government reform of vocational qualifications; however, elements of these qualifications have been retained in the EDUQAS GCSE replacements.

We must look also at the rise in the number of students taking examinations that are of a lower 'tariff' than the GCSEs and the Level 2s. The introduction of new sub-GCSE examinations seems to have rewarded students who may not have had sufficient time or specialist teaching to take the standard examinations: the most recent figures available show that in 2012, a total of 1,149 students took OCR's Entry Level qualifications in Latin, increasing to 1,366 in 2013 (JCQ, 2013) although falling back to 693 in 2022 (the year of Covid, when schools were closed) (OCR, 2022). These students, who have had their efforts recognized by external examinations for the first time, might be more easily persuaded to continue with the study of Latin at higher levels. The WJEC examinations board has also introduced Level 1 certificates in Latin, which attract some 500 candidates each year (OCR, 2022). McPherson reports on the success of this qualification in encouraging students to continue with Latin to GCSE (2017). We must also consider the fact that the examinations boards are themselves willing to develop new forms of assessment – a mark, in a way, of their belief in the health of the subject, as no examination board, mindful of the need to maximize its profits, would seek to invent more forms of assessment than it felt it had to.

School autonomy

The Blair government legislated for a new status for underperforming state-maintained schools that was designed to help them develop new identities and, with better funding and a changed leadership, seek to improve the attainment of their students. These new academies, sponsored by private investors, were allowed to vary the curriculum for their students as part of this process of improving the quality of teaching and learning. A small number of them used their new-found freedom to offer subjects outside the National Curriculum to set themselves apart from the normal state-maintained schools, in some cases consciously aping the independent/private schools. In 2011, I visited Park High School, a sponsored academy in King's Lynn, a deprived former seaport in North Norfolk, whose new principal designate declared that her academy's unique selling point would be that it would be the only school for miles around that would offer the students the opportunity to study Latin, Ancient History and Archaeology. The fact that the school opposite – still a local-authority state-maintained school and its deadly rival for attracting students – already offered Latin and Ancient History was not something lost on her: Park High was now in competition for the most motivated students in town. A Classics specialization was felt likely to be able to attract them – or at least their parents, which would come to mean the same thing. The Coalition Government (2010–15) extended academy status more widely to any school judged to be outstanding by Ofsted – so-called converter academies – and to the independently run but state-maintained Free Schools. All three types of schools are the subject of a disputed claim by the Department for Education that they are helping raise educational standards (*Times Educational Supplement*, 2015). At the time of writing, there are 2,781 secondary schools which have converted to academy status – the overall majority (Department for Education, 2022). They all have the freedom – up to a point – to vary their curricula, to extend the school day and to employ unqualified teachers who have specialist knowledge if they wish. Such circumstances can provide opportunities for unusual extra subjects such as Latin to thrive. For example, in Sidney Stringer Academy, an inner-city sponsored academy in urban Coventry, I met a teacher of modern foreign languages who had been given permission by the principal of the school to vary the curriculum and replace some English and modern foreign language lessons with an accelerated Latin course for a small, trial group with the intention of extending it in later years to a more sizeable cohort. The teacher went on to establish a successful classical languages strand at the school (Neto, 2019).

Competition between schools

All political parties seem to be in agreement at present that one of the main drivers for the improvement of standards in education is comparing students' grades in examinations on a school-by-school basis and publishing the scores in national league tables. This has had several effects. Some schools have tried to attract a better 'quality' of parents (and thereby students) to improve the school's standing. Latin has sometimes played a part in these attempts. The non-selective convertor academy where I presently teach Latin, located in the university city of Cambridge in East Anglia, promotes Latin in its local adverts because it is in direct competition with other local independent schools, all of which offer the subject themselves. The head teacher of Bishop Thomas Grant School, a local authority state-maintained Catholic school in suburban south-west London, told me that he had introduced Latin because he wanted the parents in the area to consider his school first and the other ones second. The head teacher of Dereham Neatherd High School, a non-selective local authority-maintained state school in rural Norfolk, finding out that Latin was being offered in the nearest school to his own, instructed his modern language department to begin offering it as well in an attempt to prevent parents turning their attention to his rival.

University outreach

University Classics departments are acutely aware of the need to attract potential students from diverse backgrounds. Meanwhile, access to the study of subjects such as Latin has been restricted by successive government educational policies. Early models of school liaison tended to consist of school talks given by visiting academics and the organization of summer schools in the classical languages and ancient civilizations. More recent developments have been prompted in part by the demands of government-set targets for widening participation (Lovatt, 2011). Another driver of university engagement seems to have been the 2014 Research Excellence Framework, which not only assessed the quality of research in UK universities but also measured 'productive engagements with public and private sectors' and 'direct public engagement'. For Classics, this has frequently meant outreach work in schools, such as offering taster lessons in the classical languages and offering resources, advice and facilities for the general public (Ryan, 2010). Ryan notes elsewhere that such engagement is mutually beneficial. She suggests that there may be considerable benefit in sending academics into schools where they can use the opportunity not only to supplement and enhance the classroom experience for students and classroom teacher alike, but also to develop their own pedagogical practices and understanding of the environments in which potential students of their own have studied (Ryan, 2011). While the Faculty of Classics at Oxford University has gone so far as to employ a specific outreach officer for Classics, academics and administrators in several other University Classics departments have also been given responsibility to engage with local schools and develop activities that engage with the public. This has led to some effective collaboration. There are many examples of this: the University of Liverpool's Classics Graduate Teaching Fellow Partnership has sent postgraduate students out into local state schools to teach Latin and Ancient History GCSE (Coker, 2012); the University of Swansea's Literacy Through Latin Scheme has arranged for undergraduates to be sent to teach Latin and Classical Studies in primary schools (Bracke, 2013); Eleanor Dickey recreated a Romano-Egyptian classroom based on her own research, in which local students were invited to participate in historically accurate period lessons (Dickery, 2015); and Sonya Nevin, at the Ure Museum at the University of Reading, has developed animated versions of their artefacts for use in outreach work in local schools and communities (Nevin, 2015).

Raising standards

Governments of all political persuasions have set their heart on raising standards in literacy and languages in education. The most consistent support for the study of Latin (among other subjects) to achieve these ends comes from the Coalition government (2010–15) when Michael Gove's time in office as Minister for Education

(2010–14). Support for Latin also continues from Classicist Boris Johnson, extrovert former Prime Minister: his passion for Classics remains undimmed. A flavour of his intent can be gleaned in an early interview in the *London Evening Standard* newspaper in 2008, given when he was an opposition Member of Parliament. He is reported to have said,

> I think there's a huge amount we can do in London by promoting the learning of languages including Latin. [...] I would like to see not only that but I would like to see ancient Greek. Latin can help with all languages. The government want to encourage more kids from less advantaged backgrounds to top universities and that would really help them.
>
> Johnson, 2008

The theme of Latin as a school subject that would help students access the cultural riches of the ancient world, and engender in them the ability to enhance language learning, chimed with other efforts to raise the bar of supposed educational underachievement. Once in power, the Conservative politicians got to work. Nick Gibb, Minster of State for Schools (2010–12 and 2014–15) declared his support for Latin as an academic subject that would improve students' abilities in languages in particular. In a speech in 2010 to the right-wing *Politeia* think-tank on the subject of the introduction of Latin in primary schools, Gibb said:

> Reintroducing the importance of a broad range of academic subjects as a measure of standards in our schools will provide an incentive for schools to refocus on encouraging more young people to study a language. And since we include ancient languages in that measure, this is a real opportunity for the Latin lobby to promote the teaching of Latin in schools.
>
> Gibb, 2010

Soon the casual reader might think Latin had become the panacea that would solve many of the problems facing the country. The right-wing journalist and author Toby Young (founder of the state-maintained West London Free School, where Latin is compulsory for all pupils up to the age of 14) has extolled the educational advancements which the learning of Latin conferred on students, particularly from deprived backgrounds (Young, 2011); and the newspaper pundit Harry Mount, author of a best-selling Christmas book *amo, amas, amat And All That*, applauded the return of Latin to take its place in the new, invigorating curriculum (Mount, 2010). Peter Jones, tireless supporter of the Classics and retired university lecturer, as well as columnist for the right-wing magazine *The Spectator*, weighed in with a narrowly focused report from the charity Friends of Classics that suggested that teachers valued the 'mental training' that the study of Classics seemed to offer more than its ability to support modern foreign languages (Friends of Classics, 2010).

Under Michael Gove's reforms of the compulsory KS2 Primary School curriculum, Latin has become one of the languages approved for study by all students between the ages of 7 and 11. At KS4, Latin has become included on the list of language subjects that are counted for the English Baccalaureate qualification, which is one of the accountability devices for school effectiveness. Gove saw Latin as one of the subjects that enable students from state-school backgrounds to compete fairly with their peers from independent/private schools and improve their chances of access to the best universities. In a speech to the London Academy of Excellence in 2014, he announced funding from the Department for Education to support the training of Latin teachers in state-maintained schools. In relation to appointing academics from the universities to provide leadership on these programmes, he said that,

> Academics of this calibre would be able to give state school students the extra level of stretch and challenge that privately-educated students enjoy through extra coaching and preparation. Their work will do far more to improve access to the best universities – by genuinely democratizing knowledge and robustly supporting a more meritocratic system – than any other set of academic initiatives I know.
>
> Gove, 2014

Such reforms have been successful in raising the profile of Latin as a school subject once again and making it possible to timetable it. The principal of Cottenham Village College, a rural convertor academy in Cambridgeshire, told me in 2011 that he wanted '. . . to give pupils in the top streams of the ability range the same chances I had when I was at school. I've spent the last ten years providing vocational courses. Now it's the turn of the upper ability range.'

The danger is, of course, that Latin may be seen to be in the purlieu of the right wing and as quickly snuffed-out when the political climate changes. In her June 2013 blog *A Don's Life* published in *The Times Literary Supplement*, Mary Beard reported on the public debate held at the *Life and Death in Pompeii and Herculaneum* exhibition at the British Museum:

> What came over most clearly – and clearer than I had ever seen it before – was the way we have projected onto Latin so many of our anxieties about privilege in education, teaching quality and the personality of the traditional teacher, ideas of utility, the control of the curriculum, etc. Latin in other words is so much of a symbol that it is hard to discuss it without getting involved in series of much bigger debates, only symbolically connected with Latin.
>
> Beard, 2013a

In a similar vein, Page duBois (2001) set out her challenge to overturn what she perceived were conservative US politicians' misrepresentation and misappropriation of ancient Greek culture for their own political ends. It is to try to ensure that Latin is seen for what it is rather than what politicians of any beliefs would like it to be that the subject associations are currently working closely with one another, putting together materials and lobbying all parties in order to maintain and strengthen its position in all schools today.

New initiatives

In 2021, the then Minister for Education, Gavin Williamson, announced that there would be funding for a Latin Excellence Programme, to the tune of £4 million. The programme is to be modelled on the Mandarin Excellence Programme, in which the Chinese Government and the British Council provided training for new teachers and funded teaching and assessment resources for their use with selected students in state-maintained schools in England. The announcement was something of a surprise, especially at a time of something of a funding crisis for schools in the UK. More of a surprise was the requirement for the programme to develop its own resources and assessments when plenty already existed (Hunt 2022e), The tender for the four year tender was awarded to The Centre for Latin Excellence, run from the Future Academies Trust in London. According to its website:

> Charlie [Furber, the Director of the programme] has led Classics at Future Academies since January 2017. Over five years, he has produced an entirely bespoke and inclusive curriculum suited to the demands of the state sector and he has championed the impact of direct instruction in the classroom.
>
> Centre for Latin Excellence, 2022

Sample Latin resources may be found on the Oak National Website (2022). Whatever one feels about the prospect of a very traditional 'direct instruction' approach to teaching Latin and the quality and effectiveness of some of the materials visible on the two websites, one can only hope that the programme achieves its aim of increasing the number of state-mainatined schools in England which offer Latin.

The charity Classics for All has been working with state-maintained schools in England, Northern Ireland, Scotland and Wales for something over ten years. From small beginnings, by 2021 it developed classical subjects, including Latin, with some 564 primary and 483 secondary schools (Classics for All, 2021). For primary schools, it has developed a suite of resources for teaching Latin, based on a word-roots package – maximum Classics – which has proven very popular; with secondaries, standard programmes involving the *Cambridge Latin Course* and *Suburani* have been overwhelmingly popular. Classics for All trains teachers who are already qualified in other, often related, subjects and who are able to expand a school's curriculum 'from the inside', with face-to-face training events or, increasingly, online (I must declare an interest, as being a trainer for them).

The US experience

Meanwhile, there is talk of something of a renaissance in the USA too. Provision across the whole country is about as patchy as in the UK, and not, at present, driven by any national agenda. Phinney (1989) recalls the catastrophic fall in Latin enrolments during the 1960s and 1970s as American priorities in education turned towards science and technology. The tide seemed capable of being turned, however, with the development of the Foreign Languages in Elementary Schools (FLES) programmes of the 1970s and 1980s. Latin instruction was introduced to students in inner-city Philadelphia through such programmes as Masciantonio's (1970) Language Arts Through Latin. The British linguist David Corson carried out research on what he called the Graceo-Latinate lexical bar. He believed that there existed in the English language a barrier that 'separates the users of some social dialects from a ready access to the lexis of semantic categories essential for success in education', and noted the success of these programmes in helping students make 'highly significant gains in the effective use of English throughout the curriculum' (Corson, 1982). The further success of these programmes in apparently raising general academic performance encouraged the spread of Latin to Washington DC, New York City and Los Angeles (Polsky, 1998).

Although the FLES programmes have long come to an end, Latin can be still held to be sufficiently important in raising achievement in literacy that it forms a compulsory four-year programme in schools such as Brooklyn Latin School (*New York Daily News*, 2013). In schools such as the Charter Schools, funding is dependent on results. LaFleur's (1980) research seemed to show that learning Latin improved students' SAT scores and this continues to be cited as evidence for introducing Latin. At the American Classical League Institute in 2012, a teacher commented to me: 'It's all about the power of Latin to improve the GPA [Grade Point Average]', and such anecdotal evidence seems prevalent in US thinking about what Latin teaching in schools is for. The value of SATs scores have, however, recently become less of a selling point. Latin in US schools comes under World Languages or Foreign Languages and students enrol into any one of the languages offered at the school. Thus Latin might be the only language that a student takes in a US school, and thus issues of accessibility and inclusivity are seen as vitally important. The *Washington Post* newspaper reported Claudia Bezaka, world languages programme coordinator for D.C. Public Schools, as saying Latin could 'be a game changer, in terms of the literacy of the students' and 'the great equalizer' because it was a language that students from diverse backgrounds could all start at the same place. She advocated a mixture of active teaching, making widespread use of spoken Latin, and traditional language learning techniques (*The Washington Post*, 2014). Lindzey (2002), by way of further example, has written eloquently about how she and her predominantly Hispanophone students shared excitement and interest in the exploration of the connections between Spanish and Latin. Abbott reflects this trend in trying to blend traditional and more modern approaches to teaching Latin in order to make it more accessible to students from all backgrounds, reporting:

> Educators have called for teaching Latin as a language instead of a complex translation puzzle that students must struggle to solve. When our classes focus predominantly on

teaching students about the language rather than to use the language, classrooms become stifling environments where only the most capable students can be successful … Our goal and our focus is on teaching students to read Latin, but in the process of doing so, it is vital to use other skills, such as listening, speaking, and writing, in order to meet the learning needs of students.

Abbott, 1998, p. 36

How prevalent this approach is in reality is the subject of much discussion. US Latin programmes seem to be much more wedded than UK programmes to grammar-translation courses. However, approaches which involve comprehensible input, such as speaking and listening and reading non-original authors are in their turn much more widespread in the USA. We will look at these different teaching approaches below.

Teaching approaches

The three main teaching approaches employed in the study of Latin can be broadly defined as the grammar-translation approach, the reading approach and the Living Latin approach. In the UK, course books such as the *Cambridge Latin Course*, *Suburani*, *ecce Romani* and the *Oxford Latin Course* are by far the most frequently used, which suggests the popularity of the reading approach. For example, Cambridge University Press sales figures suggest that around 35,000 *Cambridge Latin Course* textbooks are sold annually in the UK (CUP, 2015) and the Cambridge School Classics Project (2015b) claims on its website that 90% of secondary schools in the UK use its *Cambridge Latin Course*. US teachers, by comparison, seem to be advocates of a wider number of approaches. These are worth explaining here.

Grammar translation

The grammar-translation approach is a product of the nineteenth century. Grammar is laid out in chart-and-table form to be memorized by the student. Lists of vocabulary are also provided for students to memorize. Detailed notes explain the functions and forms of the language – again to be memorized. Once these tables, lists and notes are mastered, the student applies their knowledge to practice sentences, from Latin into English and from English into Latin. Gradually passages of Latin are introduced to translate into English and vice versa. The grammar-translation method conducts all its teaching in the students' own language. Typically, the emphasis is on reading and writing rather than speaking and listening. Some background material about Roman customs is presented, which may or may not support the learning of the language by providing a socio-cultural context. Eventually the student progresses to reading original literature. Several US grammar-translation course books (such as the venerable *Wheelock* and *Jenney* courses) are still in use in the early twenty-first century. In the UK, *So You Really Want to Learn Latin, Gwynne's Latin, De Romanis, Latin to GCSE* and the resources of the Centre for Latin Excellence follow the traditional grammar table/translate model. Advocates of the grammar-translation approach tend to argue that as Latin is not spoken and the end purpose of learning it is to be able to comprehend and analyse original Roman authors, the reading approach is too slow, Living Latin approaches are unnecessary, while the grammar-translation approach affords students with the linguistic tools to do the job most efficiently, especially where time is short, such as on *ab initio* university courses. In practice, in schools at least, grammar-translation courses proved to be anything other than speedy and were notorious for the boredom and horror of learning foreign languages that they induced in their students (Richards and Rodgers, 2001). Technical proficiency in knowing and being able to identify the forms of Latin does not always seem to equate to students' ability to be able to comprehend Latin – a complaint made even in 1962 by the foremost upholder of the value of traditional methods, the then President of the Classical Association, Tommy Melluish (1962a). His answer (and one which was destined never to come to pass): to encourage schools to provide more time to learn Latin rather than for teachers to change methods.

A note about translation from English into Latin

One of the traditional features of the grammar-translation approach has been the translation of English sentences and continuous passages into Latin. Strong views are held by teachers and commentators on this matter. First, as far as assessment has been concerned in the UK, English into Latin translation is not the same discipline as, for example, the free composition exercises that are often practised in modern foreign languages. A student of French, for example, may be asked to compose a letter to a pen pal about their holiday experiences. Such a student has freedom to use the vocabulary and grammatical structures which they know and with which they feel confident. A number of US teachers have written about using Latin composition in class. Dugdale suggested that, at the early stages of learning Latin, creative composition on the modern foreign languages model enriched student learning by reinforcing their cultural knowledge, their awareness of the link between language and communication, their knowledge of vocabulary and their awareness of 'how Latin works' (Dugdale, 2011, p. 3). In his article, he went on to describe some of the writing activities his students have undertaken: captions for cartoon strips, short letters to a friend, Latin 'Haiku' poems, mottoes, and inscriptions. Beneker (2006) recounts intermediate Latin classes where students wrote their own Latin stories, with instructions to include specific vocabulary and types of grammatical form from a list provided by the teacher. At university level, Davisson (2004) describes free composition Latin classes that were created to help students from diverse prior educational experiences reach a common standard of linguistic knowledge in preparation for reading original authors. At a much more advanced level, Lord (2006) recounts experiments with university students using extracts from modern speeches, poetry and novels for translation. Free composition may act as a vehicle for discussion about the Latin language, such as Trego (2014) describes in her discussion of competitive and collaborative learning in her college classroom. Gruber-Miller (2006b) advocates free composition as a way of encouraging students to think of writing Latin not 'simply as an exercise to learn correct structure or correct grammatical forms' but also to pay attention to structure and form depending on the audience. He argues that the process of writing is much more effective a tool for learning than the act of completion and that students must therefore have time to reshape their writing. He reflects,

> By submitting their drafts to peers at one or more stages in the writing process, students can tackle global rhetorical problems such as audience, topic, development, logic, and even local-level rhetorical problems such as spelling, sentence structure and word choice.
>
> Gruber-Miller, 2006b, p. 196

In these examples, then, free composition seems to have had some positive motivational impact on students' engagement with the Latin language. We must remember, however, that this pedagogical practice seems to flourish more in the university rather than the school setting. Direct translation of English into Latin sentences, as practised in the school classroom, seems, on the other hand, to be a very different matter. Unlike free composition, direct translation restricts student choice over vocabulary and grammatical structures and becomes a test of the student's knowledge of that same vocabulary and those same grammatical structures. When it becomes a means by which a student is to be assessed in national examinations, there is plenty of anecdotal evidence to suggest that it has historically been a demotivating exercise for nearly all students except a very few. If the purpose of learning Latin is to be able to comprehend and translate the Latin language and authentic Latin literature, there is no reliable evidence from the school classroom to suggest that the ability to translate Latin sentences helps. Eales, in a small-scale research project on the attitudes and responses of Year 13 students in a selective school in the UK, found that students' success at being able to translate indirect statements from English to Latin did not seem to match their ability to translate them from Latin into English, drawing him to conclude that the two practices comprised different skills for which some students were more suited than others. Regarding motivation, as Sharwood Smith ruefully commented in 1977, when translation from English to Latin made up a significant part of the UK O Level examinations in Latin,

[...] inspection of candidates' O level examination papers, if not observation in the classroom, quickly reveals that the experience of a very large proportion of Latin pupils was that of failing (because of lack of time, or of ability, or of good teaching, or of sufficient motivation, or of a combination of all or any of these) to learn precision and accuracy in the handling of elementary Latin sentences [...]. What they did learn was a worrying familiarity with red ink.

Sharwood Smith, 1977, p. 29

We must remember that Sharwood Smith's comments refer to O Level candidates in Latin. These students were likely to have been the most highly attaining students in the UK: selected by competitive entrance examination to grammar schools, streamed into Latin classes, and identified as possible entrants for the universities of Oxford and Cambridge. In 1962, Baty reported that only 27% of the total number of students in these schools who had started Latin completed the course to O Level. By the time of Sharwood Smith in 1977 the number would likely have been smaller still. Moreover, young Latinists at that time could expect to receive three or four lessons per week. Arguments for the compulsory introduction of English into Latin sentences at GCSE (see, for example, Peter Jones, 2013 and Butterfield et al., 2013) seem to pay little attention to the changes in circumstances that have occurred over the last forty years and the way in which Latin has been made accessible to a much broader range of students than ever before. While the value of free composition of Latin or of translation of English into Latin is still a source of considerable debate, the practice's conscription into national assessment bring potential problems of their own. For example, although the number of marks allocated to the assessment of prose composition in the GCSE is very small, the preparation for this part of the assessment itself and concomitant student anxiety exert a disproportionate impact throughout the GCSE years (Hunt, 2022a).

Reading approaches

The development of cognitive psychology and the theories of Noam Chomsky resulted in new approaches to teaching Latin. Course books that subscribe to the reading approach use a continuous, connected storyline of material specially written for the purpose of teaching the language. The aim is to promote reading comprehension of Latin. Language features and vocabulary are carefully introduced with scaffolding structures such as pictures and glossed words, and the socio-cultural context is integrated with the text so that the two are mutually supportive and intrinsically motivating for the student. Detailed grammar notes are kept until after the student has met examples of their kind in the reading passages, so that the passages are seen not so much as tests of what have been learnt, or places for the application of grammar rules, but as places where the language is used and familiarized through use. Advocates of the reading approach submit that grammatical understanding is inductive: through extensive reading of texts, the reader acquires their own 'personal grammar' (Gay,

2003). In practice, with the limited amount of time provided for Latin lessons in a school context, and few opportunities (if any) for immersion in the language, most teachers of the reading approach probably make use of other approaches as well. The four main reading-approach courses – the *Cambridge Latin Course, Suburani, ecce Romani* and the *Oxford Latin Course* – developed in response to demands from teachers in the UK looking for alternatives to the grammar-translation courses, are in widespread use today.

Living Latin approaches

Dissatisfaction with both the grammar-translation and reading approaches has led some teachers today to transfer the principles of modern foreign language learning to the Latin classroom. The Living Latin approach is not a new one, however. In the UK, W. H. D. Rouse, head teacher of the Perse School in Cambridge, taught his students via what was called the Direct Method in the early years of the twentieth century, giving instructions in Latin and modelling responses for students to copy and then modify as they became more experienced. Stray (1992) has written extensively about W. H. D. Rouse and recordings of the great man himself (only available in Greek at the time of writing) can be found at https://archive.org/details/grc-whdr-sounds.b. His ideas had a small, but devoted following, out of which formed the Association for the Reform of Latin Teaching (ARLT), which continues to operate today as the Association for Latin Teaching. Rouse's practices were not widely followed, however, due to anxieties about the effectiveness of the approach in enabling students to be able to carry out written translation from Latin to English and from English to Latin – the prerequisites for scholarship in the universities – even though independent evidence suggested the method delivered 'generally high levels of achievement on composition and translation in the sixth from' (Stray, 1992, p. 25). A bigger problem – and one which haunts us today, in more general terms – was that teachers, while impressed by the performances of Rouse and his colleagues with students at the annual ARLT conferences, felt they lacked the technical proficiency in speaking Latin themselves to make learning effective for their own students (Stray, 2011).

Modern enthusiasts for Living Latin approaches use a variety of methods. Some hold to the theories of Krashen (1981) and the idea of comprehensible input: a student acquires a language by performing the actions associated with it or in another meaningful context (Macdonald, 2011). In its most basic form, there are those who advocate the concept of Total Physical Response (TPR), which requires students to act out the words and phrases as they say them. Others, such as Patrick (2011, 2019) and his colleagues, adhering to the theories of language acquisition offered by Krashen (1981) and Asher (2012), advocate the use of storytelling and question-and-answer sessions, in Latin, to encourage students to engage fully in the language learning process – this they call Teaching Proficiency through Reading and

Storytelling (TPRS). Patrick has argued that Latin teachers have traditionally spent more time talking *about* Latin than actually *talking* Latin, and advocates spending most of the lesson time using the language for simple questioning and even complex discussions about original Latin literature. He says:

> TPRS [was] developed based on some very basic principles: students make progress in a language when they receive comprehensible input in the new language, when they receive it in a low-stress environment, when the material (the story) is interesting, and when the language level is just slightly beyond their current ability. Hence, TPRS will do almost anything required to make *puella* comprehensible as 'girl', including a picture, dramatizations, pointing to a number of girls in a room in contrast with a number of *pueri* in the room, or simply saying *puella significat* 'girl'.
>
> Patrick, 2011, p. 10

Clark (2013) found TPRS to be an effective way to engage students' interest – particularly among lower-attainers – but that the initial enthusiasm waned and students in her class preferred a return to more traditional approaches. Other Living Latin approaches build on the ideas of Hans Oerberg and his book *lingua Latina per se illustrata* (2011). The course book is written completely in Latin: text and notes are occasionally awarded small line drawings to illustrate objects or actions. The meaning and function of all new words and grammatical features can be inferred from the context. Through extensive listening to the text being read aloud and through reading aloud themselves, students are intended to gain understanding of vocabulary and grammar, which is consolidated by further written exercises (Carter, 2011). Living Latin approaches to learning Latin have now become much more popular in the USA and are beginning to be treated with some interest in the UK. For a full picture of the sorts of activities – far more than there is space for in a book this size – see *Communicative Approaches for Ancient Languages* (Lloyd and Hunt, 2021), which covers theory and practice in the school and college classrooms. Ancona's recent article 'Introducing a Bit of Active Latin into Your Current Advanced Latin Classroom: Usus loquendi et audiendi de Terentio Catulloque' (2022) puts to bed the idea that using spoken Latin is far too difficult except for experts, and is well worth reading.

Some Latin teachers (most notably in the USA) have taken the approach a step further and promote the idea of using Living Latin approaches to Latin not just as a means of beginning to learn Latin more fluently and for the purpose of reading the original authors more quickly, but as a means of bringing the language itself back to life. In 1995, Terence Tunberg set up the Latin *Conventiculum* or Convention at the University of Kentucky to provide opportunities for teachers to live in an all-Latin environment, with the intention, perhaps, of affording them the opportunity to improve their active use of Latin for the classroom (Tunberg, 2011). Such approaches have not always met with universal approval. In an article in the *Modern Languages Journal*, Ball and Ellsworth (1996) complained that such approaches were, essentially, pointless and doomed to failure. Who would want to speak in a language that had died out years ago when perfectly sensible ones were widely intelligible and readily available? This piece was in turn addressed by Wills (1998), who reminded US teachers of the importance of an oral element in everyday classroom teaching: its appeal to students who responded well to speaking and listening approaches to language learning, as well as opportunities to provide variety in lessons that were still focused on Latin, rather than on project work relating to learning about Roman civilization, for example. In support of the general aims of Living Latin approaches to learning Latin, the authors of the *Standards for Classical Language Learning* include an oral and aural component. Coffee, while admitting to his own preference for the grammar-translation approach, which, he believes, 'inculcates a precision of thought that benefits further scholarly study' (2012, p. 264), also suggests that the inclusion of this requirement in US Latin classrooms is largely beneficial and acts as a reminder to teachers of the importance of the spoken word in learning languages in general. He reports:

> I have seen how speaking and writing Latin can bring a much deeper and more fluent knowledge of the Latin idiom that not only significantly improves reading comprehension – ultimately the primary, first-order aim of Latin instruction – but itself forms part of the bedrock of cultural understanding that is the larger goal of classical studies.
>
> Coffee, 2012, p. 264

Comprehensible Input does not have to imply only speaking and / or listening to Latin. A number of recent innovations in Latin teaching in the USA are beginning to percolate through into the UK, in addition to the more traditional approaches of course book and translation. These include novellas and tiered readings.

Novellas are short Latin stories, written by modern authors, at A Level suitable for the beginning or intermediate student as found in the secondary school classroom, and who are not yet ready for reading original Roman authors. Generally, these books are short, have a small and repetitive vocabulary, and often support the story with illustrations and extensive vocabularies. Much like school readers, the idea is that students find the stories easy to read because the vocabulary is familiar, and the story sufficiently interesting or compelling that they wish to read it, thereby gaining in reading fluency which pays off when coming to read more traditional texts later. For further reading, specific to Latin, see Hunt (2022a, pp. 88–99; 2022c); Ramsby (2022); Shelton (2021); Piantaggini (2021); Vanderpool (2021); Conway (2021); Patrick, M. (2019); and Olimpi (2019).

Modern writers are also experimenting with making original Latin texts more comprehensible to intermediate to advanced readers (for whom the text remains extremely challenging) by tiering the text – that is, by simplifying the original and progressively restoring it as the student comprehends first, as it were, the skeleton, then the muscles, the flesh and finally the skin of the text. For examples of this practice, see Hunt (2022a, pp. 74–84), Gall (2020) and Sears and Ballestrini (2019).

Further developments include the harnessing of digital media to help with making a Latin text comprehensible: some are using sound / simultaneous reading of a text (Pettersson and Rosengren, 2021); others creating video stories in Latin (Craft, 2019). Indeed, the use of digital media is very much on the increase (Hunt, S., 2022a; Hunt, C., 2022). It makes, in my view, an important difference in pedagogy which is not just attractive to more students, but also produces better learning of Latin, because they treat it not as a cypher, but as a language spoken, written and used in a whole variety of situations.

For further resources about language learning approaches, see Section 3.

Latin in diverse communities of students

Latin for students with learning needs

A fundamental principle is that students with special educational needs must be included in the Latin classroom. Hubbard (2003) proposes that the study of Latin is not purely a linguistic one: it involves language work, literature and the study of the Roman world, all rolled into one. Few students will be equally as good at these. Each student should be able to perform at their individual best in any of them. The Latin teacher must adapt teaching for all students' abilities in the class, not expect each one to adapt themselves to the teacher's personal interest.

Hill (2006), drawing on articles by Ancona (1982), Ganschow and Sparks (1987) and Hill et al. (1995), suggests that, of the foreign languages learnt in US schools, Latin is suitable for students with special educational needs for a number of reasons: students tend to begin the learning of the language from the same point; the Roman alphabet is the same as the English one; in lessons there is more of a focus on the written word (which they can see and read), rather than on the spoken (which they only hear); the number of Latin words used in class is relatively small; pronunciation is regular; and there are some 50% of English words derived from Latin. She goes on to suggest that leaning Latin helps to promote literacy among poor readers and speakers, as most of the discussion takes place in the students' own language and may focus explicitly on the morphology and syntax of the language: students may benefit from looking at the underlying ways in which the language conveys meaning, rather than merely relying on word order. Parker (2013) noted in her research that students with dyslexia, for example, did not perceive that the learning of Latin was any more challenging to them than the learning of other modern foreign languages. Several students in the study suggested for themselves that Latin was helpful at improving their own literacy and the understanding of languages in general.

A number of authors have commented on approaches that are appropriate to use with students with special educational needs in Latin. Ashe (1998) has made many recommendations: a multi-sensory approach with the use of gesturing, speaking out, miming and acting out – especially in the early stages of learning, when the students need to acculturate themselves to the sound of words in order to internalize their meanings; a stress-free classroom environment is essential, with all students' responses valued by the teacher; short explanations, written down on the board or on hand-outs, and short, achievable tasks. Printed hand-outs save the time of students who have fine motor-skills deficiencies having to write notes, as can large A3 sheets, with lots of white space to write in large writing, rather than copying sentences from course books into exercise books. Students who are visually impaired may need coloured sheets or coloured overlays. The *Cambridge Latin Course* e-learning resources can be electronically adapted to provide different font sizes, colours and background colours. Charts and tables can be chanted and always kept to hand for reference – rather than for testing against.

Latin for gifted and talented students

There has been a tendency to see Latin as a good fit for the highest-attaining students in our schools. In the USA, VanTassel-Baska (2010) has suggested that a Latin enrichment programme offered at elementary level to verbally talented students would accelerate access to other language options at high school level and lay the foundation for higher Latin programmes and the Advanced Placement examinations. In the UK, as we have seen above, the Gifted and Talented scheme of the Labour governments seemed to provide an incentive for some schools to start up Latin where none had previously existed. Dyson (2003) reported to a US conference on her experiences teaching the *Cambridge Latin Course* to gifted and talented students in the socially deprived urban area of London's Barking and Dagenham. She reflected on three themes that appeared to challenge students: intellectual *challenge and difficulty* of the subject matter; the importance of *resilience*; and the *privilege* of doing Latin. Other teachers argue that by offering Latin to a small minority, we risk perpetuating the idea that Latin is an elitist study. Maguire and Hunt (2014) suggest that schools are more successful in promoting Latin to students and parents if it is seen as being suitable for everyone. In Maguire's case studies of projects she set up for UK primary school students to learn Latin in socially deprived areas of North Norfolk, she was anxious that the benefits of improving students' English literacy through learning Latin must be offered to all students and not merely to a few who are already advantaged.

Equality, Diversity and Inclusion

Equality, Diversity and Inclusion (EDI) (known in the USA as Diversity, Equity and Inclusion – DEI) has attracted considerable attention in recent years – and rightly so. In response to the increasing diversity of the students who study Latin, the Classics

Community on both sides of the Atlantic and further afield have taken the issue of what subjects to study, what resources to use, and what pedagogies to employ very seriously. Thinking about the students themselves, Classicists have cast a critical eye over the resources which are in use in the classroom; is there a gender imbalance in the subject matter and the authors of the texts which they read? Do the texts reflect the reality of Roman life? What do the course books say about Roman attitudes to race and gender – and do they reflect what we really know? Do they send out subliminal – or not so subliminal – messages to our students? Are, indeed, particular pedagogical practices in themselves exclusionary? I have also addressed some of these issues more fully in Hunt (2022a), but more can be found elsewhere. The *Cambridge Latin Course* is currently undergoing revision precisely for these reasons; *Suburani* was written from scratch with them firmly in mind.

For two helpful articles about teaching about race in the ancient world, see Mataya (2022) and Nappa (2022).

In terms of shifts in thinking about pedagogy, worth reading are Piantaggini's (2020) thoughts on why grammar-translation is ill-suited to teaching in the inclusive classroom. For some of the sorts of considerations given to changing teaching practices in the USA, see McGlathery (2022) and Pagain (2022). In the UK, it could be argued the monolithic nature of the examination system and its assessment approaches makes change more difficult.

Several organizations are raising the profile of women in texts, as authors and as learners. These include in the USA The Women's Classical Caucus (https://www.wccclassics.org/) and in the UK The Women's Classical Committee (https://wcc-uk.blogs.sas.ac.uk/). Lupercal (https://www.lupercallegit.org/) is a reading group of female classical authors.

The choice of texts to work with with students in today's classrooms is also under consideration. While teachers may choose course books and authors which more accurately reflect the peoples of the ancient world, the question arises of how a teacher might address difficult and sensitive issues as oppression and violence, especially in the area of Roman slavery. Hunt (2016) noted that Latin teachers were unusually placed to address many of these difficult topics and were willing to do so, provided that they had the support of their schools and parents – something which is perhaps easier to achieve in UK schools which are less circumscribed by local and national political factors than those in the USA. More recent advice has been offered by Kennedy (2022) and Witzke (2022) for the US classroom.

Teachers using Living Latin approaches are having to consider ways to modify personal pronouns in the classroom for students who identify as non-binary or trans. For some suggestions, see Cleveland and Cerulli's *Style Guide for Gender Inclusivity in the Latin Language* (2021).

Recent panels at the Classical Association and the Society for Classical Studies have produced thoughtful papers more generally on gender, race disability and LGBTQ+ issues in Classics teaching which are all worth reading: see, for example, the CUCD Bulletins 45–50 (https://cucd.blogs.sas.ac.uk/) and The Classical Outlook 96.1 (2021) for details of current developments.

2

Teaching Language, Civilization and Literature

In this section, we consider teaching methods for use with confected or made-up and original Latin texts. I have chosen to exemplify practice through the use of several case studies, drawn from observation in schools in the UK. The reading approach is the most widely used in the UK, with the *Cambridge Latin Course* by far the most popular. For this handbook to be helpful for teachers who use the reading approach (the vast majority in the UK and a sizeable number in the USA), I have decided to focus on case studies that utilize materials from this course, with an indication of which of the five American *Standards for Classical Languages* might be being addressed. However, the teaching methods described below are just as applicable to any other course where students read and comprehend any Latin texts. This book is not intended as an endorsement of a particular course.

I have chosen to include three types of case study here. These include examples of:

- effective practice from experienced classroom teachers of Latin;
- the developing practice of beginning teachers; and
- classroom interactions between teacher and students, and between student and student.

The case-study approach provides opportunities for me not only to describe real-life activities that might be applicable elsewhere in the classroom, but also to comment on their effectiveness. Case studies provide opportunities to compare and contrast different classroom experiences in a way that a continuous set of instructions might not. Different teachers teach students to comprehend Latin stories in different ways and I would not presuppose to know that there are right answers. Moreover, there is some light to be shed about how students, early-career teachers and more experienced teachers plan and deliver lessons by investigating their less meritorious experiences. Effective practice consists of engaging the students with the subject matter of the story, a brisk pace, interaction between teacher and students, opportunities for students to work independently or in small groups, and feedback from the teacher. This does not just happen: it is dependent on effective planning by the teacher.

Schemes of work

The first task of the beginning Latin teacher is to calculate how much time there is going to be to teach. They should draw up a scheme of work matching the days of the school calendar and including the following details:

- The length, frequency and number of lessons.
- Dates of fixed holiday periods (suitable for student revision or review or teacher marking of assessments).
- Dates of extra-curricular activities (such as sports fixtures, school functions and extra-mural visits).
- Dates of school assessment periods and external examinations.

The teacher needs to look at their chosen Latin course book and calculate how much time to allocate to each chapter. Remember that the full *ecce Romani* course is designed to take three years, while the *Cambridge Latin Course* was originally designed as a four- or five-year course – although teachers report success with much shorter allocations than that today. Both of these courses assume a timetable allocation of one or sometimes two lessons of about an hour each per week. US course books such as *Latin for the New Millennium* are also designed to take students through a three-year course leading to original authors, but it should be remembered that US Latin students might study Latin one lesson each day of the school week. In many cases, however, teachers will not be given as much time to teach as the course book might suggest. Corners may well have to be cut and it is unlikely that the teacher will have time to let the students do every single activity in the course book. Therefore, making a scheme of work is essential. The teacher should plan ahead and work out where they and their students want to be at given points in the year. The teacher wants to get to a suitable point in the course book, for example, where there is an obvious break to end the year; then they work out how many lessons they have until that point. They should look carefully in the course book: what appears to take a long time to accomplish might be done more quickly. In practice, however, students complete tasks much more slowly than the teacher might anticipate at the start and so they will need to factor in more lesson time than they themselves would need. They need to think what extra resources will be required. They should use already published resources wherever possible, thus saving precious time. Often they will want to make extra time for topics that they personally find interesting and enjoy. But against that, essential topics that need to be covered must take priority. Rather than skip topics, it is sometimes possible to teach a couple of topics alongside each other. This is most often easiest where the reading material delivers two for the price of one, such as a linguistic as well as a civilization point. Watson's (2011) article 'Classics, Citizenship and *Cambridge Latin Course* Stage 11' describes a case in point. As a result of reading the Latin stories in *Cambridge Latin Course* Stage 11 – stories that present further uses of the dative case in the social context of the Pompeian political elections of 79 CE – more than a third of his mixed-gender class of 13–14-year-olds reported that they had become more interested in *modern* politics than before. Watson reported:

> Latin teachers should recognize that in *Cambridge Latin Course* Stage 11 they have a wonderful resource which allows students to find out about Roman politics through their reading of Latin, and which can serve as a useful starting point for discussions of modern politics that could form a meaningful part of a Citizenship scheme of learning.
>
> Watson, 2011, p. 5

The teacher needs to consider which activities might be completed outside class, and then whether this is preparation for a lesson to follow, or consolidation of learning completed. Digital technology can often speed the process of learning at school and also at home – although there may be issues of accessibility. All of the major Latin course books now have supporting digital resources available online (see Section 3).

Above all, teachers should think of *themselves* as the most valuable resource in the classroom. That does not mean that they will 'download' subject material onto the students all lesson. They do more than merely read out the course book and mark assessments. Teachers are the key to ensuring that students make progress in their learning.

Lesson planning

> In too many classrooms teachers worry about having the students active rather than having the students thinking, and even when students are thinking, there is too often too little concern for what students are thinking *about*.
>
> Wiliam, 2014, p. xii

There continues to be a lively debate in the UK about the relative merits and successes of different teaching approaches for Latin. In Chapter 1, we examined the three main approaches that teachers tend to use: the grammar-translation, the reading and the Living Latin approaches. Sensible teachers will choose their methodology appropriately and to suit the nature of individuals in their class rather than their own, and the circumstances under which they are learning. This may vary from day to day or even within a single lesson. Although teachers with whom I have worked might see themselves as generally favouring one approach over another, like all good professionals they are apt to snatch bits and pieces from other approaches when they feel it is right to do so. In general, however, the principles given in the 1988 Department of Education and Science pamphlet *Classics from 5–16: Curriculum Matters* remain just as pertinent today as an aid to planning lessons, whether in the UK or elsewhere:

> Whatever the focus of a particular lesson may be, it should always be made clear to pupils that:
>
> - they learn Latin grammar in order to read Latin, and not vice versa;
> - to comprehend and express the writer's meaning and intention is more important than to reflect precisely the grammatical structures through which he presents them;
> - the subject matter is important, for what it tells them about the classical world and for the light which it may shed on their own;
> - an important aim of the course is an increased facility and flexibility in the comprehension and use of English.
>
> Department of Education and Science, 1988, p. 30

The learning objective

Beginning teachers need to be clear in their own minds what their next lesson is going to be about. They often describe the learning objective in terms of what *activities* the students have performed rather than what *learning* is going to take place.

If the teacher is unable to explain what learning is taking place, then they will not be able to design an appropriate lesson to ensure that it happens. The teacher also needs to know how to judge if and when that learning has taken place. Accordingly, they need to think of ways to monitor or measure what the students produce.

The following are examples of lesson *activities* – not learning objectives.

By the end of the lesson pupils will have:

- *Translated lines 4–10 into their workbooks.*
- *Completed the comprehension – questions 1–3 with the teacher, 4–10 on their own or in pairs.*
- *Written an essay on 'A day in the life of a Roman client'.*

A learning objective is measurable. It is not just the fact that a student or group of students have completed a task. The teacher needs to be able to identify what the students have learnt by what they have written or by what they have said. It needs to be some kind of *product*. In short:

- Does the learning objective define a learning outcome?
- Will it help you to decide whether students have learned anything at the end of the lesson?
- Is it something you will be able to see, hear or read (that is, you must have a way of checking if the objectives have been met)?

Counsell (2003) has compiled a useful list of words and phrases that are very helpful when thinking about learning objectives:

By the end of the lesson, pupils will be able to:

Select . . .
Extract . . .
Give examples of . . .
Relate . . .
Choose . . .
Connect . . .
Link . . .
Explain . . .
Illustrate . . .
Show the relationship between . . .
Explain the relationship between . . .
Comment upon . . .
Remember . . .
Recall . . .
Ask questions about . . .
Choose questions about . . .
Prioritise . . .
Create headings . . .
Refine headings . . .
Justify . . .
Justify their thinking concerning . . .
Explain their thinking concerning . . .
Compare . . .
Contrast . . .
Define . . .
Analyse . . .
Join up . . .
Shape . . .
Organise . . .
Reconsider . . .
Reflect . . .
Support . . .
Support a view that . . .
Evaluate . . .
Weigh up . . .
Create . . .
Construct . . .

Some of the above words and phrases might not at first sight appear obvious ones to choose when you are planning a lesson to teach students Latin. Perhaps the beginning teacher might feel more comfortable using them when teaching Roman civilization or even Latin literature. But I think that these phrases are just as valuable when one thinks about planning lessons on grammar, or preparing students for looking at a Latin story in the original.

Assessment for learning

The teacher should make sure that they know what they want the students to understand by the end of the lesson sequence and what evidence there is of students' progression at each stage. Two main forms of assessment are possible:

- *Summative assessment* is for making judgements about students' attainment: it is an assessment *of* learning at a particular point in time.
- *Formative assessment* is for making improvements in learning: it is assessment *for* learning.

Summative assessment means no more than checking off what the students have attained through written translations and comprehension tasks, essays, exercises, tests and quizzes collected in and marked. The purpose might be to gather data about the level of students' attainment in end-of-term or end-of-year examinations, for certification, or to provide rank-orders of students in a class or year group. But the teacher should not wait for exercises to be completed or for homework to come in and then find out too late that the students did not understand after all. Formative assessment – or Assessment for Learning (AfL) – is defined by the Assessment Reform Group (2002) as: 'The process of seeking and interpreting evidence for use by learners and their teachers to decide where the learners are in their learning, where they need to go and how best to get there.'

Formative assessment is common practice among good classroom teachers. Black and Wiliam (2014) set out the principles of formative assessment as follows:

The research indicates that improving learning through assessment depends on five, deceptively simple, key factors:

- the provision of effective feedback to students;
- the active involvement of students in their own learning;
- adjusting teaching to take account of the results of assessment;
- a recognition of the profound influence assessment has on the motivation and self-esteem of students, both of which are crucial influences on learning;
- the need for students to be able assess themselves and understand how to improve;

At the same time, several inhibiting factors were identified. Among these are:

- a tendency for teachers to assess the quantity of work and presentation rather than the quality of learning;

- greater attention given to marking and grading, much of it tending to lower the self-esteem of students, rather than to providing advice for improvement; and
- teachers not knowing enough about their students' needs.

Black and Wiliam, 2014

As the early-career teacher gains experience, they will carry out much informal formative assessment throughout the lesson. At the beginning, however, formative assessment is something that needs to be built into the lesson, and even experienced teachers need to ensure that regular formative assessment takes place on more formal occasions during the lesson sequence.

The lesson sequence described below in **Case Study 1** shows how each activity builds on the next and allows the teacher at regular points to monitor and informally assess students' growing understanding. Thus the teacher has not just built up a sequence of activities for the sake of providing variety or promoting an element of fun to what might seem an otherwise somewhat dry topic – adjectival agreement. Rather, they have also built in moments when they can check on students' understanding of the underlying concepts *as they go along* rather than at the end, as would happen usually in the case of a summative test on what had been learnt. (In each of the following Case Studies, I have indicated which of the '5 Cs' the example might pertain to, for US readers.)

The class comprised twenty Year 9 students who had reached Stage 15 of the *Cambridge Latin Course*. Up to this point, although they had met many adjectives in the narrative context, there had not yet been any formal discussion about adjectival agreement.

Case Study 1: The Lindens School

Lesson sequence on Adjectival Agreement (Communication / Comparisons)
The first part of the lesson was designed to get the students to notice and then explain how and why adjectives agreed with their nouns, using simple nominative singular examples.

Resources:

- Laminated and enlarged photocopy of image from *Cambridge Latin Course* Stage 15.
- Post-It® notes.
- Photocopied list of adjectives and nouns (jumbled).
- *Cambridge Latin Course* Book 2 (US Unit 2) (for the dictionary).

The students identified the people in the picture and found the appropriate noun from the list. They wrote the noun in Latin/English on a Post-It® note and stuck it on the picture in a suitable place (see Figure 1). They next chose an appropriate adjective from the jumbled list and wrote it next to the noun that they thought it best described. The focus of the activity was on consolidating vocabulary and alerting students to note that the ending of the adjective sometimes does and sometimes does not match the noun ending. This was the focus of the rest of the lesson.

The students were asked to indicate which noun–adjective pairs they chose and to give reasons. The students found the noun vocabulary relatively easy to identify by looking at the picture. They also found choosing the adjectives relatively easy for the same reason, once they had checked the meanings. No student at this stage noted that the adjective–noun pairs sometimes appeared

Figure 1 Student matches adjectives and nouns.

to have the same endings (*ancillae perterritae*) and sometimes did not (*multus sanguis*). When the teacher asked them about this, the students started to notice the endings, but none was able to explain any further why this might be the case. The teacher then asked if the students recalled anything about the formation of adjectives in their modern foreign language study. Several were able to recall that in French adjectives matched their nouns and, with prompting, said that they agreed in gender and whether they were singular or plural. The teacher checked again if that was an opinion widely held. The students agreed that it was, although their knowledge was hazy.

The teacher then asked the students to look back at their pictures and Post-It® notes to see if they could identify how the adjectives and nouns were matching, if not just by the appearance of their endings. The teacher instructed them to use the *Cambridge Latin Course* grammar tables to observe the adjective and noun patterns. As each student found a pattern, the teacher asked them to repeat to the rest of the class what they had said and modelled the examples on the interactive whiteboard (IWB). The students gradually came to notice that the adjectives matched with their nouns: in every example, the adjective–noun pairs were both nominative and singular, while their genders also matched.

It was interesting to note that at this stage the students were not at all worried that some adjectives were from a different declension type to that of the noun (for example, *multus sanguis* or *vir perterritus*). Knowing to which declension a noun or adjective belongs is only important in writing Latin (something these students would never be asked to do) or for later recognition of adjective–noun pairs that were separated in original poetry, for example. Thus the teacher focused on that which was necessary for these students at this particular stage in their learning – that is, giving the students the resources to work out for themselves how the words agreed, with oral support from the teacher and consolidation on the whiteboard.

The teacher decided that the moment was right to move into the section of the lesson where they would be able to identify whether the students had understood the concept of adjectival agreement and were able to explain it back to them with further examples drawn from different cases.

The second lesson was designed to help the pupils explain how adjectives agreed with their nouns in three ways, using examples from different cases.

Resources:

- Set of cards – adjective words (blue) and noun words (beige).
- *Cambridge Latin Course* textbooks (to check genders).
- Screen shot of adjectives table (*bonus -a -um*, *fortis* and *ingens*) on IWB screen (to cross-check endings).

The lesson started with the teacher checking that the pupils knew that adjectives agreed with their noun in three ways: gender, number and case.

The teacher modelled the process that the students were to follow. One student held up a noun – *bestiarum* – and was asked to explain, by reference to the screen shot on the interactive whiteboard, that it was feminine genitive plural. The teacher then explained that his adjective had to be feminine genitive plural as well. The teacher demonstrated this with the adjective card *maginficarum* and got the students to translate the whole adjective–noun phrase. They repeated this process again, but this time with the adjective *ingentium*. They explained that although *bestiarum* and *magnificarum* happened to look the same and both were feminine genitive plural, so were *bestiarum ingentium* – even though they didn't look identical. The teacher indicated this on the screen shot, so the students could see that adjectives from the *bonus -a -um* type and from the *ingens* type had different endings.

The teacher then handed another noun card or an adjective card to each student and explained that they had to find the matching pairs in the classroom. The students then moved around the classroom to match up their adjective and noun pairs. The activity was achieved fairly quickly as the adjective–noun pairs were quite easy to identify – for the most part the teacher had chosen adjective–noun pairs that were from the same declension. Next, the students came to the front of the classroom in their adjective–noun 'pairs' and explained to the class why they thought their words matched. After the first few students' slightly halting explanations, the other students started to understand what they had to do and made their own increasingly confident presentations. After three or four pairs of students had correctly identified the matched words and explained their reasoning, the whole class became confident to talk about gender, number and case agreement; several used the table of adjectives on the screen to check they were explaining the points properly. Although this section of the lesson took some time – maybe fifteen minutes or more – the whole class was focused on the activity and listening intently, partly because they wanted to support their friends, partly because they knew that they were going to be asked to explain to the rest of the class, and partly because they wanted to check they had understood and show it to the teacher. Once the explanation had been given some six or seven times, the teacher was reasonably sure that the whole class had got the underlying concept and were able to explain it.

In discussion afterwards, the teacher and I agreed that the matching-up part of the activity would have been improved further if they had given more thought to the nouns that they had chosen. The teacher had very sensibly chosen vocabulary that was found in the reading material that the students were soon to undertake, thereby using the experience of the present lesson to support future learning. However, they had not thought sufficiently carefully about the particular words they were using. The cases of some words were ambiguous, as far as the students were concerned. Examples of these were: *flos* (third declension, masculine = a flower) was mistaken for an accusative plural from the second declension; *agricola* (first declension, masculine = a farmer) was mistaken for a feminine noun; and *domus* (fourth declension, feminine = a house) was mistaken for the nominative singular from the second declension. Some of these ambiguities might have revealed some interesting and valuable discussions; however, looking at what were for the students at this stage of learning exceptional examples would have detracted from the overall learning objective. We did agree that ambiguity did potentially have a purpose, if suitable adjectives rather than nouns were chosen. Ambiguity is not the same as confusion and could have led to interesting discussions with the students to reveal more of their thinking about agreement. How could one engineer the activity so that the task becomes slightly more demanding yet strengthens the original learning objective? We looked at the length of time the students took to complete the adjective–noun matching. Once the pupils have found their pair, the task was soon over. But if, for example, the teacher had included the adjective *ingentes* along with the nouns *domini* and *puellas*, there would be sufficient ambiguity to challenge the students to explain which of the two nouns they thought the adjective should agree with and why. This would have been particularly useful for the teacher to ascertain how well the students had understood the concept of adjectival agreement.

The well-chosen activities built on student knowledge throughout. The activities engaged students in independent as well as collaborative learning; they built on the students' prior learning experiences both within and outside the classroom; they utilized teacher input at appropriate times; and there were opportunities for the teacher to check the progression of the students' learning through student feedback. In terms of assessment for learning, the teacher was able first to check students' understanding of the meaning of adjectives, then the concept of adjective, ideas about agreement (first gender, then number and finally case), and finally to provide opportunities to discuss ambiguities and how to resolve them through reference to grammar tables and building knowledge of the declension forms. Every one of these steps was not *assumed* by the teacher to have taken place and to have passed by without practice or checking. Traditional summative assessment, such as that carried out by a test in class or by homework, would have revealed any errors of understanding or confusion only afterwards – and it would have been difficult for the teacher to have been able to work out which element the student had found challenging. Meanwhile, the chance for immediate feedback and, where necessary, correction would have been lost. By using assessment for learning, by contrast, the teacher had been able to monitor students' understanding along the way and allowed them to remain confident about students' progress during the lesson.

Written translation as assessment

Can students' written translations be used for informal assessment of learning? Beginning teachers I have taught have often asked whether it is simply enough to expect the students to 'translate the story' – as if writing a translation from Latin into English is all that is required to show that the students have learnt something. The point is that a written translation of a passage is insufficient on its own for the teacher to tell whether the students have actually understood anything. How many times has the teacher 'translated' a Latin text all the way to the end and then had no idea what it was actually about? There are further problems. The teacher who expects the students to hand in a completed written translation at the end of the lesson has no idea how the students achieved it. Is it by chance, or by design? Do the students really understand the new grammatical features that they have translated? Is it guesswork? Did they copy off their neighbour? Also, it seems to me that merely writing a translation from Latin to English during the lesson is a colossal waste of a good learning opportunity. What extra has the teacher brought to the learning in that lesson? How much has the individual student learnt from others in the class? How much opportunity have they been given to ask questions, deliberate and think of alternative ways of thinking about the topic – if all they do is sit for twenty minutes or more and write a translation? There will come a point when the student will be expected to write a translation down from Latin into English – and maybe the other way around too. The most common form of assessment of understanding of Latin is still the formal written translation from Latin into English. But that may be for later – in the assessment part of the course – the one that has been planned ahead for. At the moment, teacher and students are in the teaching and learning part of the course. A written translation is only one of many ways to reveal student understanding – and can be a pretty poor one at that. We will have a look at some transcripts of students working on a written translation later in this chapter to see the sort of challenges they face and the lessons that we as teachers might learn in order to improve our teaching.

Variety of activity

Beginning teachers are often concerned that there is insufficient variety of activity in a lesson and that the students will become bored or too passive. As a result, the lesson plan consists of different sorts of activity almost for their own sake. Different sorts of activity can be important. For example, they may facilitate a specific learning objective that cannot be achieved by any other method, or they may provide the extra motivation that is needed for effective learning to take place. A set of different activities may be the ideal way in which knowledge and understanding is constructed through the lesson. A sequence of different activities, each building up knowledge step by step, can be a very effective way of planning a lesson. In the same way, planning a set of different activities that look at the same topic from slightly different perspectives may be a useful way to increase the depth and detail of understanding. But the teacher should first of all consider whether they are merely thinking of things to do rather than of the underlying learning process.

It is essential, therefore, that the teacher knows the resources sufficiently well. If the teacher makes their own resources, they must serve the function properly and not provide distractions from the lesson objective.

Building on prior knowledge

The students' prior knowledge is a good place from which to begin. At the start of the lesson, make a link with what they have been taught before. This is useful for you to gauge their recollection and understanding of what you taught them. If it turns out they do not remember, then you have the option of recapitulating briefly or starting all over again. The prior knowledge of the students is not restricted to that which has been taught in previous Latin lessons. From September 2014, when the new Primary National Curriculum came into force in England, secondary school Latin teachers will know that all state-educated students will have learnt about some Roman historical events, perhaps some classical mythology, a modern foreign language, and maybe even Latin itself. Students' awareness of the Roman world may also have been stimulated by visits to see Roman artefacts at local museums and sites of interest or by television programmes, films and even computer games. The teacher should be alert to recent news about Classical finds and aim to incorporate them into classroom discussion wherever possible. In general, however, the teacher must ensure that the link between previous and present learning is clear both to themselves and to their students.

Thinking about teacher language

The teacher should plan which words to use. The learning objective and the stages by which it is reached are articulated by the use of language. I do not just mean the technical terms we use for talking about grammar – accusative, indirect statement and so on. Nor do I just mean the language we use when talking about literature – such as *simile* or *tricolon*. With this vocabulary the teacher has to take care that the students understand the application of the word as well as its meaning – something that is quite challenging in itself, as we shall see later. What I do mean – and what is rather more important – is the *choice* of English or Latin words when the teacher is instructing the students or modelling an example.

Beginning teachers often fail to make the different parts of a lesson explicit to the students. This is not simply an act of kindness – to share what is obvious in the teacher's head with the class – it is about shaping the students' understanding of the topic: the purpose of the activity and its place in the sequence. You need to think very carefully about how you articulate each stage of the learning process. Phrases such as 'What we have just been looking at is . . . Now we are going to . . .', 'Well, I think we have all got the idea of . . . Now we are going to do something slightly different with that same material . . .', and 'Do you remember how we . . .? Let's have another look at this point, but looking at it in a different way' are prime examples of articulating the sequence of activities in a lesson. In fact, if the beginning teacher thinks of such phrases at the planning stage, it will often lead to a better understanding of the order and purpose of activities themselves. If the teacher cannot explain to the class why they have done something, then it is fairly clear that the activity was not necessary or poorly thought through.

The precise words that the teacher uses when modelling an example are also important. When teaching a grammar point, the teacher should always try to go from the concrete to the abstract. By this I mean that the teacher should model whole Latin sentences rather than phrases or words, drawing on examples which the students have already seen in practice or which use vocabulary with which they are already familiar. These sentences should always be in Latin rather than in English, as the students are being taught how to analyse Latin, and English grammar can sometimes be ambiguous – especially to students for whom it is not the mother language. They should start with what the sentence *means* before they begin to analyse how the meaning is *conveyed*. Unless the students need to write Latin, there is little point in telling them how to form it if all they have to do is recognize and understand the form of the part of speech. It is better to use sentences rather than single words, and better to use vocabulary which is familiar to them and which is regular. This ensures the learning focus is on the feature that the teacher desires.

Case Study 2 is an extract from a lesson where the beginning teacher has not planned the language they are going to use in their explanation of the meaning of the gerundive. The class consisted of fourteen Year 10 students who had been studying the *Cambridge Latin Course* for two years.

Case Study 2: Beechtree School

Lesson on gerundives (Communication / Comparisons)

Teacher: Right. Today we are going to learn about [writes on board as they speak] *gerundives*. Now, gerundives are quite hard. There are three types but I'm going to teach you the easiest one – so there's nothing to trip you up – unlike the rest of Latin, which is always trying to trip you up with some little difficulty or other.

Mandy: What's a gerundive?

Teacher: That's what I'm going to tell you. Now, the gerundive is formed from the second of the four principal parts of a verb. So here we have our typical verb [writes it on the whiteboard as they speak], *porto, portare, portavi, portatum.*

Olivia: Do you want us to write this down?

Teacher: Not yet, not 'til I say.
            [The students start to copy the note into their books]

Teacher: Now, we have to take off the *-re* off the infinitive here [writes]. Can anyone remind me what the infinitive means?

Mandy: Does it mean 'I . . .'
Teacher: No. Remember – the *-re* ending means, means?
Olivia: *To.*
Teacher: That's right. *To.* So we take off the *-re* . . .
Austen: Why have you written *portatum*? It's usually *portatus*.
Teacher: That's because, that's because it's the supine.
Austen: What's that?
Teacher: It's a part of the verb, a part – well, you don't need to know at the moment – you don't need to know . . . the Cambridge Latin Course shows it as a PPP, a PPP, and so does the GCSE vocab list, I think, yes, I think it does. But that's not the way dictionaries show it, no, they don't . . .
Mandy: What does it mean?
Teacher: The infinitive?
Mandy: The gerundive?
Teacher: Yes, yes, I was coming to that. You take the *-re* off and add *-andum*. There [writing on the board] we've got it.
Olivia: [copying into her book] *-andum*. What's it mean?
Teacher: It means 'something needing to be done'.
Olivia: Shall we write that down?
Teacher: Yes, if you want to. [Pause] Now I'm going to teach you the easy way in which the gerundive is used, because it's a horribly complicated one otherwise. Let's say we had a sentence like this [writes] *ad regem necandum* – what does that mean?
Simon: There's a *king* in there.
Teacher: That's right! There's a *king*. Now there's another word in there that we all know really well, isn't there? Isn't there? [Pupils nod]. It's, it's . . .
Austen: *ad.*
Teacher: That's right, that's right. *ad* – it means, it means . . .?
Austen: [Triumphantly] *to.*
Teacher: No. Not here, not here – it means *for the purpose of*.
Austen: Oh.
Teacher: So this sentence here means *For the purpose of killing the king*.
Olivia: But I thought it meant *needing to be somethinged* – where's the *needing* bit?

The main problems in this lesson extract stem from the teacher's preference for an explanation of the *formation* of the gerundive rather than its *meaning*. The phrase they choose – *ad regem necandum* – would be made more comprehensible to the students as a clause expressing *purpose* if it had been attached to a main clause. Seeing the clause in its context would have made many of the questions unlikely and could have led to better discussion of different ways to translate the phrase. The teacher confuses the students from the start with contradictory statements about the difficulty of the construction ('quite hard') but its apparent simplicity ('the easiest one'). There is much irrelevance, from the lengthy explanation about the formation of the gerundive to students who never need to write one, to the notes about the meaning of the infinitive and the difference between the supine and the perfect passive participle. This last seems to indicate a lack of familiarity with the course book and the examination specifications that the students themselves are using, and perhaps reflects the teacher's own hazy memory of writing Latin at university. There is also inconsistency: the teacher uses a different verb to model the formation of the gerundive (*porto*) from the one in the sample phrase (*neco*) and their first explanation of the meaning of the gerundive ('*something needing to be done*') given in response to Olivia's request for clarification fails to match up with their second ('*for the purpose of*').

The teacher's mixed messages perhaps belie some of their own insecurity about the construction. They seem to externalize their personal anxiety to the students. The resultant lack of clarity of exposition makes the teacher appear ignorant and demoralizes the students. The teacher attempts to use students' responses as a way of monitoring their understanding of the various stages of the explanation. But the teacher does not seem to have planned the most suitable questions to ask, or what to do when the responses are not as expected.

A common feature of beginning teachers is that they find it difficult to pitch the language they use at the right level for their students. This is exacerbated when they are teaching perhaps four or five lessons a day with students ranging in age from 11 to 18. They may recall their own university experience of discussing highly complex grammatical and literary features, and sometimes forget that their students are still at school. In the same way, they sometimes use language that is too simple, forgetting that although the vocabulary and grammar in the early stages of learning Latin are relatively simple, the students have a much more developed use and understanding of their own language. The language the teacher uses therefore needs to be consistent, non-patronizing, clear and concise.

Differentiation / adaptive teaching

Differentiation can be defined as the process by which curriculum objectives, teaching methods, assessment methods, resources and learning activities are planned to cater for the needs of individual pupils. In the UK, the term 'differentiation' is considered by the Department for Education to comprise the ways in which the teacher adapts their teaching, rather than adapts the resources, to the needs of their students, particularly with regard to lower attaining students and those with Special Educational Needs. It therefore prefers the term 'adaptive teaching' to that of 'differentiation' and refers to this new nomenclature in its Initial Teacher Training Core Content Framework (Department for Education, 2022). For a good resource for thinking about inclusive and adaptive teaching, although not Latin-specific, see

Westwood (2018). When planning a lesson, differentiation should be an integral part of the planning process. The teacher should consider from the start the stage of learning that the individual students have reached and what skills and abilities they have. The teacher should then consider what materials are suitable for the students in order for them to achieve the learning objective. To me, therefore, differentiation is not about the students doing different things, it is about the students doing the same thing differently. There are a number of differentiation strategies that can be employed.

Differentiation by outcome

Beginning teachers often find it easiest to think of differentiation in terms of the framework:

- All students must . . .
- Most students may . . .
- Some students might . . .

The following **Case Study 3** lesson utilizes this approach.

Case Study 3: Tiptree School

Class reading of Cambridge Latin Course Stage 25: venatio I and II (Communication / Connections)

The class rapidly reads the story *venatio* together with the teacher – a fast-paced story about a terrible accident at a crocodile-hunting party. There is a mixture of oral comprehension questions from the teacher, with a particular focus on specific Latin phrases and vocabulary that enhances the storytelling. After the reading, the students write a personal response to the story, entitled 'How does the story hold the reader's interest?'

The teacher's expectation is that:

- **All** must recall the main features of the story: the locations where the action takes place, the process by which the Ethiopians catch crocodiles, the details of the accident that causes *Barbillus'* boat to capsize, and the reactions of the crew to the situation. This is the minimum expectation.
- **Most** might be able to do the above, and also will be able to explain how the elements of the story generate interest for the reader. They refer to specific parts of the story and explain why they are especially interesting to the reader: which are descriptive (the Nile marshes), full of anticipation (the astrologer's warning; the preparation of the crocodile bait), excitement (the killing of the crocodiles) and horror (the capsizing of *Barbillus'* boat and his wounding). Latin words or phrases may be referred to, but without any specific reasons.

- **Some** may be able to the above, and also will quote Latin words and phrases that are explicitly used to emphasize the parts of the story. This is the maximum expectation.

In differentiation by outcome, all students are given the same resources and activity. They work at their own level and achieve different levels of outcome. Such an approach depends on the students all being able to access the same materials. The teacher would rather like the students to be able to analyse how the use of Latin words and phrases enhances the reader's interest, but is not over-anxious if most of them do not. In essence, this form of differentiation is the same as that employed in a summative assessment exercise, when the teacher wishes to rank students by the success they achieve in completing the same task. As a way of helping students improve their learning, except by perhaps rewarding those who perform well and embarrassing those who do badly, differentiation by outcome is not considered to be a particularly successful way.

Differentiation by outcome is easy to achieve for the teacher. However, it can lead to some students never being able to improve their knowledge and understanding, as they are not given the extra or different resources they might need. This sort of differentiation is primarily focused on the final product not the student's learning process. Accordingly, it is better to consider the following forms of differentiation when starting to plan a lesson.

Differentiation by product

Differentiation by product is when the teacher sets the same task to all the students, but they are allowed to respond to it in different ways. In some cases, students are allowed autonomy of choice; in others, the teacher allocates specific tasks to students, ensuring that the task suits each particular student's learning needs. More demanding tasks can be set for some students. The important thing to remember is that the individual student products combine at some point in the lesson sequence so that all students are able to contribute to the overall learning objective.

For example, different students might work on different types of response to the same piece of Latin literature. In the Latin class discussed by Downes et al. (2012), for instance, students were reading *Regulus* from the *Cambridge Latin Anthology* (Pliny 2, 20). In the first part of the lesson, the class was divided into three groups, ordered by the row in which they were sitting in the classroom:

> The first row reflected on the way *Pliny* manipulates our feelings against *Regulus*, which I felt was the easiest question. The middle row was asked to think about the way that *Pliny* adds pace and immediacy to his story. The final row had to consider the portrayal of *Verania's* superstitious nature.
>
> Downes et al., 2012, p. 26

In the second part of the lesson, the three groups took it in turns to present their ideas to the rest of the class.

The success of this type of differentiated activity relies on sufficient allocation of time to enable the student groups to make their presentations to each other. The students, by listening to each other, accumulate the different responses and gain a more fully rounded understanding of the same piece of literature. Another example might be where individual students present information about a topic in different formats. Students might choose a newspaper article, a poster, a poem or even a radio interview as a way of responding to the events of a gladiatorial display, for example. The important thing is that the different student products all contribute to an overall understanding of the same thing. They are not ends in themselves. In order to achieve this, students either need an opportunity in the lesson to showcase their own products formally, or work alongside one another, ideally collaboratively, in order that they learn from each other.

Differentiation by input

Differentiation by input relies on the teacher providing different resources to help students achieve the same task. An example might be for the teacher to provide an extra vocabulary list for some students, or for there to be an extension question to challenge the higher-attaining students.

There is some debate as to whether providing extra information like extra vocabulary is 'fair'. But to my mind questions of fairness only apply when students are being asked to complete some form of summative assessment, in order to rank their performance. In the majority of cases, teachers are finding ways to improve students' capabilities. We know that some students progress faster and further than others, and that learning is not linear. Some students need extra support at the start or at different times along the way. A student who does not 'get it' from the beginning should not be left to fossilize and progress no further. Accordingly, I recommend that extra resources are made available. These extra resources might not amount to very much, but they may be *just* enough to achieve what is necessary to give confidence to a student not to give up.

Below I present a case study of a teacher trainee's experiences when they prepared an extra resource for students in my Year 7 class of thirty-one mixed-ability students who were in the very early stages of learning Latin in *Cambridge Latin Course* Stage 3. A cloze exercise (or gap-fill) can be a useful way to focus the attention of students on particular items. Typically, a cloze exercise will consist of a translation of the whole story, missing out certain words that have a common theme, such as tenses, cases or particular syntax. They can form a diagnostic for the teacher or practice of a new feature. The teacher trainee in **Case Study 4** proposed a cloze exercise as a support for the lower-attaining students in the class.

Case Study 4: Hollyoaks School

Differentiation using a cloze exercise with Cambridge Latin Course Stage 3 (Communication)

The class had reached the story '*pictor*', which is practising the use of the accusative case in the first, second and third declensions. The teacher trainee had detected from earlier lessons that overall the students' knowledge of vocabulary was weak, and in some cases very poor indeed. The teacher trainee had not taken into consideration the fact that the reading approach purposely exposes students to a large vocabulary at a pace, and it is unlikely at this stage of the students' learning that they would have learnt all the words they had met so far, let alone find it easy to pick up the new words in the passage. Nevertheless, the teacher trainee decided to measure the success of the students' ability to comprehend Latin by getting them to write a translation of the passage into English. Inevitably their knowledge of vocabulary was preventing them making the progress that the teacher trainee felt was desired. They had noted that the higher-attaining students remembered more of the Latin vocabulary, but, when they did not remember it, they made good use of the *Cambridge Latin Course* dictionary. Meanwhile, the lower-attaining students had difficulty both recalling the meaning of the vocabulary words and retrieving them from the dictionary. Often, when they *did* find the meaning of the words, they seemed to find it difficult to remember the words they had just looked up when they were flipping back and forth between dictionary and story. This rendered it even more challenging for these students to translate the passage into English.

The teacher trainee focused on the use of the dictionary and decided that a suitable way to help lower-attaining students reach the same goal as the higher-attaining ones was by creating a cloze exercise for the same passage. Thus the higher-attaining students would translate '*pictor*' direct from the Latin to the English, while the lower-attaining ones would receive the passage half-translated, with gaps to complete in English (see Figure 2).

Once the cloze activity had been completed and the results taken in, the teacher trainee realized that they should have gone back to basics. What had seemed to be a suitable differentiation strategy had turned out not to be the case at all. The lower-attaining students did not seem to have found the cloze exercise any more straightforward. Although there were fewer words for the students to 'look up' in the dictionary, progress was just as slow as before. What the teacher trainee had not realized is that for the student to understand which word had been missed out, they still had to read every word in Latin and understand their meaning, just as in the case when they had simply to translate the words into English. The only difference seemed to be in the number of words that they actually had to write down. But the process of comprehending the whole passage was as slow and painful as it had been in the first place.

pictor, the artist

1) Read the story on page 29 and fill in the gaps.

The artist comes to _____

The artist is _____

Celer knocks at _____ .

Clemens does not hear _____ .

The slave is in _____ . Celer shouts.

The dog hears _____ and barks. Quintus _____ the dog.

Quintus comes to the door. _____ opens _____ .

Celer _____ _____ and enters the house.

Metella is in _____ . Quintus calls _____ .

Metella enters _____ . The artist _____

_____ .

Metella takes _____ into the dining room.

2) **Now finish off the translation from line 8 to 13 in your books.**

FIGURE 2 Cloze exercise for *Cambridge Latin Course* Stage 3 'pictor'.

This led the teacher trainee to rethink what had caused the lack of progress initially. The fact that the cloze exercise had not helped the lower-attaining students to make it easier for them to progress through the passage now drew their attention to focus on the efficacy of the student output – the translation – as a measure of success. In the case of the higher-attaining students, the output was a word-for-word translation into English of the Latin text. For the lower-attaining students, the output was a partial translation of the same passage. But this left the teacher trainee in a quandary. Was it *right* that the lower-achieving students had somehow to do less to get to the same point as the higher-attaining ones? It did not seem so. But then the lower-attaining students had *not* got to the same point as the higher-attaining ones anyway. As a way of facilitating progress to the same point, the cloze exercise had been a failure. It was then that the teacher trainee realized they should be thinking also about the *process* by which students of all attainments achieved the translation. That was of more interest. The teacher trainee now recalled the difficulties they had observed the lower-attaining students experiencing in previous lessons. There were several things of note:

- Students did not find it easy to recall vocabulary, to look the words up in the dictionary, and to carry them back with them to the passage ready for translating the whole sentence.
- Students seemed to lose their place in the Latin text, and missed out words and even sentences.
- Students seemed to be unclear about the difference between nouns and verbs. So, for example, the words *pingit, pictor* and *pictura* were often confused, which did not facilitate translation.

It now seemed obvious. For the lower-attaining students, progress was slowed by two factors: the practical issues of using the dictionary and following the text, and the conceptual understanding of word types. The first practical issue could be dealt with simply by one of the following: suggesting that the students work in pairs, one with the dictionary to look up words and the other with the text open; providing students with a complete vocabulary list for the text; providing students with two book marks, one for the dictionary and one for the text. The second practical issue could be dealt with by providing the students with a photocopy of the story (sometimes enlarged), so that they could cross off the words, sentences and phrases as they translated them. The third issue was to be achieved by the teacher trainee being more explicit in class discussion about how the students should be able to recognize Latin nouns and verbs and model how they are used in the context of sentences.

The teacher trainee successfully identified the sticking point that was holding back the lower-attaining students from successfully completing the task. They found that for the lower-attaining students it was not so much new differentiated resources that were necessary but the better use of already existing resources. As the lower-attaining students were using pretty much the same resources as the higher-attaining ones, they felt that there was parity of fairness in the class: after all, the lower-attaining students were less likely to fossilize in their learning this way, suffer less demotivation from being seen to have different sorts of activity, and ought to begin to improve in their learning. The teacher trainee also saved a great deal of time and energy having to make whole sets of differentiated worksheets.

Sanchez reached a similar conclusion in her article evaluating four differentiation strategies in her Ancient History class. She wrote:

> I began this study thinking of differentiation in terms of tasks, but have learnt that differentiation is more about directing learning than teaching, and that optimal learning happens when conditions are in place for students to learn actively. [...] I was guilty of being attracted to the more concrete and simplified concepts of differentiation by task and by outcome. Instead, I realized that is was not so much the activity that the students performed, but the way in which they learned. [...] I have learned to spend less time focusing on the tasks in class and more on how I can create the *right conditions for independent learning*. This had been a concept that I had originally found intimidating in its vastness, but I can now appreciate it as a prerequisite for successful learning.
>
> Sanchez, 2014, p. 29

After experimentation in the classroom, both Sanchez and my teacher trainee learnt that differentiation should be conceptualized not in terms of what the student products consist of, but in terms of what the teacher does to facilitate and develop learning processes.

Differentiation by questioning

The most frequently used form of differentiation is differentiation by questioning. Of all the differentiation examples, this is the closest example of adaptive teaching as promoted by the Department for Education. When the teacher asks a question of students in the class, they adapt the question type to the needs of the student. In the classics *triadic* type of questioning (teacher asks question – student responds – teacher confirms response), it may be that they ask what they perceive to be simple factual questions of lower-attaining students, and more searching conceptual questions of higher achievers. Although this is a form of differentiation, it does not achieve much more than the teacher feeling satisfied that justice has been served. However, the point of differentiation is that students of all abilities are able to achieve or learn to achieve the same learning objectives.

Accordingly, while the initial question may indeed be a straightforward one, the way in which the teacher carefully structures the follow-up question – or preferably a series of questions – is vital to support and develop the students' learning yet further. Such 'dialogic' teaching (Alexander, 2004) has a huge part to play in supporting the low-attaining and extending the high-attaining students. With dialogic teaching the question is not just designed to provide an opportunity for the student to 'get it right', instead it requires:

- **interactions** which encourage students to think, and to think in different ways
- **questions** which invite much more than simple recall
- **answers** which are justified, followed up and built upon rather than merely received
- **feedback** which informs and leads thinking forward as well as encourages
- **contributions** which are extended rather than fragmented
- **exchanges** which chain together into coherent and deepening lines of enquiry
- **discussion and argumentation** which probe and challenge rather than unquestioningly accept
- **professional engagement with subject matter** which liberates classroom discourse from the safe and conventional
- **classroom organization, climate and relationships** which make all this possible.

Alexander, 2004

Case Study 5 below contains some of my own comments on the transcript of an early-career teacher's questioning of students and identifies moments when the teacher could have made greater use of differentiated questioning. The fifteen male students were in their third year of learning Latin. They had started translating the passage 'amor omnia vincit' from *Cambridge Latin Course* Stage 29 around the class. What is interesting about this extract is how the teacher seems to be unsure whether they are providing too little or too much support. This makes the teacher appear resistant to the idea of offering anything but the minimum and they do not offer the students strategies to comprehend meaning or praise them when they do succeed. In essence, the problem seems to stem from the fact that the teacher has not yet worked out what the activity is for beyond turning it into some sort of English. They do not see the opportunities within the text for teaching students of differing attainment. It is this lack of clarity in the teacher's mind that is making them hesitant about how to support the students' learning and challenge and thereby motivate them. The teacher is also anxious about the progress the students are making – anxiety that is transferred onto the students, resulting in a classroom environment that is not conducive to effective learning.

Case Study 5: The Willows School

Reading Cambridge Latin Course Stage 29, 'amor omnia vincit: scaena tertia' (Connections)
Here are the original Latin lines:

Bulbus:	*Gutta, volo te haec vestimenta induere. volo te personam Vilbiae agere. necesse est nobis decipere Modestum, quem brevi exspecto.* [The teacher starts with a brief outline of what the passage is going to be about]
Teacher:	It's different from what the usual stories are about – it's kind of like a play rather than a story about something . . . and it's like the other stories . . . this one is a love story . . . [The teacher asks Jonny to read the Latin out loud. Then they ask Hanif to translate the story into English out loud]
Hanif:	*Gutta* . . . [pauses]
Teacher:	*volo?* Remember: he is speaking . . .
Hanif:	*I want . . . I want this . . .*
Teacher:	Not *this.*
Hanif:	[to teacher] What's *te?*
Teacher:	What's that? *te.* We had *te* before . . .
Hanif:	*I want you . . .*
Teacher:	[confirming] *I want you . . .*
Hanif:	I don't know what *induere* means . . .
Jordan:	[interrupting] *Endure.*
Teacher:	Not *endure . . .*
Benedict:	[noticing the gloss at the side of the text] *To put on . . .*
Teacher:	Yes. *To put on.*
Hanif:	*I want you to put on these clothes.*
Teacher:	[asking next student to continue] Michael? [Michael reads the next section aloud in Latin]
Teacher:	[cross] In *English*, please – clearly not listening!
Michael:	*I want . . . you . . .* [pause]

Teacher:	[referring to the gloss] It's given on the right.
Michael:	. . . *to play the part of Vilbia. When* . . . *nobis* . . . erm . . . I know . . . I've forgotten *nobis. It is necessary for you to* . . .
Teacher:	Not *tibi* – *nobis!*
Michael:	*It is necessary for us to* . . .
Teacher:	We've had *quem* . . .
Michael:	Oh. *For. In a short time* – *I expect in a short time* . . .
Teacher:	What's happening?
Rocco:	He's getting his friend to dress as a woman.
Teacher:	I'm bringing out some sheets – you can write on the sheets. Timothy, what am I going to ask you to do?
Timothy:	Stick it in.

The teacher's introductory comments are designed to offer a way into the story for the students. The initial premise is not revealed, but there is the promise of excitement. It is a love story. But the teacher leaves the students in considerable doubt about what the love story might consist of. Although this might be deliberate – to whet their appetite for more, the comments are rather more than ambiguous: they are confusing. It would have been better for the teacher to have said something like: 'The story is set as a play. This will allow several of you to take the parts of the characters. We haven't met these characters before – but I can tell you that one of them is in love with someone – and that the path of true love, as we know, is never easy. There's going to be an element of *deception* . . . and it's a *comedy*.'

The teacher is right to ask a student to read the passage aloud. This allows a little time for the students to prepare themselves briefly before they are asked to translate. An even better approach would have been for a lengthier passage to be read, in which some part of the action mentioned by the teacher in their introduction might be revealed, thus encouraging the students to believe that the passage is worth reading. At the end of such a reading, students might be asked an overarching question to check their understanding of some of the main points in the story but which leaves enough room for closer inspection to reveal the details and correct misunderstanding. Such an overarching question needs to be carefully thought about beforehand. It has to get the students thinking about the passage in such a way that a quick skim read will start the process of them wanting to look into it in more detail. Such a question might be: 'Something strange is going on here – can you tell me what it is?', followed up by 'What does *Bulbus* want *Gutta* to do? What does he want to achieve?' The story is a vehicle for learning the language: it is not just a story to be read (enjoyable though that might be). The students are interested first in *what* it tells us about these Romans, and then as a check on the understanding of the language, *how* the Latin tells it. That this is partly happening is most evident when Rocco realizes what is going on in the story and he says, 'He's getting his friend to dress as a woman.' It is a wonderful moment of revelation for the students as a group and an opportunity for the teacher to explore Rocco's line of reasoning and sense of expectation. The teacher could have capitalized on his observation by asking him to explain what he thinks is going to happen next, which could have led into further opportunities to interrogate the text for more details.

Questions that challenge the students to look closely at the text and to predict events and the outcome of the story are powerful teaching tools. Yet the teacher is focused on merely getting through the text as quickly as possible and restricts their questioning to helping students recall items of vocabulary. Take Hanif and Michael's fumbling attempts to translate their three Latin sentences: both students focus exclusively on the meaning of the individual words rather than on the syntax of the sentences. The teacher ought to have thought more about the questions they asked in order to get the students to compare the three sentences to show how they are similar. Here they are one under the other, with some highlighting to indicate the similarity in structure of each:

> <u>volo</u> **te** haec vestimenta <u>induere</u>.
> <u>volo</u> **te** personam Vilbiae <u>agere</u>.
> <u>necesse est</u> **nobis** <u>decipere</u> Modestum, quem brevi exspecto.

As you can see, each sentence follows the typical *Cambridge Latin Course* fashion – with a pattern set up, followed by a disruption of the pattern (main verb + accusative pronoun + infinitive (× 2)/verbal phrase + dative pronoun + infinitive).

The teacher does not, however, make use of this sentence patterning as a tool to teach the students. As far as they are concerned, merely translating the words will suffice. In the same way that they have failed to show an interest in the development of the story and how that might motivate the students to read further, they have failed to use the Latin in front of them to teach the students how to comprehend it. Hanif easily recalled *volo* but then stumbled at the next word. The teacher's repetition of *te* somehow enabled Hanif to recall the meaning, but then he fell again at the next hurdle – the word *induere*, which Benedict helpfully supplied by looking at the gloss. Hanif's agony over, the teacher moved on to the next line. In this simple sentence, Hanif did indeed put the words together to make his sentence, but he remains none the wiser as to how he might have got there if the teacher and the helpful Benedict had not been present. Next in line, Michael plunges in successfully with *I want you* and then flounders a while until he is rewarded by the whole of the rest of the phrase being presented to him in the gloss. He struggles with the relative clause until he gets some sort of understanding about what it means, even if he seems to be grammatically insecure in both Latin and English. He does not, however, translate the sentences at all in a way that shows he has really understood the *meaning* of the Latin, before the teacher moves off into the security of a written activity.

What sort of things could the teacher have done? Just at the point when Michael had said '*I want you*', the teacher could have referred Hanif and his classmates to the exact same type of phrase as had occurred in the previous line. They could have recalled to the class how Hanif had naturally looked for the infinitive *induere* to follow on from *volo te* and they could have instructed Michael and the class to look for the equivalent in his sentence – *agere*. This use of the infinitive in these types of clause could have been consolidated with the next one, which follows the phrase *necesse est* – *decipere*. Thus the teacher is thinking not so much about getting through the passage as quickly and painlessly as possible, but thinking ahead about what learning opportunities there are within the text. When Hanif struggled with his sentence, the teacher should have been alert to the possibilities of the text to check, correct and consolidate with subsequent students. By involving all of them in a hunt for similar phrases or grammatical features, the teacher could both support those who were struggling as well as stretch those who were already following the meaning of the text but who were perhaps not looking as closely as they could at the syntactical features and the exact meaning of the Latin.

Differentiation by intervention

Differentiation by intervention is when the teacher realizes during the lesson that some students need a different approach, different resources or use of resources, different questioning styles or types of questions, or even modification of the task during the lesson in order for them to be able to complete the task.

Differentiation by progressive questioning

Differentiation by progressive questioning can take place during a class discussion or when using a worksheet. In a class discussion, the teacher can ask more straightforward questions of lower-attaining students and, building on their responses, direct more challenging questions to the higher-attaining ones. It is important that the questions directed at the lower-attaining students are explicitly linked to the more challenging ones. Similar progressive questioning can be used on a worksheet, with more straightforward questions at the start and more challenging ones towards the end. However, the teacher needs to be careful to set out the questions in such a way that lower-attaining students are led into completing some of the more challenging questions.

Differentiation by grouping

Differentiation by grouping is when the teacher groups the students according to their prior attainment, their gender, or some other classification.

Differentiation by task

Differentiation by task is when different students are given different tasks to complete. Some teachers think that it is reasonable for the tasks not to be related to a common topic, though I disagree. I believe that the point of differentiation is to ensure that all students in a class – each in their own way – are able to access the same topic. Some will take longer, some will require extra resources, some will need a different sort of questioning, some might even perform different tasks – but all activities should contribute to the same understanding overall.

Process not product

Differentiation, therefore, needs to be thought of not so much as an add-on – some extra activity for the higher-attaining students and something easier for the lower-attaining students. Instead, it should be considered as a normal part of the planning of a lesson sequence. The teacher should consider the process of learning as well as the end product. They should aim to provide the right conditions, resources and teaching approaches that will facilitate every student's access to the topic, enabling them to make a contribution to the overall learning objective.

Universal Design for Learning

Universal Design for Learning (UDL) is defined as 'an instructional framework that seeks to give all students equal opportunities to learn, by providing multiple means of representation, of action and expression, and engagement' (Cooper-Martin & Wolanin, 2014, p. 1, quoted in Westwood, 2018). In UDL, students would engage with the teaching and materials in multiple ways, including the use of written materials, watching films and videos, listening to podcasts and so on – something that a number of Latin teachers and organizations are beginning to experiment with post-Covid (when digital resources became much more widely-used) and also in recognition of the variety of students who make up the student body. Coe and Hunt (2022) collated some practical suggestions for adaptive teaching Latin literature, but the subject is only beginning to receive serious attention in schools. There is, however, a much stronger recognition, for example, of being aware of the needs of neuro-divergent students in the universities, which is beginning to filter down into the school classroom (see, for example, the organizers of the Asterion website, whose mission is to raise the profile of neurodiversity, to celebrate the achievements of neurodivergent Classicists, and to tackle barriers to inclusion through support and training (https://asterion.uk)).

Teaching Latin through stories

The most common resource used by teachers to teach students Latin is the Latin story. I deliberately use the word 'story' rather than 'passage' or 'text' because I think it helps us conceptualize that the object through which our students are going to learn is something that conveys *meaning* first. 'Text' implies a series of individual words that might be utilized in a different, primarily linguistic way. Depending on the course book, this story might be made-up Latin or an extract from an original author.

There are two ultimate aims: one is for the student to have developed the necessary knowledge and understanding to be able to comprehend a passage of Latin that they have not seen before (known as an 'unseen' or an 'at sight' passage); the other is for the student to be able to comprehend Latin literature in the original. Comprehension of Latin stories has traditionally been tested by oral or written translation into English, by answers in English to questions asked in English (or occasionally Latin), by analysis of the grammatical or stylistic features of the story, or by making a personal response to it. This section explores teaching strategies and examples of how to teach with a story in the earlier stages of learning Latin.

There are many activities a teacher could use to expose students to a Latin story, including:

- listening to the story being read;
- reading the story aloud;
- translating the story orally;
- writing a translation of the story;
- answering questions on the story;
- skim-reading the story for clues about character, setting and narrative;
- analysing the way the Latin is constructed;
- watching a dramatic performance of the story;
- performing the story;
- representing the story through creative activities;
- comparing different translations or representations of the story.

Before we look at some of the sorts of activities that the teacher might employ, we should consider the students' learning preferences.

Thinking about cognition

The traditional approach to learning Latin was, as we have discussed in Chapter 1, the grammar-translation approach. There has been a very small resurgence of interest in the grammar-translation approach in UK secondary schools and much of the teaching in independent preparatory schools (for students aged 5–13) is based on it.

But it is noticeable that where these grammar-translation courses are being used, it is (to my knowledge) mainly among students in the academically selective sector. Teachers in most other schools in the UK seem to prefer the reading approach – reading course books that they perceive to be more accessible to a wider range of students. By contrast, in the USA the grammar-translation and reading approaches have equally strong adherents, with the Living Latin approach in a strong third place, as we have seen. Students very rarely get to choose the course book that will be used in class, and so, the teacher needs to be aware of the variety of students in the classroom and plan the way in which they are going to teach and their students learn appropriately. Deagon (2006) warns of what happens if the teacher privileges one learning style, such as the grammar-translation approach, over another:

> Traditional Latin instruction, emphasizing a strong orientation to grammar and meticulous attention to detail, favours a particular kind of student: one who learns well sequentially, is field-independent (i.e. sensitized to subtle differences such as case endings), puts high value on memory work and rules, prefers abstractions to concrete realities, and prefers to study alone. [...] The brightest students with these learning styles will be able to adapt to the needs of a traditional course, but others will become bored and not want to continue, or become alienated from a language they may have been initially interested in learning, describing it as 'too hard' or 'useless'. This situation must be remedied if Latin is to be taught effectively, and, bluntly, if it is going to continue to be a viable language in today's schools and universities.
>
> Deagon, 2006, pp. 33–34

In the same chapter Deagon (2006) refers to 'cognitive styles' and how the teacher should be aware of the different 'types' of learner and tailor teaching accordingly. Howard Gardner's (1983) theory of multiple intelligences has also been popular in the past as a way of thinking about how teachers structure learning and resource materials by taking into consideration the supposed 'learning styles' of their students. More recently, Gardner's theory has come under criticism as having no basis in empirical evidence (Riener & Willingham, 2010) and the present guidance in the Initial Teacher Education Core Content Framework from the Department for Education in the UK is to tell teachers to disregard it (Department for Education, 2022). On the other hand, we should also remember that when we are teaching a group of students in the classroom, teaching and learning is very much a collaborative venture: each student will learn something new or learn how to learn something new from the Latin passage or exercise by working with and listening to the experiences and practices of the teacher and the other students. Teaching and learning does not take place in a social vacuum. The teacher therefore should be prepared at all times to adapt their teaching to the needs and interests of all students in the class and remember that a great deal of what and how students learn may well be tacit rather than explicit. Teachers need to adapt their teaching to their students, not provide different sorts of materials for different students to use.

At the time of writing, in the UK Department for Education and Ofqual recommend that teachers take note of cognitive science in their teaching practice. Much is made of cognitive load theory, retrieval practice and interleaving. (Department for Education, 2022), with reference made to Rosenshine's Ten Principles of Instruction (2012) and others. One has to be careful, however, in that much of the cited research is not classroom-based but experimental, and almost none of it pertains to learning languages, let alone classical languages. There is much to be said for reducing the cognitive load when teaching languages (by, for example, providing interlinear translations while explaining grammar, or by providing multiple forms of supplementary support materials, or manipulating the text – see examples in this book and in Hunt (2022a)), the danger is that government-approved fads (see Learning Styles themselves from twenty years ago!) do not last long or are misapplied. I worry, for example, that the current encouragement for retrieval practice works well only up to a point, as far as language is concerned – and this mostly on the word level (recall of vocabulary or morphology) rather than on the phrase and sentence level. So, to be short, while it is important to know vocabulary, it is not enough merely to recall it; the student needs to have plenty of practice using it or seeing it in context with other words, as part of something which makes meaning. Time spent on retrieval practice takes time away from using it or seeing it in context. For those interested in retrieval practice in the classroom, non-specific to Latin, see for example Jones (2019).

The next section investigates approaches to teaching students to comprehend Latin using the sort of stories that are common in reading-approach course books. Grammar-translation course books tend to have a regular set of instructions for the student (and teacher) to follow. Procedure and purpose are written out: there is a focus on learning vocabulary lists and grammar tables; a translation is to be completed; practice exercises to be done. Instructions for students throughout *Latin for the New Millennium* – which describes itself as providing 'a fusion approach to Latin combining the best practices of the reading method, the traditional grammar approach, and a cumulative vocabulary foundation' (Bolchazy-Carducci Publishers, Inc., 2014) – leave them in little doubt what they are supposed to be achieving at any one point. But even with this course book, with its Latin reading passages and conversational Latin dialogues, there is as much scope for teachers to vary the style of learning, as is normal with courses such as the *Cambridge Latin Course, ecce Romani, Suburani* and the *Oxford Latin Course*, which more fully adhere to the reading approach.

Latin aloud

The importance of hearing and seeing the words is the best place to start. One reason for allowing students to hear Latin being read aloud is, of course, that its literature was written originally to be heard by an audience. Fifty or so years ago, Thompson gave an impassioned warning against the deadening effect of Latin teachers' preference for the written word and silent translation, and it still holds true today:

> One of the first things we must do is to rid our pupils (and ourselves, if necessary) of the notion that language is something distinct from literature and that its study is pedantic and even inhumane. [...] This demands that we as teachers insist on the utmost accuracy in pronunciation (both for ourselves and for our pupils) as being of vital importance if the full literary value of ... Latin verse and prose is to be gained by the boys and girls we teach.
>
> Thompson, 1962, pp. 20–21

Thompson recognizes that reading aloud can play a part in linking language and literature together in the students' minds. It is, however, only one reason why it is important. Much more so is the role reading aloud plays in learning language itself.

Latin has a regular and easy pronunciation, compared with many other foreign languages, and its alphabetic system is the same as that of most students learning it. Nevertheless, students in the early stages of learning still need to develop the 'hearing eye' and the 'seeing ear'. An item of vocabulary that appears simple to the teacher – *appropinquabamus* – can be incomprehensible at first to the student: a collection of syllables without rhyme or reason. The teacher needs to realize that students' internalization of vocabulary will normally be a long and slow process. Spotting words in a story spoken by the teacher is challenging for students when they are still unfamiliar with them. The teacher needs to read the story aloud, not too fast, and with a consistent pronunciation, while the students follow it on the page, perhaps repeating it aloud themselves. In general, students should develop the ability to 'see' words that have been heard. Rendall reminds us of the steps a student of modern foreign languages takes between first meeting a word and learning it:

- First they have to be able to match sound and meaning to the written word.
- Then they must be able to pick out the correct written equivalent when they first hear the word or phrase spoken.
- Then they have to be able to visualize the word when they hear it.
- They have to be able to distinguish between correct and incorrect versions of the word or phrase.
- And then finally they have to be able to produce the correct version both orally and in writing, checking all the time with the internalized version now carried inside their head.
- When they can do all this, they will have learnt the word.

Rendall, 1998, p. 12

Through frequent practice of seeing and hearing and perhaps repeating vocabulary, students will come to internalize the meanings and start to recognize and understand the significance of morphology. I go into the importance of asking students to listen to Latin and to read it aloud in Hunt (2022a). Accordingly, at all stages the teacher should make use of the learning potential of reading Latin aloud – whether by the teacher or by the student. Guides are available in most course books for teachers unsure about how to pronounce Classical Latin, and recordings of the stories used in most widely used course books are available in digital form. Details of these are given in Section 3 of this book.

Teaching not testing

The teacher should be sure they know *why* they are going through a story. If the teacher falls into the mentality that it is merely procedural (that it's 2.30 pm on a Thursday and they are in the room with the pupils with a Latin book in front of them – what else is there to do than *go through it*?), then they should *think again*. The aim in using stories is *not merely to get to the end*.

A very common activity that I have seen in classrooms is students silently writing a translation from Latin to English. When asked why the teacher is getting them to do this, the most common response is 'to practise'. 'To practise what?' The response to this is frequently circular: 'To practise unseens'. (In the UK, Latin texts that students have not seen before and that are set for silent, individual written translation into English are common features of summative assessment practice. In the USA, these are sometimes called 'at-sight' passages.) But practising unseens is not a learning activity – or if it is, it is only one particular kind: learning how to pass an assessment based on translating an unseen. And most of the time, the errors a student makes only get corrected once the teacher 'goes over' the text in class, or, more frequently, after they have corrected it and handed it back some days later. I worry in particular about this when I see students silently translating one of the stories from the beginning of a stage or chapter, *before they have been taught anything*. The stories in books that use the reading approach are there not as *tests* but as *teaching and learning tools*. Teaching students to comprehend Latin stories generally needs teacher input at most stages, but especially at the start when a new language feature is being presented. Some teachers believe the idea of the reading approach is that students will learn the new language point inductively for and by themselves. And sometimes they do. But for the most part they do not, or they only get it partly right. The teacher cannot afford to take the risk. And did the student get it right by design or by accident? How much can the teacher be sure that the student is internalizing the correct way to go about the business of learning to comprehend Latin? The early stories in a new stage or chapter are designed to alert students to a new language feature that the teacher must use to probe, develop and consolidate through further reading and examples together with the students. I have come to believe that this is one of the defining differences between the approaches of the grammar-translation course book approach and that of the reading-comprehension / comprehensible input: in the former, the Latin passage is written as a test on the new language material presented before it; in the latter it is the start of a conversation about the new language material. This means that the pedagogical approach for each has to be different: the former is a test bed for material, the latter a learning programme – and that difference will highlight the amount of support that the teacher will need to give to the student.

Clues about how students comprehend a Latin story

First, we will look at what we can learn about how students 'do' a written translation. It is a good place to start from, as we can build and develop our teaching strategies if we know the sort of things that students think about when they do such an activity. **Case Study 6** is a transcript of the discussion between two students working together on producing a written translation from Latin into English.

Case Study 6: Cedarbridge School

Written translation from Latin to English (Communication / Cultures / Connections)

The following transcript affords some insight into the way in which students go about the process of translating a continuous Latin passage. Mike and Sian are in Year 10, in the third year of learning Latin. They are of average attainment and have chosen to continue with Latin to GCSE examination after one year's compulsory lessons. They are translating the passage *'fons sacer'* from *Cambridge Latin Course* Stage 21. All the students have already read lines 1–11 together and through class discussion have established the historical and social context in which the piece is set. They know that British *King Cogidubnus*, feeling ill, is asking the advice of his friends, the Romans *Salvius* and *Quintus*, about whether he ought to visit the Roman baths at *Aquae Sulis* to seek a cure. The new language feature – the perfect passive participle – has been the subject of preliminary discussion through the reading of model sentences in the previous lesson, but it has not been mentioned by the teacher in the context of this lesson.

The teacher has asked the students to make a written translation of the remaining lines (lines 12–20) in pairs.

Sian: *aegroti* . . . *Ill people* . . . or [said sarcastically] <u>peasants</u>.
Mike: Huh! I just wrote the Latin!
Sian: *Many who drunk* . . . *biberunt* . . . there's no *bat* – past tense – . . .
        *who drunk from the fountain, the water, the water from the fountain
        – got better afterwards.*

Mike:	[unintelligible]
Sian:	Is it? Erm . . . it's *fountain*, a *fountain* or something – no. Oh, I don't know.
Mike:	I don't care, but I should. [Looking at the story] *The Roman architect – missus –* Let's see what *missus* is.
Sian:	Check to see if it's in the vocabulary first.
Mike:	See if it is . . . [checking in the vocabulary].
Sian:	What?
Mike:	Sian, I have no idea – oh *send* . . . *send him to me.*
Sian:	*a me missus – A Roman architect, send him to me . . .*
Mike:	Something about *He* . . .
Sian:	*He can build the perfect bath* . . .
Mike:	*Baths* or *bath? He builds* or *he can build?*
Sian:	[nonchalantly] Back in the day when they built the perfect bath.
Mike:	*Builds* or *built?*
Sian:	*prope stat templum* . . . *Near the bath . . . of the goddess . . . Near the baths stands the temple of Sulis.*
Mike:	What does *prope* mean?
Sian:	*Near the baths.* I just said it.
Mike:	*a meis fabris. fabris, fabris* or *fabis?*
Sian:	*fabris –* we did it yesterday – it's *fabris – workmen.*
Mike:	What does it say?
Sian:	*Me craftsmen build –* wait! – is it *big building* or *building . . . my . . .*
Mike:	It's *meis – me . . . me . . . me . . . m-e-i . . . m-e-i . . . m-e-i..*
Sian:	*I build . . .*
Mike:	*They will build me, build me, build it for me . . .*
Sian:	*I . . .*
Mike:	*They built it for me . . .*
Sian:	*By me . . .*
Mike:	*It was built by my craftsmen.*
Sian:	Oh! *Built by . . . by craftsmen. I honour the goddess.* Wait! *saepe. Often, I often honour the whatever.*
Mike:	*The goddess, I often honoured the goddess. I often honoured the goddess . . .*
Sian:	*fortasse . . .*
Mike:	There are so many of these words which I used to know but I forgot . . .
Sian:	I know the words! It's annoying! I'm not able to . . . [starts to look up words in the dictionary] . . . erm . . . *fortasse . . . fortasse . . .* I knew that word, I just knew that word! [Reading the letters of the alphabet in the dictionary] B . . . C . . . D . . . F . . . *Perhaps.*
Mike:	[to a friend] Sian's working so I'm taking a rest.
Sian:	*Now, perhaps the goddess can heal me.* Oh, OK. *Perhaps she . . .* (this is fun) . . . *can heal me. Salvius can go . . .* No. *You are a man*

who can, . . . *You are a man* . . . [to herself] (apparently Salvius is a man) . . . *clever. You are a very clever* . . . or it says right there [noticing the word gloss at the side of the story] . . . *You are a man of great cleverness* – [to herself] is that a word? *volo. I want. You. To. Give me advice. You are a man of great cleverness.*

Mike: Yo! I need to catch up! [Mike starts to copy down Sian work]

Sian: *You should . . . must . . . quid . . . quid* . . . I don't know what *quid* is . . . *What . . . should I do? . . . facere . . . What should I do? . . . What should I do? . . . You are a man of great wisdom* . . . Yes. *melius, melius* . . . is *will . . . miracle . . . It is better you to . . . to be . . . .it is better for you . . . better for you to . . .*

Mike: Is this a complimenting thing – *You are a man of great wisdom, a man of great . . .?*

Sian: *It will be better for you to will do . . . to do a will.* Oh! [looks surprised]

Mike: He's going to die.

Sian: . . . *better to make a will.* That's a bit depressing. Basically he's saying you're going to die.

Teacher: You have one more minute.

Sian: [drawing] Sad face 'cos that's sad.

Note: All spellings, punctuation, crossings-out and errors are the students' own.

Sian's written translation:
'It is in the town of Bath', said Cogidubnus. 'many sick people, who drunk the water from the fountain, recovered after. That Roman Architect, ~~send him~~ sent by me, he ~~can~~ builds the perfect baths. Near the baths stands a temple of the Goddess Sulis, built by my craftsmen. I often honoured the Goddess; now perhaps the Goddess can heal me. Salvius, you are a man of great cleverness; I want you to give me advice. What should I do?'

  'You are a man of great wisdom,' he responded. 'It would be better for you to make your will.' ☹

Mike's written translation:
'Is in the town of Aquis Sulis', said Cogidubnus. 'many sick people, who drunk ~~from~~ the ~~water~~ water, got better afterwards. A roman architect, ~~send him to me~~ sent by me he can build the perfect bath. Near the temple bath for the Goddess Sulis, ~~they were both built it~~ it was built by my craftsmen. I often honoured the goddess, ~~now he perhaps~~ now perhaps the Goddess can heal me. 'Salvius, you are a man of great ~~cleverness~~ cleverness; I want you to give me advice. What should I do?'

  'You are a man of great wisdom,' he respond. It will be better for you to make a will

Below are some observations and comments about the students' dialogue and their written translations and how they might help us to think about teaching strategies.

The story is not written purely to introduce new vocabulary. The vocabulary is a means of providing a sufficiently interesting narrative for a new language topic. Yet these students are spending the majority of their time gathering and understanding vocabulary in order to make sense of the story rather than on recognizing and understanding the new language point. The students' use of vocabulary gathering strategies is not methodical, however, and looking words up in the dictionary takes them a lot of time. Sian's sudden recollection that there is glossed vocabulary (*'You are a very clever . . .* or it says right there: *You are a man of great cleverness* – [to herself] is that a word?') reminds us yet again of how students forget the help that is already provided. Students often need reminding that the title of the story, incidental images and glossed vocabulary help to scaffold understanding of the written story. Sian's frustration at not being able to remember words ('I know the words! It's annoying! I'm not able to . . . erm . . . *fortasse . . . fortasse* . . . I knew that word, I just knew that word!') belies the fact that the effort required in physically looking the word up while repeating it back to herself again and again is a good way to learn it. The students' sharing of responsibility, with Sian doing most of the looking up while Mike helps with the translation, is also worth noting. If the purpose of the activity is for students to use whatever resources they can – and that includes each other – to come to a conclusion about what happens in the story, then sharing responsibilities is an effective way of achieving this. Students can learn a lot from each other.

Mike seems to sound out the Latin word when he is trying to recall the meaning of a word from memory; he seems to do the same when he is looking for a definition from the dictionary. Seeing, hearing and sounding a word is helpful and reminds us of the importance of the oral/aural in Latin learning.

It takes the students time to recall words. Teachers often expect instant answers from students, especially in the type of lesson where the students translate one by one round the room.

The students also repeat phrases to themselves – fragments of translation – until a 'best fit' is found. Thus Mike's *'They will build me, build me, build it for me . . .'* and Sian's *'melius, melius . . . is will . . . miracle . . . It is better you to . . . to be . . . it is better for you . . . better for you to . . .'* slowly grasp at the meaning by trying out various permutations. This 'building up' of meaning sometimes occurs when the students try to translate on their own. It also occurs when the students work together, as the two of them bat ideas back and forth until the 'eureka' moment. This method seems to be the main strategy for translating. Once the vocabulary has been recalled, they juggle the words around until they make English sense. They are helped in this in two ways:

- By using their own common sense when they think they know what the meaning of the sentence is. Sometimes they do this on their own, and at other times they share their thoughts – 'borrowing the other person's brain', as one of my teacher trainees called it.

- By following the underlying storyline that supports their understanding of the meaning of the passage. This is perhaps particularly evident if we consider Mike's comment about what he calls the complimentary phrase, 'You are a man of great wisdom' and by both students' recognition at the end of the passage that one of the main characters will die.

The students are alert to how much the grammar affects meaning but are rather imprecise about checking. Sian notes that *biberunt* does not have the usual imperfect ending – *bat* – but then, perhaps, through insecurity in understanding the terminology, declares after all that the verb is not in a past tense. Nevertheless, she still translates the verb as a perfect *they drunk* [sic], and the other verbs correctly too. The story is composed of significant pieces of direct speech. This gives the biggest clue to the fact that many of the verbs are in the present tense. But neither student checks their hypotheses. Mike tries out various ways of dealing with the phrase *thermas exstruxerunt* ('*Baths* or *bath*? *He builds* or *he can build*?'). He is clearly aware that such things as singular and plural and the precise tense of the verb are what matters. The guesswork evident here alerts us that we need to remind students from the earliest stages of the importance of accuracy and where to look to check.

The students rely upon a number of individual signpost words. When they start to translate the phrase *a me missus*, they find the new language feature – the perfect passive participle – not easy to translate at first. Mike starts with recalling the vocabulary, doing his usual trick of repeating the words to himself: '*a meis fabris. fabris. fabris* or *fabis*?' Once they know the vocabulary, Sian merely repeats the words in the order in which they appear in Latin: '*Me craftsmen build* – wait! – is it *big building* or *building . . . my . .*', which Mike proceeds to work on: 'It's *meis* – *me . . . me . . . me . . . m-e-i . . . m-e-i . . . m-e-i . . .*'. Sian's attempts '*They will build me, build me, build it for me . . .*' seem to be rejected as being nonsensical: no-one can be said to be built. The students have not noticed that *aedificatum* agrees with *templum* – which might be one way of resolving the sense of the phrase. Instead, Sian recalls that the word *a* means *by* and Mike remembers the meaning of the word *fabris*. The two of them put the words together and unlock the meaning of the whole phrase:

Mike: *It was built by my craftsmen.*
Sian: Oh! *Built by . . . by craftsmen.*

The students intuitively reach consensus on how to translate the new language feature – the perfect passive participle. The signpost words themselves release the meaning of the phrase. This suggests that students comprehend Latin more successfully when they think in phrase lengths rather than in simple words. This is a feature of how the reading approach works. The teacher should teach students to identify which sorts of vocabulary signposts are the most effective at unlocking the meaning of phrases as an aid to translation. The students, by struggling to make sense of the new language feature, have become alerted to it and the teacher will provide consolidation using the exercises that follow in the course book.

The teacher allows the students sufficient time to complete the comprehension of the story. If the story is worth starting, then it is worth completing. The teacher who states 'it doesn't matter if you haven't finished' risks demotivating the students who have been led to believe that the piece was worth reading. Furthermore, the story is meant to be read as a complete narrative. Not only will it contain just the right number of language features that the course book authors have decided are necessary to achieve the learning objective, but also the student needs to comprehend all the elements of the story to gain the reward for the trouble of reading it. The students' sudden grasp of the significance of the will in this story quite shocks them – Sian is moved to draw a 'sad face' at the end of her work – and would not have been achieved if they had been stopped prematurely. My teacher trainees named this the 'penny dropping moment', when the pieces of the jigsaw all fitted together. Teachers should be wary, therefore, of trying to improve the pace at which students complete a task like this by splitting the story into sections, with different students or groups of students assigned to different parts. Often events in the middle or end of a story are dependent on students' understanding of what has happened in the earlier parts; sometimes the significant new language features are grouped together in one part of the story and not the others, causing one group of students to be challenged more than another. If, for reasons of time or efficiency, the teacher wishes to split the story up, it is best for them to work with students on the first part all together (as is the case with lines 1–10 in the lesson recounted), with the students working on the next section by themselves or in groups, with further consolidation – perhaps with contributions from the higher-attaining students – of the final few lines, where the 'penny drops'. The shared experience of this moment leads to a feeling of achievement – not just for having got to the end, but for having realized the point of the story.

Reading philosophy argues that language is learnt as part of a cultural and social mixture not as an abstract concept. Vocabulary is met in the context of a real world and is thus easier to remember and think about because it is pinned to a memorable and interesting narrative event. It becomes meaningful because the recall and use of it has purpose. Motivation and engagement through reading to find out culturally important information and to find out what happens in the story are therefore very important to the reading course. Karsten (1971) provides a very good round-up of the sorts of comprehension questions that might achieve this. At the same time, the reading of the story itself serves to introduce, underpin, reacquaint and reinforce the new language features. The reading course requires careful plotting of each individual language feature in its own context. Each linguistic feature is introduced separately, or occasionally compared with another direct equal (e.g. imperfect and perfect tenses) – so the reading course builds up sentences from the smallest units to the larger, step by step. The student sees new grammatical features in the context of phrases and sentences rather than stem and individual morphological changes. The concepts of gender, number and case, tenses, subordinate clauses and so on, can be more easily absorbed through seeing examples in a longer setting – where there is more support from context – rather than through concocting or translating sentences using charts and tables. Language is, after all, a conveyor of meaning not just as a series of linguistic puzzles.

Latin round the class

Teachers often ask students to translate a Latin story out loud around the class. This has the advantage that it is the students who do most of the talking rather than the teacher, and there is no doubt that students may learn from each other in this way. But it is not to be relied upon. Argetsinger, discussing first-year US college students of Latin, points out:

> Even some very good students … when they are forced to sit 'idle', or to listen to other students struggling with material they already understand, … become bored … This sense of boredom may contribute at least as much to the attrition rate in Latin programs as the sense of confusion or inability to master the material that some other students feel.
> Argetsinger, 2006, p. 69

We know that students in a classroom, who on the whole have been allotted Latin rather than chosen it, might not be as peaceable as bored undergraduates fulfilling their language course requirement; school students are also rarely allowed to abandon class. The teacher's request for individual students to provide a translation, word for word, of a story that has not been seen before, in front of their peers, at short notice, can be terrifying. Almost certainly a student who does not know how to translate a Latin sentence will be little wiser from hearing another student do so, whether haltingly or effortlessly: they are either reading ahead to prepare for the next question, in a state of nervous excitement that they might next be asked, or merely resting quietly because they have been asked already and are unlikely to be asked again. Various ways have been suggested to take the sting out of this kind of student performance before their peers, most of which involve students preparing the story before presenting responses in class. The first aim should be to provide a comfortable setting in which all students' voices can be heard, where difficulties about their understanding can be expressed to each other and to the teacher, and they can learn new strategies when others have failed. Deagon (2006) suggests, for example, that pre-reading exercises for grammar or for information may be useful for students who have different learning styles. However, the time when this pre-reading takes place can affect the learning outcome significantly. It is not clear from her account when such pre-reading activities might take place. One can assume that they are meant to be part of the lesson itself, where such prior discussion has particular saliency and where the teacher is personally able to monitor and guide learning. By contrast, taking the pre-reading out of the classroom context bears the risk of the students having insufficient support from the teacher at the first and most significant stage in the process of comprehending a Latin story, as Natoli reported of his own experiments with the flipped-classroom model with a university beginners' Latin class:

> What was missing was active, in-person modelling that is so crucial to an introductory language course. Learners simply did not have the tools to interpret not only the Latin grammar and syntax, but also the way in which to approach the language itself.
>
> Natoli, 2014, p. 39

The teacher needs to create an opportunity for the students to work cooperatively with one another and with the teacher either on a pre-reading activity based on the Latin story or simply on the Latin story itself. Social interaction and the construction of knowledge through group work is the key idea, following the familiar idea of the *Zone of Proximal Development* (Vygotsky, 1978). There are, of course, some potential problems that can occur: students may not know enough to be able to help their peers; they may make errors; or individuals may refuse to work with one another. The teacher's responsibility therefore is to monitor and provide support where necessary; to use plenaries to ensure progress is being made; and to assign particular tasks (such as scribing or dictionary use) to named students in the groups.

Very simple but effective activities can be adopted in small groups – things which are never fully 'performed' in front of the class, but which help the students gain confidence. Mini-whiteboards seem to be good ways of encouraging the more reticent students: the impermanence of the writing encourages greater expressiveness and risk-taking. They also allow easy drafting and redrafting of ideas. Several students can be given different coloured marker pens to show that they have each made a contribution. Simply reading the story in Latin to each other before class also helps: they gain a little understanding of the story and can follow the discussion in class as they have been given the opportunity to skim the Latin and practise out of the spotlight. At the end, students might be asked to feed back their responses to the whole class, with an appointed spokesperson from each group (who, having discussed the ideas with the other group members, should feel that they are speaking with greater authority than if they had been asked on their own); or the groups are reconfigured in such a way (such as by 'jigsawing') that they share their knowledge with each other. Group activities can often be very productive, but it must be emphasized that the teacher's role is not just as a facilitator. One of the purposes of group activities is to provide students with the time and the resources (which include each other as well as any printed material and, of course, the teacher) in a mutually supportive atmosphere to prepare for further whole-class comprehension and discussion of a Latin story.

Dialogic teaching and Latin

Bakhtin (1984) argued that the main way in which we develop thought is through 'dialogic talk'. Students learn by listening and responding to what others say until they are able to make the pronouncements for themselves. The teacher should therefore ensure that there is plenty of rich and stimulating material to talk about in the classroom and be prepared to teach the students not just the *what* but also the *how* to talk about it. Alexander (2004) argues that this 'dialogic teaching' can be a very powerful tool to improve students' knowledge and understanding.

Case Study 7 provides a transcript of a very simple exchange between teacher and students as they discuss a picture of gladiators fighting. It illustrates how the teacher uses a number of simple questions to encourage the students to look closely at the image and to make inferences about the action in the scene from what they are able to see.

Case Study 7: The Pines School

Students and teacher discussing an original Roman artefact (Cultures / Connections / Comparisons / Communities)

Teacher:	We've got this picture here. There's an image of two gladiators. Let's start with this: which one do you think is winning? The one on the left or the one on the right? Who's winning?
George:	The one on the left.
Teacher:	The one on the left. Why do you think that one?
George:	Because he's attacking.
Teacher:	He's attacking. Right! How do you know he's attacking? Come on, show me.
George:	He hasn't got his sword, and, like, he hasn't got his shield, and . . .
Szilvia:	Some, some gladiators don't actually have shields . . .
Christopher:	The other one doesn't have a shield . . .
Teacher:	Does this one on the left-hand side here, the left-hand side, does he have a shield?
George:	No.
Teacher:	No.
Katy:	It's on the floor.
Teacher:	It's on the floor.
Katy:	He's dropped it to start attacking . . .
Teacher:	So do we think he has dropped his shield and he's now attacking with his little dagger, or . . .
Szilvia:	Maybe his hand's been cut off . . .
Teacher:	I don't think his hand's been cut off . . .

Habiba:	Why's there a hole?
Teacher:	We'll come to the hole in a minute? Pretend the hole doesn't exist. So we've got a man on the left-hand side. He's got a dagger. His shield is on the floor. Do you think he is winning or do you think he's losing?
George:	He's losing.
Teacher:	Now we think he's losing. Why do we think he's losing? Because . . .
George:	The other one's standing on it.
Teacher:	That's right. The man on the right is standing on the shield, stopping the other one from picking it up. It looks like he's winning, doesn't it?

I give this as an example because it is easier to tell what is going on from the dialogue about a picture than from the dialogue about a Latin story. Notice how the teacher probes the students' responses and, by keeping some of the options open, encourages them to rethink some of their initial ideas. The dialogue is mostly focused on one student, but others are welcome to contribute. Irrelevant responses are batted away politely. The teacher draws the discussion to a close with the confirmation that the students' understanding of what the scene represented was correct. The teacher knows where they want to get to: it is not chance.

In her book on the teaching of mathematics, Lampert describes the essence of the dialogic teaching model and why it is successful:

> In each interaction in a public discussion, a teacher can use a student or a student's connection with some mathematics to teach the student while also teaching the class as a whole. At the same time, she might also teach a particular group of students like 'those who finished problem C' or 'those who are not yet facile with times tables'.
>
> Lampert, 2001, p. 174

Lampert identifies three choices she needs to make during the discussion: choosing the question herself, choosing who will respond, and choosing whether another student can make a contribution. When a student responds, she continues:

> There are several subsequent moves that can be made to turn that response into a resource productive of teaching and learning:
>
> - when an assertion is made, choosing to stay with the student who made it and requesting an explanation;
> - when an assertion is made, choosing to stay with the student who made it and suggesting my interpretation;
> - when an assertion is made, moving to other students and requesting a counterspeculation;
> - when an assertion is made, moving to other students and requesting an explanation.

Whichever of these actions is chosen, the teacher can then continue by

- Asking additional students to comment on another student's thinking;
- Rephrasing a student's explanation in more precise mathematical terms and asking them to comment; or
- Creating a representation of the student's talk on the chalkboard.

Each of these acts of teaching makes more potential resources available. Students can take advantage of them as opportunities to study, and the teacher, to teach.

Lampert, 2001, p. 175

Such an approach can also be very effective in Latin teaching, especially with a story that contains a richness of discussion points. So rich, perhaps, that the teacher needs to ensure that they draw on only the most important ones, which they need everyone in the class to understand. When initiating such a dialogue with a class of students, it is important to engage them with specific questions and to think ahead about the sort of responses one might receive and how to deal with them. At first, the following aspects should be taken into consideration:

- What happened before this story? How might the outcome of previous stories affect the students' understanding of what happens in this story?
- What happens in this story that is essential knowledge to maintain the story thread?
- What happens in the next story? How is it connected to the present one?

The answers to these questions could be about socio-cultural features, language features or both. Time needs to be factored in to allow students to recall the prior learning that this lesson builds upon, to consolidate what has been learnt and to prepare for the next lesson: the students need to know that the lesson is part of a sequence of learning.

Next, the teacher should look for the learning opportunities within the story itself: what is this story for except as a *tool for learning*? Merely *reading it through* and *getting to the end* is not enough. The Latin in course books – whether it is authentic or made-up – has usually been written by the authors or chosen by the editors to develop students' understanding of language features first and foremost. The narrative provides the rich, socio-cultural background in which the more abstract language features are embedded. Therefore, the teacher needs to maintain a balance between thinking of the story as something that motivates the students to read the Latin for meaning, and also as something that teaches them how to develop knowledge and understanding about the language itself. If the authors or editors have chosen wisely, all the stories will help achieve both of these aims. Some suggestions are given below of the sorts of things the teacher needs to look out for. I have subdivided them into external and internal features: the first are those which are not part of the actual Latin story, but are accessories to it, around the edges and elsewhere in the course book; the second are those features that are contained within the Latin story itself.

External features

Line drawings and photographs often appear on the same page as the story or in near proximity. Sometimes the authors of the course book have selected images which are directly relevant to the stories and which can be used to stimulate the students' curiosity to read the Latin. The teacher might ask the students to examine a picture for clues about the story, or point out that a particular artefact has a role to play within the story that they are about to read. Alternatively, as the story is read, students may be referred to the picture to act as a visual reminder of what is going on.

Students should be directed to the title of the story, which will help prepare them for what the reading is about. The title often gives away clues about the main characters in the story, including the names of people and places mentioned in the story. This simple strategy is helpful, of course, when the student is translating an unseen/at-sight translation.

Word glosses often give students some guidance as to the shape of the whole story: the teacher might set them the challenge to predict what the story is about. Vocabulary given in the gloss can have different purposes. It may contain new or relatively rare vocabulary that aids understanding of the story, or specific types of vocabulary that help support the learning of new syntax features. As the students internalize the vocabulary, it is gradually withdrawn and replaced by new examples.

I recommend that students should learn early how to use a dictionary. Different course books use different ways of presenting the information at the start (for example, the *Cambridge Latin Course* does not give the traditional nominative and genitive singular and gender of nouns at the start), and the teacher should teach students the meaning of dictionary entries as required. The same goes for the use of grammar tables and charts: students should be taught how to interpret and use the information in them. But too much the other way – the memorization of tables and charts – can lead to disaffection and boredom and a loss of interest in the story itself.

Internal features

Genre can often be helpful to students when reading a story. Course book authors and editors try to include different literary genres for the sake of variety in the stories, and also because they allow greater variety in the type of language used (such as increased use of the present tense and first and second person verb endings in dialogue-type stories). Short plays, dialogues, ghost stories, political intrigues, travelogues, wills, letters, prayers and incantations, stories that are comic or tragic or both – all of these provide opportunities for teachers to alert students to the effect that genre may have on the style and content of the story and how this might help comprehension.

Vocabulary is clearly important to understanding the story. Vocabulary knowledge and reading comprehension are very closely related to one another (Stahl, 1990,

Tutorial on how to use the CLC !

quoted in Nation, 2001, p. 144). But it is not essential for a student to know all the vocabulary before they can comprehend the story. It can be a two-way process: vocabulary helps reading and reading helps vocabulary (Chall, 1987, quoted in Nation, 2001, p. 144). The teacher should take the view that developing students' vocabulary knowledge is a means to an end: that of comprehending the story. Thus they need to decide which words are significant – for to give equal time to all will be a Herculean task and risks the students being confused by having to take too much in. Rather than focus mostly on the meaning of every item of vocabulary, the teacher should look for patterns and links between lexical items across the story that serve as markers and opportunities for learning or for consolidation. We will look more at learning vocabulary in other ways later in this chapter.

The same approach should be used for learning about grammar. The story acts as a vehicle for the new grammatical feature as well as providing opportunities to practise previous ones. Typically, it will contain two or three examples of the same feature, each of which follows the same or very similar patterning. There then follows a disruption of the pattern, which the student needs to have their attention drawn to if they have not already noticed it for themselves. The cognitive challenge of trying to solve the problem by comparison with what has previously been learnt drives the learning process. The teacher therefore needs to think carefully about how to deal with each stage of this process: setting the students up to recognize and understand the pattern, and then developing their understanding with the new example. I recommend that choosing a small number of examples before the lesson to serve the specific purpose of the teacher will achieve greater understanding than any number of examples chosen at random as the lesson progresses.

The reading-comprehension approach is designed to develop students' abilities to comprehend original Latin. It is important to remember that the students are learning Latin grammar in order to read Latin, not reading Latin in order to spot Latin grammar. (It seems odd, therefore, that current GCSE and A Level questions ask students to do precisely that.) Sometimes teachers feel that the story itself provides all the material required for the student to understand the new language feature; at other times they may feel the need for some more formal instruction and consolidation through practice exercises. All widely used course books provide these, but they differ in the order in which they place them in the sequence of activities. *Suburani* and the *Cambridge Latin Course* put the formal grammar-input 'About the Language' section *after* the stories. It follows the principle that explanation follows reading: the students need only be taught the formal, more abstract aspects of the language once they have met concrete examples in the context of meaningful stories. The teacher must make sure, therefore, that they *do* make that explicit connection between the reading of the stories and the explanation of the language features. The *Cambridge Latin Course* does refer each time to this fact, by repeating the phrase 'as we have seen', but students do not always pick up on it. The *Oxford Latin Course* has its reading materials at the front of the book and its language explanations at the back, which makes the connection between the two quite challenging physically if not intellectually. With the other reading approach courses, the connection tends to be made more explicit within the text of the book itself. *ecce Romani* and *Latin for the New Millennium* offer quite lengthy explanations about the new language features contained within their reading material. While these course books subscribe to the idea that students should first experience Latin through reading a story, they tend to offer their own explanations about the new language features earlier than that of the *Cambridge Latin Course* and *Suburani*. All the course books tend to use familiar vocabulary and sentences from the just-read stories. This maintains focus on the language feature and is important to remember if the teacher decides to model their own examples for the students.

In short, then, the sequence of activities will probably take the following pattern. Ideally, this should be achieved over no more than two back-to-back lessons of, say, 45 minutes each, depending on the length of the story and the complexity of the language feature:

- Recall of students' prior socio-cultural and/or language knowledge.
- Comprehension of the story, to elicit meaning.
- Drawing attention to selected language features embedded in the story.
- Checking that students are able to sum up the story and can show what they have learnt.
- Anticipation of the next stage of learning.

In the follow-up lessons:

- Formalization of the new language feature and consolidation of learning.

Reading a Latin story round the class is still a high-risk venture, even with the best-made plans. The following classroom examples show some further simple ways to help support the teacher and the students as they read.

Motivating students to read

The teacher should let the students know why they are reading a particular story. This does not mean, however, that every last detail needs to be given away. Although teachers are encouraged to make learning objectives clear to students at the start of lessons, this does not necessarily mean that the precise process by which students will achieve them needs to be made explicit. A well-judged and interesting question or piece of tantalizing information can often be sufficient to indicate the purpose of the lesson. For example, in **Case Study 8** below, the teacher used a simple sketch to introduce the two stories *Vilbia* and *Modestus* from *Cambridge Latin Course* Stage 22.

Case Study 8: The Grove Academy

Year 10 students studying the parallel stories Vilbia and Modestus in Cambridge Latin Course Stage 22 (Communication / Cultures / Comparisons)

The teacher had already prepared the whiteboard before the students entered the classroom (Figure 3). The stick figures on the left represent the characters from the *Vilbia* story (*Vilbia*, her sister *Rubria* and ex-boyfriend *Bulbus*) and those on the right from the *Modestus* story (*Modestus*, his sidekick *Strythio* and some of his ex-girlfriends). A simple spider diagram for each story is used to frame the way in which the teacher wants the story to be read. The learning objective is for the students to reach conclusions about the way in which the two characters are drawn. During their reading, the students are to look for Latin words and phrases that provide evidence about the characters of *Vilbia* and *Modestus*. This evidence is to be categorized by what *Vilbia* and *Modestus* say about themselves, what they say about each other, and what others say about them.

As the students and the teacher read the stories together, the teacher added extra vocabulary to the drawing. Words were added to the pictures themselves to help students follow the narrative. Extra pictures were also added (such as the brooch which *Vilbia* is showing to *Modestus*). The black cloud hovering over *Bulbus* on the far left of the board, had been drawn in right at the start but without comment by the teacher to act as an incentive for the students to find out by reading what it was. A number of words were deliberately placed at the bottom of the board: you can see the interrogatives prominently collected on the left to act as a reminder.

The whiteboard is a vital piece of teaching equipment, not yet, in my view, superseded by the interactive whiteboard. Here the teacher is using it to the full: as a place to set out expectations about what the story will consist of, a

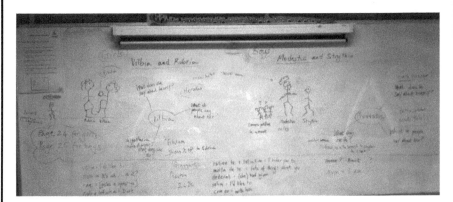

Figure 3 Whiteboard being used as stimulus to enquiry and as collective classroom memory.

place to help the students construct the events in the story, and a place to gather and sort particular items of vocabulary. The board acts as a place to store student contributions and build knowledge for the whole class: it is the collective classroom memory of the lesson. An interactive whiteboard could be used to save the annotations made on the drawings for the following lesson, but in this case was not available. It might be reasonable for one lesson to be given over to the *Vilbia* story and another set aside for the *Modetus* one. This would then allow the students to compare the characterization in the two stories. In fact, the teacher arranged this lesson so that half the students read *Vilbia* and the other half *Modestus* at the same time. The whiteboard then became the centrepiece for each group to feed back to the other as the teacher collated their responses on the board. The teacher skilfully selected questions that focused precisely on the original characterization questions, and swapped the questioning between the two groups to gain the most provocative observations: the *Vilbia* group were aghast when they heard of their deception by the braggadocio *Modestus*. At the end of the lesson, the students were instructed to write brief character sketches on the two characters, referencing original Latin quotations.

As noted at the start of this section, there are many alternative ways of getting students to comprehend Latin using a story-based approach. The case studies that follow are examples I have seen used in the classroom.

Reading for a purpose: learning about language and socio-cultural content

The following two case studies both feature the same story, '*Felix et fur*' from *Cambridge Latin Course* Stage 6 (which introduces the imperfect and perfect tenses) and indicate different ways a teacher might use it. The first example (**Case Study 9**) is from a teacher trainee who wanted students to show that they had understood the meaning of the story through the storyboard technique. Typically for a beginning teacher, the initial planning focuses on the final student product. The students' lack of success caused the teacher to remind herself of the importance of thinking more about the process of learning than about the final product. The other example (**Case Study 10**) takes as its focus the opportunity afforded by reading the story with the teacher for students to gather historical information from the story and use it to reflect upon ancient and modern attitudes towards enslavement.

Case Study 9: The Alders School

A storyboard approach to help students understand the story 'Felix et fur' from Cambridge Latin Course Stage 6 (Communications / Cultures / Connections / Comparisons)

The teacher trainee wanted to use a storyboard on which their students could write their understanding of the events of the Latin story '*Felix et fur*'. Using a storyboard, students usually draw a series of pictures that illustrate the events they have read about, with Latin or English subtitles. The teacher trainee was anxious, however, that some students might spend more time on making the illustrations than could be justified, while others who were not good at drawing might be demotivated and produce poor quality work. One of the ways to ensure that the task was not too open-ended was to restrict the number of frames the students could use to six. The teacher trainee was also concerned that for the students to show their understanding of the Latin they would need to select Latin phrases from the story and write them as subtitles for each of the six frames, drawing a picture for each of the Latin phrases as a kind of disguised written translation. The teacher trainee now needed to think about speeding the whole activity up, as it now looked as though reading the story, comprehending the meaning, selecting the six best phrases and making the drawings would take as long as writing the whole thing out in English – something they had rejected in the first place as being too similar to their normal approach. The answer seemed to be to provide a photocopied storyboard with a set of six alternately arranged frames, three of which featured a picture with a space to write the Latin subtitle and the other three of which featured a Latin subtitle with a space for the picture. The frames were arranged in a sequence to reflect the chronological arrangement of events in the Latin story. Now that the storyboard had only three – not six – pictures to fill in, the teacher trainee reasoned that those students poor at drawing would be more inclined to complete the task.

The lesson itself gave mixed results. Few students were able to complete all six frames. A number of issues arose. Naturally enough the students looked at the pictures first rather than the Latin story and tried to identify what was going on. They were not always able to identify what the pictures represented (although the teacher was an accomplished artist), and this frustrated them in finding a corresponding Latin phrase. Students then turned to the Latin story. The process of reading, comprehending and selecting Latin phrases for three out of six pictures was exactly the same as that which would have been needed for six – except that some of the students were disappointed by having found the teacher had got there first and drawn a picture for them. Some of the pictures seemed to fit with several of the Latin phrases, not just one specific one. Did it matter which one they chose? Meanwhile, the chronological arrangement of the frames did not seem to help, as the skills students had to employ to identify a Latin phrase from a whole story to match the drawing or make a drawing to match a Latin phrase were completely different to one another. Each one was challenging enough in its own right. But to have both going on at the same time was even more challenging, and the students were confused as to what was the best approach. Furthermore, the students who had poor drawing skills were just as disinclined to draw three pictures as they would have been to draw six; they did not know that the original plan was for them to draw six, and so couldn't show their pleasure of having only to draw three. The lower-attaining students found the activity just as hard to complete as if they had undertaken a written translation into English – they still had to comprehend every word in the story. The students who liked drawing saw the pictures as an opportunity to show their creativity, but this took their attention away from rendering the Latin accurately. These students were more likely to have left the class with (good and bad) memories of drawing the picture rather than thinking about the meaning of the Latin story. The whole process took much longer than expected and there was insufficient time at the end of the activity to do anything more than collect the storyboards in. Looking at them it was not clear to the teacher if the features drawn were properly referencing the Latin or not. Some of the pictures were undoubtedly attractive, but contained elements of a story that were not originally there or missed elements of the story that were there. The teacher was disappointed that despite their best efforts the storyboard did not seem to have achieved its intentions.

In the discussion that followed, the teacher and I identified a different place to start from. What evidence was there that the students had comprehended what had happened in the story *Felix et fur?* What did the evidence of them filling in the frames suggest about their learning? Was the storyboard idea worth pursuing, and how would it change if it were to be used again? We revisited the idea of a simple storyboard that contained six identical frames. We concentrated on three possible layouts:

- *Layout 1*: Six empty frames for pictures to be drawn by the student with corresponding Latin phrases selected from the story by the teacher.
- *Layout 2*: Six pictures drawn by the teacher with corresponding spaces to write the Latin phrase selected from the story by the student.
- *Layout 3*: Six empty frames for pictures to be drawn by the student with corresponding spaces to write in a Latin phrase selected from the story.

At last the teacher stopped worrying about whether the students would be interested in or motivated by the activity. Instead, they began to consider what learning objective each of the layouts would likely achieve. Layout 1 seemed to be the least beneficial for learning. The teacher would already have made the Latin choices and when the students drew the pictures they would be little more than turning the phrases into a visual rather than written translation. Layout 2 seemed better: if the teacher drew their own pictures, lesson time could be spent much more fruitfully on the students interrogating the Latin rather than honing their illustration skills. The teacher would be careful to choose pictures that would force the students to make their selection from the story as a whole, and which either tested the students' ability to find the phrase that was an exact match or left deliberately ambiguous to allow the students some autonomy of choice. In either case, compared with Layout 1, Layout 2 made the students read the whole story rather than rely on it being turned into pre-digested chunks. Layout 3 was at first considered to be even better as a concept, except for the fact that it would take longer to complete. At this stage, the teacher still considered Layout 3 to provide the 'fun' opportunity for drawing that the they had originally thought would add to the students' enjoyment. But was drawing pictures from the story the 'fun' thing that students wanted? Wasn't this somehow a concession to the lower-attaining students – something that didn't involve them writing? Or could it be considered a challenge to the higher-attaining students? On further reflection, the teacher realized that Layouts 2 and 3 asked students to do exactly the same thing: to read through the story to select six Latin sentences. Drawing pictures of the six Latin sentences did not add anything to the original process of making the selection. Thus Layout 2 was finally considered the best: it provided enough visual support to motivate the students to make their selection from the whole story and was the most efficient in its use of time.

During our discussion, the teacher completely re-thought their approach to the storyboard teaching approach. They stopped thinking about it as a means of providing some form of variety and motivation, and saw it instead as a means of highlighting what the student needed to use the story in the course book for. Looking more closely at the story the teacher began to reconsider whether it was really as long and challenging as they had previously thought. And it was at this point that they realized that the whole point of the story in the course book was to *make* the students *read* a lot of Latin. The teacher counted the grammatical elements of the story:

- 24 lines consisting of a story framed within a dialogue;
- Number of verbs: two present tense verbs, 15 imperfect tenses (all third person singular, apart from one), 15 perfect tenses (all third person singular);
- Number of subordinate clauses: two *postquam*, three *quod;*
- Six adverbs.

The course book did not contain *too many* stories, or *too many long* stories after all! The teacher's thoughts had until now turned on the idea that their role as teacher was to find the fastest and least painful way of getting through them by developing lots of different types of resource. They now realized that the stories were written to serve particular purposes and were actually *just the right length* to do so and contained *just the right number of examples* to enable the students to learn. Not only was the teacher wasting their own time in making resources, they were making resources that *reduced* the impact of the learning process that the stories in the course book were designed to achieve. If the students skimmed through twenty-four lines of Latin in order to pick out six phrases to match the pictures, how could they be sure that the students had understood the different tenses, the adverbs, the simple subordination – all the things that were now staring them in the face whenever they looked at the Latin story? Now the teacher could see how to make use of the framing conversation: the opening could be teacher and students working together to set the internal story in context; the closing lines would resolve any lingering questions in the students' minds about the identity of the baby – and it was essential to allow time to look at these lines before the end of the lesson, as they might lead into a very interesting discussion about Roman attitudes towards enslavement. The teacher could draw the students' attention to the way in which the imperfect tenses in the first part of the story tended to set the scene, while the repeated *erat* and *aberat* verbs reinforced each other and introduced the idea of the compound verb. The teacher noticed that the imperfect and perfect tenses that were concentrated in the main part of the story were all regular -*bat* and -*vit* endings. This, the teacher realized, gave students the optimal chance to recognize the different forms (and for them to check that they had) and translate them appropriately, guided by the exciting events in the story itself. Some of the imperfect verbs could be translated in different, more nuanced ways, something that could be explored with the higher-attaining students. There were plenty of chances to teach new vocabulary, especially the adverbs, all of which (apart from *ferociter*) followed the same pattern. The teacher had come to recognize that the key to learning Latin through the reading approach was not for the students to read the Latin and get to the end by one means or another, but that they needed to prepare the lesson by pre-digesting the story to discover the learning opportunities contained within it and find ways to make these explicit to the students. If they were to use the storyboard approach again, the teacher would need to satisfy themselves that it enabled the students to learn better than if they had read the story together in class. This seemed unlikely.

Case Study 10: Chestnut School

Reading for socio-cultural content with Cambridge Latin Course Stage 6 'Felix et fur' (Communication / Cultures / Connections / Comparisons)
The socio-cultural content inherent in Latin stories can help to engage and motivate students. Let us look again at the story '*Felix et fur*' in *Cambridge Latin Course* Stage 6. Why might we read this story? The teacher could use it to remind the students of the tiny off-the-cuff comment towards the end of the *previous* story '*Felix*': '*paene lacrimabat, sed ridebat*'. Why *did* Felix almost burst into tears, but then begin to smile? Finding this out is as good a reason as any for the students to be motivated to carry on with the story – and the story does not disappoint with its tale of attempted kidnap and violence. But

that might not be incentive enough. How about wanting to find out why Felix was set free by his ex-master Caecilius? That got a mention in the previous story as well. Now that *is* an incentive to want to read on. While reading the story, the students will consolidate the tense endings that have been discussed previously and come across the revelation that a citizen of Rome entrusted his own son to the care of an enslaved person. This could lead to a discussion on what the thief might have been planning to do with the baby had he been successful in stealing him, and might broaden out further to talk of people-trafficking in modern times.

To accomplish all of this will mean the teacher taking a dialogic approach to teaching and learning. The teacher cannot leave it to chance that the students will pick up on all these points – let alone consider them thoughtfully. So, they are going to have to conduct a lot of the story orally – but not all of it (there may be one or two lines they want them to do on their own, in their books or on whiteboards). But as soon as the teacher asks the students to translate word for word aloud in class, it stops being learning and instead becomes testing. So they have to be careful if and when they ask the students to do so. There are plenty of other tests the teacher can use later in the stage.

The following are some questioning approaches that worked well:

- Some can be quick-fire comprehension questions: When did this dialogue take place? What question did *Quintus* ask? Who told the story?
- Some questions can be more searching: it says that *Felix* was on his own – *solus*. Why was this? Where was everyone else (allow a few minutes to answer)?
- One can use a storyline approach: *nemo erat in villa nisi Felix et infans* . . . where did this scene take place? *nemo* – what's that? – *nemo erat in villa nisi* . . . can you give me a good way to say that? Who is mentioned?
- One can ask cultural questions: Do you find it odd that Caecilius would have left his son and heir alone in the house together with an enslaved person? What might this suggest about the relationship between Caecilius and the enslaved person?
- Even some grammar questions (but only after translating/getting the story – the whole point of a narrative story book is that the grammar is learnt in the context of a story, not in abstract): How do the tenses of the verbs in lines 11–16 express the way in which the action took place? Stage 1: what happened – the thief entered; he looked around; he entered; *Felix* heard; he was working; the thief began to carry; the child wailed; *Felix* heard; he hurried. Stage 2: the perfect tenses express single, one-off actions, or sudden actions; the imperfects express continuous actions. That's all – no tables or charts, not lengthy '*how to form the imperfect*' verb sessions. Leave that until later. Move on through the story . . . the story is so exciting the students don't realize they are practising and consolidating the verb endings.

- The story is exciting! The teacher might know exactly what is going to happen – they might have read the story four, five, fifteen times. But this is the first time the students have ever read it. It *is* exciting!
- Can the students give the teacher some details about how the fight ended? How did the story end for *Felix*? Was this a good reward? Can the students explain the 'surprise' ending?
- What do the students think would have happened if the fight had ended badly for *Felix*? What might have happened to the baby (he could have been held to ransom or, more likely, sold into slavery)? Could such a fate have befallen *Felix* himself? Students will be sure to spot the irony here.
- What do students know of human trafficking today? How does this story help them to reflect on such issues?

Now that seems to me to be a far more interesting thing to do with this story – we are developing the plotline, learning masses of sophisticated material about enslavement and freedom, and something about checking our verb tenses along the way. Isn't that why we study Latin?

Addressing gender issues through the story

In the last few years, since the first edition of this book was written, the ways in which the commonly-used Latin course books have under-represented and misrepresented Roman women and their lives have come under scrutiny (Churchill, 2006; Upchurch, 2014; Joffe, 2019; Amos, 2020). It was this criticism in mind that the Cambridge School Classics Project published a revised US 5th edition in 2016 and a revised UK 5th edition in 2022. The US 5th edition will, I believe, be further revised to merge it closer to the UK 5th edition. Reasonable criticism centred around the facts that in the US and UK 4th editions, Roman women were somewhat absent from the main stories, and, when they were present, lacked the sort of agency which we know from the sources and the archaeological record they did possess – apart from significant responsibility in running the household, women worked in small and larger businesses, for example. In the US 5th edition, small changes were made to provide more examples of Roman women from Pompeii, to give them stories of their own: 'Lucia' was added to Caecilius' family and received a number of her own stories; the artist 'Celer' became 'Clara'; and, among other small changes, 'Metella' was given more of an active role within the story. Sadly her character – and Lucia's – were both killed off at the end of Book 1 when Vesuvius erupts and many of the main characters in the continuous narrative perish. While these small changes went some way to satisfying readers in the

US, it was felt that the changes had not gone far enough. In particular, the character 'Melissa', an enslaved woman in an early story 'venalicius' ['The Slave Dealer'], remained – the cause of concern among many educators for its 'sexism and misogyny' (Joffe, 2019, p. 4). The recently-published UK 5th edition takes the changes a considerable step further: Metella and Lucia have even stronger storylines (and I am not aware at the time of writing whether they survive the eruption of Vesuvius and go forward into the next book); and the Romans' 'voices' (in translation) are represented in the background information in such a way that it makes it easier for the course book to distinguish between the authentic 'Roman' voice and the modern authors' interpretations. Moreover, the 'venalicius' story has been completely rewritten, such that the focus is not so much on the men bartering for the enslaved woman, but more on the feelings of powerlessness that the enslaved woman has and her sense of anxiety as she goes to her new home with Caecilius. Of course, good teachers will always find ways of bringing out the real lives of the slightly cardboard cut-out figures in a beginners' Latin course book: they will be alert to their students' thoughts and feelings and touch lightly or more seriously on the issues that arise from the conversations which inevitably flow from discussions about the meanings of the stories that they read with them. But a good course book should not make that more difficult than it needs to be – it should not get in the way and it has a responsibility to teachers and learners alike not to obfuscate, blur or otherwise misrepresent the Roman world. The new 2022 UK 5th edition of the *Cambridge Latin Course* has done that well.

Recently published is the Latin course book *Suburani* (Hands Up Education, 2021), using a reading-comprehension approach broadly similar to the *Cambridge Latin Course*. Being written from scratch in the 2020s, this book has been able to incorporate much up-to-date knowledge and understanding of the peoples of the ancient world, and also to be able to respond to the needs and interests of the range of students and teachers in the classroom today: the stories feature a number of strong female leads, from various backgrounds: Sabina, for example, whom we meet right at the start of the book, is a teenage girl from a distinctly lower-class, non-traditional family. She and the other characters, many of whom provide examples of the ethnic diversity of the Roman world of the first century CE, meet with high adventure in a number of quite gritty situations, Feedback from teachers has so far been good and a second book in the series has recently been published.

In the US, there is perhaps more flexibility of what resources to use, there being no national examinations such as the UK GCSEs, Some teachers have chosen not to use published course books, but instead have drawn on original sources, lightly-adapted as required, This 'untextbooking' approach clearly allows teachers to choose authors and stories of a wider range than those traditionally in use: (see, for example, Ash, 2019). Stories written by Roman women are more frequently found in later Latin writing, and subject matter can be found which is less dominated by 'great men' narratives.

Again, some US teachers have started to write their own short stories and to publish them. These 'novellas' I refer to elsewhere in this book; but clearly there is the opportunity here for teachers to borrow stories from antiquity or even contemporary times which may feature women more prominently.

I also address gender issues more fully in Chapter 6 of *Teaching Latin* (Hunt, (2022a).

Case Study 11 uses the Latin story to encourage students to consolidate a recently introduced language feature (the dative case) while at the same time investigating a socio-cultural issue (the roles and responsibilities of Roman women).

Case Study 11: Greenfield School

Addressing gender issues in teaching Cambridge Latin Course Stage 9 'in taberna'. (Communication / Cultures / Connections / Comparisons)

Here's another story-based approach: '*in taberna*' from *Cambridge Latin Course* Stage 9. The lesson was devised by a teacher in response to the fact that students in the all-girl school rarely were exposed to the range of roles and interactions that Roman women had in the stories written in their course book and were getting a false impression. Churchill (2006), quoting Pope, identifies the *Cambridge Latin Course* as having the poorest gender balance of all the course books in the first two years of learning Latin, with only three major female characters in the whole of Book 1, while Upchurch (2014) found that in her mixed-gender class of Year 9 students, the names of the female characters, let alone their actions, seemed to be 'invisible' to the students. Churchill's suggestion is a long-term solution to the problem:

> 'Made Latin' that is the stuff of many students' first – and dare I say only – encounters with the language may be revised to represent women in more active roles . . ., as subjects of verbs as often as objects, in activities other than domestic roles, and of worth and significance beyond their physical appearance.
>
> Churchill, 2006, p. 90

To address this, the US fourth edition of the *Cambridge Latin Course* Unit 1 (UK Book 1) has already revised images of women to present the two most prominent female characters in less stereotypically passive roles, and the US fifth edition (2015) has introduced new, strong female characters. But in the UK, we still await the revision of our own *Cambridge Latin Course* Book 1, and so the problem remains. Upchurch (2014) is not convinced that most teachers are sufficiently concerned as to make use of the opportunity the problem offers to make students question the representation of the female characters in the *Cambridge Latin Course*. She suggests that as well as revisions to the Latin stories themselves, more English background material ought to be provided to show the extent of the roles and activities of Roman women. I too have suggested ways in which students might use resources such as museum artefacts to help them investigate the role of the *Cambridge Latin Course* women (Hunt, 2013a). However, both of these suggestions involve the teacher going beyond the Latin story and devising extra activities. The following activity was therefore built by the teacher around one of the pre-existing Latin stories 'in taberna'.

The twenty-four Year 8 students had read all the stories up to this point in *Cambridge Latin Course* Stage 9. *In taberna* is a story that consolidates the use of the dative case in the context of two Roman women (*Metella* the materfamilias and *Melissa* the enslaved girl) buying a toga in the market from the merchant *Marcellus*. They choose a toga and haggle with the merchant about the price until eventually the deal is struck.

The teacher began by using a hook: they suggested to the students that the title of the story *in taberna* was inadequate and that they were to think of changing it to make it reflect the events of the story.

First, the story was rapidly read aloud, first by the teacher and then by the students. In this way, the teacher was able to emphasize the importance of phrasing to bring out the direct and indirect object. Thus:

- *Metella Quinto* [slight pause] *togam quaerebat.*
- *Marcellus feminis* [slight pause] *togam splendidam ostendit.*

The teacher also gestured with the verbs, especially ones that experience has taught us cause difficulties – *tradidit, dedit* – and also noted their present tenses on the whiteboard: *tradit – tradidit; dat – dedit.*

As the teacher and students read through the story, the teacher asked focused questions on particular linguistic and cultural features. They did not ask questions about every single word, or even every single sentence, assuming that the meaning of some of the sentences would be self-explanatory once they had been read. The teacher quickly told the class the meaning of some sentences; sometimes they would translate half of a sentence and ask the students to complete the translation; for others the teacher asked the students to translate the whole thing. But in each case, the focus was on the importance of the verb in fixing in the mind the concept of the indirect object and checking that on each occasion the students translated it. The English 'concealed' indirect object – '*He showed the women the splendid toga*' can wait for now. The teacher wanted the students to see the pattern and gain confidence in spotting it and translating it for themselves: in every case where it occurred, the teacher wanted the pupils to translate the dative as 'to' or 'for'.

Another thing to keep an eye on is the price of the garment being sold. As some pupils are unlikely to have the cultural knowledge to understand what 'haggling' involves, it is a good idea to have someone in the class explain it or the teacher explain it in the case of drawing a blank. It's a good idea to keep a 'score' on the board of the prices that each of the protagonists asks. The teacher drew attention to the fact that *Marcellus'* price dropped from 50 denarii to 40 denarii in the first stage. *Melissa's* role is very interesting, and again the teacher drew the students' attention to this. *Melissa* started the haggling: she began with a ludicrously low price, 10 denarii, and then she increased it to 15 denarii. So the upshot of the first part of the negotiation is that the man dropped his price in tens, while the enslaved girl increased hers in fives. The intervention of *Metella* was represented by the teacher as supposedly unexpected. Suddenly, however, *Metella* stepped in and sealed the deal, offering 30 denarii. So *Marcellus* dropped from 50 to 30 denarii, while *Melissa* raised her bid from 10 to 20 denarii. They compromised by meeting in the middle.

The teacher then asked the pupils to look back over what bargaining methods *Melissa* had used to get to this stage. With a little probing, they were able to point out that she had used intemperate language to cajole *Marcellus* – '*hercle!*' and '*furcifer!*', and she had complained that the first togas displayed in the street were dirty. The teacher elicited responses from the students as to how they perceived Melissa's actions. The students responded (in *their* words) that she was powerful, strong, sassy, feisty.

The teacher then encouraged the students to look at *Metella's* intervention and consider why she had remained silent up to that point and why she chose to intervene when she did. Melissa seemed to be making good progress, so why didn't she let her beat Marcellus down even further? Why didn't *Metella* do all the bargaining from the start? This led to a discussion about the social status of *Melissa* versus *Metella*, and the roles that entitled them to play. *Metella* wanted to buy the toga as a present for her own son. So she was the one with the cash – but perhaps *Melissa* was more adept at haggling and using intemperate language, as she was an enslaved person. It would be unfitting for *Metella* to sully her reputation with such public outbursts. Other suggestions included that *Metella* was tired with the transaction taking so long, and so slapped down the money to get the toga before *Melissa* spoiled the whole thing. The students also picked up on the fact that *Marcellus* thanked *Metella* at the end and addressed her as *Madam*.

A valuable discussion had taken place: the students were now more aware about social status and the effect it had – the basic idea of enslaved person and citizen had been raised using an example of actions relating to their statuses; it opened up an interesting debate about the roles of women and the power they had; and in a sense it began to look at the *Cambridge Latin Course* story as an item of literature – as a resource not just of datives but also of socio-cultural information. If students are alerted to these possibilities, then they will see what Latin is for.

The teacher returned to the original question. What would they now entitle '*in taberna*'? Student responses showed a renewed understanding of the role and status of Roman women and the relationship between enslaved person and *domina*.

Using information and communication technology to teach Latin

Information and Communication Technology (ICT) is progressing very quickly and it is highly likely that individual resources will have been rapidly overtaken even before the publication of this book. Latousek's (1998) overview of practice already feels like another world, with no mention of the internet, social media or tablet computers, smartphones or apps. The guidebook produced by CIRCE by Classics teachers for Classics teachers suffers a similar fate (Morgan, 2005). For a fuller treatment of practical examples of using digital technology in the Classics classroom at the school and college level, I should also draw attention to Natoli and Hunt's *Teaching Classics with Technology* (2019) and Chapter 7 of Hunt's *Teaching Latin: Contexts, Theories, Practices* (2022a). Accordingly, rather than provide a description of programs that will quickly go out of date, I will draw attention to the more generic ways in which ICT is having an effect on student learning in Latin, and then pick out a number of specific resources that are having the most significant impact on teaching and learning. Website resources that maintain up-to-date information about the use of ICT can be found in Section 3 of this book: not only are they able to keep up with developments in 'real time', but they possess additional functionality to connect with other websites and video demonstrations of ICT in use. Of course, the Covid-19 pandemic has ushered in a whole new digital learning experience for teachers and learners of all kinds. Schools rapidly had to adjust to distance teaching and learning, at short notice and without much support from school leaders. It was a phenomenally steep learning curve, not without its problems (see Hunt, 2020b). However, for the most part, the impact on practice has been largely beneficial as teachers worked out new ways to deliver material, to engage with students, and to monitor and assess performance. Much of what has been learnt has become standard practice in only a few short years (for examples of practice and useful websites, see Lamb, 2020).

Evans (2009) reports that the use of ICT in classrooms has more of an impact on students' attainment in modern foreign languages than other subject areas, including History and English. This is primarily due to the ability of ICT to introduce rich and authentic audio-visual material in the target language into the classroom with ease. Some of the examples to which he draws attention are directly applicable to students learning Latin, such as teacher-directed PowerPoint presentations of and about language, multimedia presentations about cultural topics and, increasingly, student-produced resources such as media presentations and recordings of their own. Teachers know how motivated students are to use ICT both inside and outside the classroom, even when they using it on their own. But ICT can enhance the interactions that take place in the classroom and lead to even greater and faster progress for all students. ICT should not, however, be introduced into a lesson without due thought and consideration. Effective practice can involve both the most up-to-date and the most traditional teaching methods. As Counsell and Haydn (2003) note:

> Teachers do not generally confine themselves to a single method of teaching throughout a lesson. They do not write on the board for an hour, or have pupils working from the text book for an hour. Why should computers be any different?
>
> Counsell and Haydn, 2003

Thus the most effective lessons blend learning styles and methods to appeal to the students' interests and needs, and also to make the fullest use of the resources and functionalities of the ICT. Lister (2007a) comments:

> One could move some aspects of classroom teaching online (for instance, vocabulary tests and language reinforcement exercises) to create space for aspects of the course that require whole-class interactive teaching (for instance, explaining grammar points and reading the set texts).
>
> Lister, 2007a, p. 5

The most simple – and some of the oldest – software still in common use related to grammar and vocabulary drill-and-practice programs. The format usually corresponds to simple question-and-answer, right-or-wrong feedback and a pre-set or randomized sequence (Latiusek, 1998). Goodhew (2003) claims that such programs take the drudgery out of learning vocabulary or charts by rote and allows more time in the classroom for doing interesting things, as the activities can be completed at home.

Course books such as *Wheelock's Latin* and *Imperium* have their own dedicated drill-and-practice programs. These programs are simple to use and have some features that the older programs such as those by *Centaur Systems* (Morgan, 2015) do not have, such that they are better at retesting students on the words they cannot recall. Some programs are able to monitor students' progress and feed information back to the teacher, thereby saving the time needed to create mark sheets. The main disadvantage of drill-and-practice programs is that they inevitably function as testers rather than teachers of students. If the programs are used at home, they also do not replicate the classroom environment in which learning most effectively takes place – where the interaction between teacher and students builds knowledge and understanding together.

In UK classrooms today, data projectors and interactive whiteboards are almost ubiquitous. Regarding teaching methods for Latin, these two devices have perhaps had the most significant impact: almost always the course book story or original text is displayed on a screen or interactive whiteboard and the teacher makes constant reference to it, pointing out key words and phrases, highlighting them with a board marker or stylus. My own teaching of *Horace Odes* to a class of 18-year-old students using a wireless mouse, data projector and interactive whiteboard showed the viability of this approach and the opportunities it afforded for teacher–student interaction and co-construction of knowledge (Hunt, 2008). Cox's comment that the ability to annotate a digital text 'without damaging any hard copy' (2007, p. 16) seems to see the value of the activity in too simplistic terms: it is not the protection of the original hard copy that matters, so much as the affordance of the digital text to be written over again and again if necessary, and for the text to be cut, copied and pasted in different sequences, for it to be sliced up into sections and to be otherwise digitally manipulated – all of which help students understand what is being said and how the author is saying it and why they choose to say it in the order that they do. I rarely see this, however: instead, teachers seem intent on simply replicating the static page as seen in the text book on the screen, rather than using the affordances of the word processor to manipulate sentence structure and morphology in real time on the screen. Furthermore, an interactive whiteboard allows the teacher to save the results for later use or for forwarding to students by email, lending greater efficiency to the lesson and allowing more flexibility in recalling and recasting what took place in prior learning (Hunt, 2013c). This is a powerful tool – no longer does the teacher have to keep reminding students where to look, which line or which word; they can point to it for the whole class to see. The pace of working seems to be faster and the students more attentive, and there is more efficient use of time than when using the book alone. For an example of how the teacher might use the interactive whiteboard actively with their class when teaching language while using a narrative text, see Hunt (2019).

Good practice, nevertheless, seems to blend traditional printed resources with new technology: the teacher might have students view the interactive whiteboard, work on a passage of their own from the printed course book, look up references on a tablet or other device, create flashcards, or self-test vocabulary. Regarding software designed specifically for learning Latin, the *Cambridge Latin Course* and *Suburani* are by far the best-resourced course books (although *ecce Romani* and *Latin for the New Millennium* have built their own digital resources in response to the huge demand for online materials in the USA). The *Cambridge Latin Course* and *Suburani* have all their stories and exercises available in digital form on their respective websites. These include morphological analysis tools, digital dictionaries, practice exercises and the like. Each digitalized story is presented in exactly the same format as the printed course book version to optimize this type of blended learning technique. The *Cambridge Latin Course* digitalized stories also contain a very useful *Explorer Tool*. Teachers have reported different strategies for using this tool with whole-class teaching methods. These include its use as a:

- *Teaching tool*: by selecting the words to click on, the teacher can provide sufficient scaffolding for the students to understand a phrase, sentence or new grammar feature, and to recall the words from prior knowledge or to use the context and surrounding words to hazard a sensible guess;
- *Diagnostic tool*: by hovering the cursor over individual words, the teacher can check if the students are able to recall them, only clicking on the word if they are unable to; and

- *Assessment tool*: the teacher asks individual students to recall the meaning of words over which they hover the cursor: if a student provides a wrong answer, there is an instant corrective.

The *Explorer Tool* interface is very easy to use. Further functionality is afforded by the following features:

- Each time an item of vocabulary is clicked, the meaning as it appears in the *Cambridge Latin Course* dictionary is given.
- Grammatical analysis can be turned on or off.
- When desired, a further button on the screen lists all the words that have been clicked on.
- These words can then be turned into a type-it-in vocabulary test straightaway.

Innovative practice with the *Explorer Tool* and whole-class teaching includes teachers:

- allowing students to come to the front of class to demonstrate their knowledge by clicking on particular words;
- allowing students to use the *Explorer Tool* for themselves while the class as a whole uses printed course book material;
- allowing small groups of middle- to low-attaining students to access the *Explorer Tool* one at a time throughout the lesson;
- encouraging individual students to peer teach the rest of the class by using the support that the *Explorer Tool* affords them.

The *Explorer Tool* is frequently used to support students while they are reading, comprehending or making a written translation of a Latin story either individually or in pairs or groups. The increasing prevalence of tablets and other devices in the classroom facilitates this and the *Cambridge Latin Course* e-learning materials work on all platforms, including smartphones. Despite the students' access to the e-learning materials, the teacher should be clear in their minds about how using the *Explorer Tool* will be of benefit. Some teachers express concern that the *Explorer Tool* makes learning Latin vocabulary too easy, something upon which many students themselves appear to agree (Laserson, 2005; Hunt, F., 2018; Titcombe, 2022). But this would only be the case if the purpose of the *Explorer Tool* was to facilitate the learning of Latin vocabulary – but it is not. The *Explorer Tool* developed from a program originally created for undergraduate students of Classics at the University of Cambridge who were struggling to read and comprehend course texts in their first year of study. It was found that 70% of their time was spent looking up words in the dictionary and only 30% reading the texts (Lister, 2007b). The *Explorer Tool* is designed to help students develop reading fluency by providing them with the opportunity to read much greater quantities of Latin than had previously been the case; learning of vocabulary will also occur by this method, but this is not the main way in which it happens (Nation, 2001). Current research at Cambridge University, with partnership schools, is investigating how students use the Explorer Tool in the classroom in various different combinations with teacher, each other and alone, and also with what intended purpose. Two factors are presently emerging: the significant increase in engagement with the text for lower- and middle-attaining students, and the near doubling of speed with which the text is comprehended. In fact the e-learning resources provide vocabulary testers, word-sorting activities and language manipulation exercises as various ways of developing students' knowledge and understanding of vocabulary.

Innovative practice with the *Explorer Tool* and individual student or small-group learning includes teachers:

- allowing students to skim a story for meaning, before feeding back to the rest of the class;
- allowing students to use the *Explorer Tool* for deep reading of selected passages;
- encouraging students to take responsibility for their own learning by getting them to test themselves or each other on the vocabulary they have clicked on;
- encouraging students to keep a list of the words they have clicked on for later revision or review.

The *Cambridge Latin Course* used to publish a DVD which contained mini-documentaries about aspects of Roman life, dramatized versions of the Latin stories with Latin subtitles, audio recordings of all the stories, and *Rachel* the 'talking head' who dispensed grammar information. Sadly, with the new UK 5th edition, the DVD will no longer be published as a stand-alone platform. However, many of the resources have migrated (or will soon migrate) to the improved Cambridge Latin Course websites. Current Latin teaching practice in the UK, where the *Cambridge Latin Course* is the most popular course, has been profoundly affected by the availability of the e-learning materials and is all the better for it.

The course book *Suburani* also has many similar digital offerings to those mentioned above, including a morphological analyzer and digital dictionary of its own. Additionally, the online digital offer provides, the opportunity for teachers to check in on students' work completed online and the number of attempts at exercises. It also offers a self-marking scheme, which reports back to the teacher. Suburani crowd-sources many of its worksheets, which are sent in by teachers themselves and made freely accessible on the website.

When I first began using ICT in the classics classroom in the late 1980s, I was keen to develop and show off my own skills (there were incentives for teachers in the vanguard of using ICT in the classroom at the time). How many PowerPoints did my poor early students have to sit through! How many times were they forced to watch a crackly video made up of stills taken from the pages of assorted textbooks scrolling past in time to music! Now I think differently. It is through students making something for themselves that the most effective learning takes place. Standard software packages offer students many different ways to engage with Latin texts, and the socio-cultural environment and increasingly straightforward computer interfaces make the process engaging and achievable in a lesson or two. The advent of tablets and smartphones adds another dimension. The BBC (2014) reported a study by the educational technology charity *Tablets for Schools*, which suggested that around 70% of UK schools used them. Apps seem even more intuitive than the software found on a PC computer and the students can use them in the classroom – there is no need to pre-book a separate computer room. It is no longer the teacher's job to spend time explaining to students how to carry out a task: they are able to comprehend the program or app quickly and concentrate on the production of material rather than the mechanism of how to achieve it. The following are the sorts of activities that teachers have reported as being successful at engaging students with the classical world:

- *Movie-Maker*: students made a short video of themselves re-enacting the final voyage of Pliny the Elder in 79 CE as Vesuvius erupted.
- *Animation programs*: students used animations to recreate/recast stories read in class; or as representations to the rest of the class of the events which they were in the process of reading. Figure 4 shows a student creating an animation, using the iPad app iMovie to recast the final stages of the *Cambridge Latin Course* Book 1, where Caecilius is found semi-conscious by the faithful Clemens.
- *E-books*: students went on a coach trip to a Roman site. During the journey they learnt how to use the e-book app on their iPads; on site they took photos and notes, while on the journey back to school they completed their own e-guidebooks.
- *Movie-trailer* app: students made a movie trailer involving stills, text and short video clips to represent the culmination of a sequence of stories read in class.
- QR *codes*: students can read QR codes scattered around the classroom or school on a 'treasure hunt' style information quest (Downes, 2013); or they create and upload their own QR codes to take them to information on their i-Pads.
- *Videos*: students recorded each other and the teacher in real time as they explained a new grammar feature. They saved them to a digital folder.
- *Pinterest*: students and teacher shared image resources in preparation for project work (Atkinson, 2012).
- *Text manipulation*: students cut, copied and pasted, rearranged, précised, annotated, coloured, and added images and hyperlinks to original Latin texts and translations of texts, to show their understanding of the structure and narrative elements of a story (Paterson, 2012).
- *Audio-recording*: students created recordings of plays, readings and interviews with characters from the stories they were reading, using standard recording software such as *audacity* or apps.

- *ORBIS*: students used the University of Stanford website to explore travel in the ancient world, making comparisons with the experience of modern travel (Pike, 2014; Arcenas, 2019; Morrice, 2021).

Published films and documentaries provide many opportunities for students to visualize the ancient world, aid recall of scenes they have read, and act as a springboard for discussion about the choices film-makers make (camera angles, plot conventions, costume, storyline), which encourages critical reflection on the same choices the ancient author made (Paul, J., 2013). Easily accessible *YouTube* clips can be downloaded to illustrate key themes and ideas (Paul, D., 2013). If their spoken skills are sufficiently good, teachers can use video clips from any source with the sound turned off, and narrate from a script or extemporize the narrative in Latin. These so-called 'movie-talks' can form the basis of new interactions between teacher and students and enhance comprehensible input (Ramahlo, 2019; Hunt, 2022a, pp. 55–56). Students can get a sense of the world of Classics 'out there', beyond the immediate realm of the classroom.

Virtual learning environments (VLEs) have been shown to be beneficial to students. Moss (2013) reported the positive impact of a VLE on the attainment of her second-year US college level students, who were able to access and review class notes and digital versions of the notes they had made together in class on a Latin text. Smith (2012) describes the positive learning outcomes that his sixth-form school students enjoyed when they were able to use a VLE to gather together resources, to discuss and reflect on texts for study. Eaton (2013) describes how teachers can utilize the functionality of the VLE to present multimedia information to students in formats that include *YouTube* videos.

In a school VLE, students and teachers worked together on a shared digital text, for analysis and / or literary appreciation (Lewis, 2019; Travis, 2019). Outside formal education, a group of learners generated their story over a period of time using their knowledge of the language based around a subject which interested them personally, under the guidance of an expert teacher (Schwamm, 2019).

Computer games seem to be inspiring a new generation of students and their principles and approach can be harnessed to teach Latin and the classical world. For example, Sapsford et al. (2013) devised an interactive games-based program that tells a story about the lives of Roman characters in Latin. Even the mere *terminology* of computer games can have a motivational effect (Pike, 2015).

Social media often receive less attention in the classroom due to concerns about privacy and the threat of cyber-bullying. However, some schools have their own password-protected internal systems, such as *Edmodo, Fronter* or *Firefly*, whereby students and teacher remain within a protected and safe 'zone' to set and grade homework, discuss topics and share resources. Reinhard (2009) discusses some of the practicalities of setting up a Classics membership-only social network – a *Ning.* Some

Figure 4 Student animating the death of Caecilius from the *Cambridge Latin Course*, using an iPad.

teachers have taken to *Twitter* to keep students abreast of developments in their schools and to alert them to events and newsworthy items.

Distance learning via e-tutoring or video-conferencing allows learning of Latin in places where an expert teacher is not physically present, and by students who are not in mainstream schooling due to geographic isolation or sickness, for example (Mead, 2014). Reliable communication between students and the specialist online e-tutor is essential for effective learning (Lister, 2007b; Walden, 2019). Lessons learnt during the Covid lock-down have has a significant impact on approaches used today in online teaching. Hardware and software have rapidly become assimilated into practice, with Zoom, Microsoft Teams and other platforms proving their usefulness. The Cambridge School Classics Project has had a highly-successful long-standing distance-learning course for GCSE and A Level Latin (Walden, 2019; Kilbey 2014). many individual tutors have seen the potential of online teaching for reaching out to students of all ages, in areas where there is no other provision for Latin teaching in schools. During the lock down, Oak National (2022) put up its own Latin course freely available online. For teacher training, the charity Classics for All (2022) has made increasing use of video conferencing, and runs an online annual Summer School. The authors of the *Cambridge Latin Course, Suburani* and *De Romanis* regularly offer training sessions on their websites. Social media, such as Twitter and Facebook, offer tips and advice from practising teachers and advisers. Teachers and students have a digital medley from which to choose.

Latin vocabulary acquisition and learning

We looked in Section 1 at the evidence of the possible benefit afforded by studying Latin to the learning of English. This section deals not with how Latin helps learners improve their English but is instead concerned with how to help students learn Latin. Nation's survey of studies of language teaching and learning strategies, *Learning Vocabulary in Another Language* (2001), can assist us in thinking about approaches that might be applicable to Latin. There are two stand-out issues. First, the frequency of study of Latin vocabulary is important: learners of Latin appear to need to encounter items of vocabulary as many as seven times (and sometimes more) before they can assimilate them into long-term memory (Nation, 2001). Second, the ability to comprehend Latin is dependent on students knowing most of the vocabulary already. In English academic writing, the reader is required to know as much as 95% of the vocabulary in order to make sense of the whole piece (Laufer, quoted in Nation, 2001). I think it not too much a stretch of the imagination that to comprehend original Roman literature, it is essential students of Latin similarly acquire sufficient vocabulary.

The first issue – frequency – seems to point towards the student reading as much Latin as possible, following a course that presents new vocabulary in a systematic and manageable way, with the teacher actively drawing attention to the vocabulary. In other words, the teacher should not be leaving vocabulary learning to *chance*. This is especially important when Latin words undergo so many morphological changes that students in the earliest stages of learning Latin are confused as to whether different forms are indeed the same word. The second issue – that of learning sufficient numbers of words to make sense of an extended Latin story – can be achieved by the reading approach, although traditional vocabulary learning and testing still has its place.

Individual items of vocabulary will be much more easily remembered and assimilated if they are viewed within the context of a phrase or sentence, not as individual words. Thus extensive reading of continuous writing is probably better than short, self-contained sentences. The teacher needs to make a judgement about the vocabulary of a story, because that will affect the importance they attach to the students' learning of it. The students need to know which words are more or less important, and why. Some Latin words appear more frequently in Latin literature than others – and indeed more frequently in some genres than others. The Dickinson Core Vocabulary list provides a helpful guide to the more-frequently found words (https://dco.dickinson.edu/vocabulary). Some words may be more important than others for understanding the story being read in class; other words provide more opportunity for learning about grammar or word patterns or socio-cultural topics. The teacher should be sufficiently familiar with the vocabulary in the story to ensure the students' optimal progression through it, without them becoming bewildered or anxious. Similarly, the teacher needs to think carefully about how the students will access new vocabulary in order to be able to comprehend the story. Long opined that Latin and Ancient Greek 'are the only field in foreign languages ... which forces a student to look up every word he doesn't know in the dictionary. It's killing our discipline' (quoted by Kitchell, 2000) – and this still reflects a good deal of classroom practice today wherein more time is spent looking up words than on comprehending the meaning of the story in which they appear. There is a feeling among Latin teachers that the lengthy and laborious process of looking up words in a dictionary is an aid to vocabulary retention – a view, it seems, shared by the students themselves (Laserson, 2005). But transcriptional evidence I gathered of students working together on making a written translation of a Latin story suggests that apart from being a very time-consuming practice, students frequently fail to find the right words in the dictionary, are confused by the multiple meanings given there, and also fail to make the right connection *between* the words they have looked up either because they have poor memories or because they lose track of the meaning of the whole sentence or phrase. This affects the highest-attaining students as much as the lower-attaining ones. This observation is upheld by Bartelds (2022), whose research (for ancient Greek) suggests that students need to be taught how to use dictionary entries rather than be assumed to understand how to use them for themselves. The comment of a high-attaining student is typical of the dangers of this approach when using the dictionary: 'Yeah . . . I, I write down the Latin, I write down the words that I translated and then I just put them in order, in the way that they make sense, so, they don't always have to make sense' (Hunt, 2013b).

Teaching students dictionary skills and the conventions employed by dictionaries is important. However, it is debatable if looking up every word in the dictionary is the most effective method for students to acquire new vocabulary. In a meta-analysis of dictionary usage in second language learning, Zhang et al. (2021) found that dictionary usage was a significant predictor of success in language learning, that it did not seem to matter if paper-based or digital dictionaries were employed, that monolingual entries were more effective than bilingual (that is, where Latin entires are defined by Latin synonyms or phrases, such as those provided in the course book *Lingua Latina per se Illustrata*), but that the recall of vocabulary in intentional learning fades rapidly unless other means of recall and practice are utilized. The following additional methods are discussed in brief below:

- Reading stories
- Practice exercises
- Living Latin approaches
- Total Physical Response
- Visuals
- Vocabulary tests
- Information and communication technology
- Quizzes and games
- Derivations.

Acquiring vocabulary through reading

A good reading approach course book subtly blends the introduction of new vocabulary and grammar with an interesting and motivating storyline. Some of these course books – such as *ecce Romani* and the *Oxford Latin Course* – provide lists of vocabulary to be learnt before the students try to comprehend the story. Others, such as *Latin for the New Millennium*, *Suburani* and the *Cambridge Latin Course* are based on the principle that the subject matter of the stories themselves is sufficiently motivating and interesting that students will rise to the challenge of wanting to work out what the words mean; accordingly, vocabulary is carefully introduced in manageable amounts, with additional glossing and other contextual material such as pictures and supporting English text. Nation (2001) draws a distinction between two types of reading for developing vocabulary. The first aims for *vocabulary growth* and is achieved through extensive reading, with stories set at a level one step above the student's comfort. This is typical of the approach used in reading courses: the cognitive challenge of trying to recognize, recall and learn the meaning of words is helped by the large amount of reading that is involved: students need to read *a lot*. The second type of reading aims to improve reading *fluency*, with its stories set one step below the student's comfort. Reading approach course books contain stories that follow this model too; for example, vocabulary from an earlier section of the book is repeated and familiar phrases reappear to consolidate what has already been learned.

Take, for example, the way in which the *Cambridge Latin Course* introduces new vocabulary. The socio-cultural context of each stage is developed from the start using a photograph that stimulates interest in the subject matter of the following stage. Next, a set of line drawings is used to accompany model sentences. The line drawings support understanding of new vocabulary, which, in turn, serves as a vehicle for the new grammatical feature. Each line drawing matches exactly the meaning of the sentence – down to the expressions on people's faces and representation of the fixtures and fittings of Roman life in the first century CE. This is done not just to create a course book that is an accurate historical representation (although that is a fine thing); it is so that the teacher can use the picture as a support to help the students understand what the new vocabulary means.

The teacher needs to teach the students how to take the guessing out of learning to comprehend Latin. Most students, when meeting an item of vocabulary for the first time, find an image aids their understanding: the Latin words *atrium*, *palaestra* and *murmillo*, which have little to do with everyday student life in the twenty-first century, clearly need some visual support. However, common-or-garden Latin words with straightforward English equivalents are also understood better when accompanied by an image. For example, we ought not assume that every student in the classroom knows what an altar is, or a gladiator for that matter. Students who do not immediately recognize or understand the meaning of a new word can be directed to look at the picture. By asking questions such as 'Can you see what they are doing?', 'What sort of expression do they have on their face?', and 'Would you like to receive this present?', the teacher can provide the extra stimulus to take the guessing out of what the words mean.

New items of vocabulary that have obvious English derivatives are often easily recognized: 'It looks just like the English word' – although care should be taken, as we shall see later. Sometimes it is necessary to tell the student the meaning of the word: after all, this may be the first time they may have encountered it, or they may not be able to recall it at the moment of being asked. In which case, rather than *testing* them on something they do not yet know or do not know well enough, it might be better to *teach* them the word or *remind* them of it. The teacher's judgement and how they respond to the student's needs are paramount. Moreover, the pictures do much more than support the learning of individual new words: they create in the student's mind a view of what it was like to be a part of the Roman world, how all the different aspects of Roman life connected together. Knowing what it was like in Roman times is a great aid to recalling vocabulary – rather than thinking of words as isolated one-on-one meanings, the socio-cultural background binds them together in a meaningful context; one word often provides a strong clue to the meaning of the next or preceding word, or does so when seen in a particular context. A modern language teacher is able to do this quite easily, because the topics of early language lessons consist of the familiar – both the objects themselves and the situations in which they appear. In Latin, the words are frequently beyond the experience of most of the students in the classroom.

The stories that follow the initial sentences often repeat any recently encountered vocabulary early on, as a link between that which was supported by the pictures and what now is not. Glossing at the side of the story now takes over as the support mechanism. Some reasons for the use of glossing are:

- to introduce new vocabulary that will assist with the reading of the passage;
- to remind the student of newly met vocabulary;
- to place vocabulary in a new context;
- to provide a different meaning of an item of vocabulary that is specific to that passage;
- to show patterning in the use of a new language feature; and
- to provide sufficient words to help students focus on the new grammatical feature.

The teacher who understands the reasons for glossing will know that one of them is not helping students to 'cheat' – the authors will have been judicious about what they chose to include in the gloss as a means to help the students learn. During the reading of the stories the teacher should be alert to the potential for vocabulary gathering and understanding. After a preliminary reading, the teacher should ask the students to interrogate the text for word groups and word families – not 'first declension nouns' or even just 'verbs': students need a more concrete way of recalling vocabulary – a decent skeleton on which to hang the flesh. I have observed students dismembering, as it were, a story and laying out the nouns, adjectives and verbs in neat rows. Some Latin course books continue to advocate this approach. Even better still, after reading a story, or possibly during the process of doing so, the teacher could ask the students to gather words and phrases that describe the behaviour of a particular character, or which set the scene in which the action takes place, or which describe the nature of a particular event or circumstance. By attaching the vocabulary to a person or scene or event, the student is not just vacuuming up adverbs or participles (that is, recognizing words as parts of speech rather than as meaningful items of vocabulary) but thinking deeply about the meaning of individual words and phrases and how they pertain to the situation at hand – the interesting story they are reading.

Learning vocabulary through practice exercises

Following the reading of the stories, the students should complete a series of practice consolidation exercises. Nation (2001) notes a difference between the impact that incidental and intentional reading have on vocabulary acquisition. He reports that gains in vocabulary via incidental reading will be small unless much reading is done. As a follow-up to the reading, further gains can be made by the use of practice and consolidation exercises. In general, exercises consisting of sentences that contain meaningful associations between words are more effective at helping students acquire vocabulary. Such exercises might consist of the student choosing a word from a list to complete the meaning of a sentence, eliminating incorrect words from a list, or substituting one word for another. Learning from vocabulary lists is more effective if students have to do something active with them, such as ordering or reordering them, or spotting the odd ones out. Exercises that follow a story should build on the same items of vocabulary and the same grammar features encountered there: other features may serve to confuse the student.

Learning vocabulary through Living Latin approaches

In Section 1, we saw how the Living Latin approach to teaching Latin has been adopted in many US classrooms. There is, however, plenty of scope to employ some of the principles of the Living Latin approach with other teaching approaches, especially in the case of learning vocabulary, where there is less pressure upon the teacher to be a competent speaker in Latin. The main course books all contain sections where spoken Latin is encouraged: *ecce Romani* has its '*reponde Latine*' questions; the *Cambridge Latin Course* Worksheet Masters booklet contains many examples of aural exercises; and *Latin for the New Millennium* (written by Minkova and Tunberg, 2008, experts in and proponents of Living Latin approaches) contains – as one would expect – numerous exercises and activities that require the student to read aloud, answer questions, write and even hold conversations in Latin. But learning vocabulary through hearing or saying the words does not have to be as structured as the course books make out. I have already alluded to how important it is for the student to hear and say Latin words in order to internalize them; similarly important, the role the teacher has in reading Latin aloud, with correct phrasing to show the connection between different parts of speech (noun and adjective pairs, for example) and between different syntactical features (such as main and subordinate clause). Few teachers seem to ask students to read Latin aloud for themselves – whether it be whole sentences or individual words – and I have almost never heard a teacher dictate a passage of Latin to their students. But wouldn't each of these activities be a way to help students learn vocabulary? After all, there are plenty of other Latin resources available that consider hearing the words to be important; for example, audio-recordings of course books are routinely available and, in the case of the *Cambridge Latin Course* DVD (sadly no longer published, but copies still exist), dramatic reconstructions of the stories with Latin subtitles. Students themselves regularly suggest the strategies of getting a friend or relative to test them, or of recording vocabulary on their smartphone to listen to as they fall asleep. Perhaps this is indicative of a consensus that Living Latin approaches do have a place – that is certainly the case with the learning of modern foreign languages, and not *just* for the purpose of speaking to another person. Other approaches include asking students to read passages of Latin to one another, or to make their own audio-play on a smartphone or tablet. What is important, regardless of the method used, is that the teacher models a consistent pronunciation and, when asking students for information about a Latin story or text, gets them to practise pronunciation by speaking the word or phrase in Latin. Many of the digital resources that accompany the Latin course books mentioned above contain audio recordings to assist students and teachers with pronunciation.

Learning vocabulary through Total Physical Response

The combination of repetitive physical actions and hearing and saying Latin vocabulary seems to aid recall. This method can be useful at any stage in a course – students of all ages enjoy the entertaining aspect of acting out teacher commands – but it is especially useful in the early stages of learning Latin when the teacher introduces or reinforces particular word types, such as commands, adverbs and concrete nouns. The teacher should start with the simple verbs that are encountered at the start of a typical course book. Some teachers prefer only to use the imperative forms; others use the forms of the verb given in the stories themselves. Thus the teacher might command, '*state!*' or '*dormite!*', or use the forms '*stat*' or '*dormit*' as they think appropriate. A list of words should be drawn up and used regularly, adding to the list as the sequence of lessons goes by. Adverbs (*lente, celeriter,* etc.) and nouns (*fenestra, porta, mensa, sella,* etc.) can be added – whether those encountered in the course book or others that are to hand in the classroom; either way, it will encourage students to take an active part in the lesson. Some US practitioners advocate that as much as 25 minutes per day be spent on Total Physical Response with beginning Latin students (Toda, 2014). I have met with success with this method of reinforcing vocabulary with middle- to low-attaining students in Year 7.

Learning vocabulary through visuals

A picture is often helpful to help visualize the meaning of a word and to recall it from memory. Some Latin courses use pictures and line drawings explicitly to illustrate the context in which the Latin stories are set and to assist students learn new vocabulary. The *Cambridge Latin Course* is the most successful at this: the photographs and line drawings that are a feature of the course book, and closely integrated with the stories were specially commissioned. *Ecce Romani*, the *Oxford Latin Course* and *Imperium* include drawings and photographs as a useful stimulus to the recall of vocabulary. *Latin for the New Millennium* and the grammar-translation courses include generic photographs that tie in only loosely with the historical or social events referred to in the texts: a stock image of Erasmus or a photograph of the Duomo in Florence (as presented in *Latin for the New Millennium*, Book 2) is, however, something of a challenge for the teacher to use as a vehicle for language learning.

There are, of course, many ways in which a picture may assist students learn language. The teacher can consider the picture as being either a *preparation* or as a *support* for the process of acquiring new vocabulary. Let us take by way of example **Case Study 12**: the line drawing of *King Cogidubnus* at the pyre in the *Cambridge Latin Course* Stage 15 'caerimonia'.

Case Study 12: Green Lanes School

Using an image to help students acquire vocabulary (Communication / Cultures / Connections / Comparisons)

There is a line drawing of a scene from the Latin story 'caerimonia' that is worthy of investigation by the teacher and the class. The teacher could, in advance, make a copy of the image and then display it on the whiteboard through a data projector; alternatively, the teacher could make a quick sketch of the main features of the scene. Best of all, however, the teacher could ask the students to describe the scene as they sketch it on the board, thus ensuring active engagement with the different elements of the picture: How many people are there? Are they all of the same age? What are they wearing? What are they doing? And, without giving away the plot, what do they think is going to happen in the story? The teacher added to the picture on the whiteboard items of vocabulary that they knew were going to be encountered in the story, such as *rogus, fax, lectum,* and *effigies,* for example. Although not widely encountered and almost certainly new to the students at this stage, knowing what these Latin words means is essential for understanding the narrative. It is likely that they would hinder rapid comprehension of the story; even their meanings – pyre, torch, couch and image – might need to be explained if the teacher did not prepare the students beforehand. By carefully choosing which words were essential at the start and which words could be added as the story progressed, the teacher was able to aid understanding and develop vocabulary knowledge. Therefore, only at the relevant points in the story did the teacher add the words *principes Britannici, flammae, liquabant* and the particular adjective *cerata* to the noun *effigies*, which had been written up earlier. Finally, at the climax of the story, when the eagle flies out of the wax image, the teacher asked a student to add *aquila* to the whiteboard.

Learning vocabulary through information and communication technology

The information and communication technology (ICT) used to help students learn vocabulary is constantly being updated. Details of the use of the latest technologies in the Latin classroom can be found in the pages of the *Journal of Classics Teaching* (see especially Hunt, 2013c; 2104b; Adams et al., 2014; Walker, 2015; Cleary, 2022) and occasionally in the online journal *Teaching Classical Languages*. I will focus on a small number of common applications, which will serve to illustrate some methods in widespread use.

Several Latin drilling programs are available. Drilling programs, which usually ask students to type in the correct Latin or English meaning of a given set of words, are the sort of things that a computer does best: it takes some of the drudgery out of revising vocabulary and can take place at the time of a student's choosing, thereby freeing up lesson time for the teacher to do something more interesting (Goodhew, 2003). Details of such resources are given in Section 3.

The downloadable vocabulary testers available on the website of the *Cambridge Latin Course* and *Suburani* course books are significantly better. First, they do not require the teacher to input any words, the task already having been done by the authors of the course, and every word encountered on the course is available for testing. They also offer two alternatives: a multiple-choice or a type-in the meaning version (see Figure 5). Both of these can be Latin into English or English into Latin; the number of words, their source within the course and a time limitation can all be individually set to meet the student's needs. The interface is very clear and easy to use and feedback is instant. Students have commented that they find the multiple-choice version an effective way to *learn* new vocabulary and the type-in the meaning version

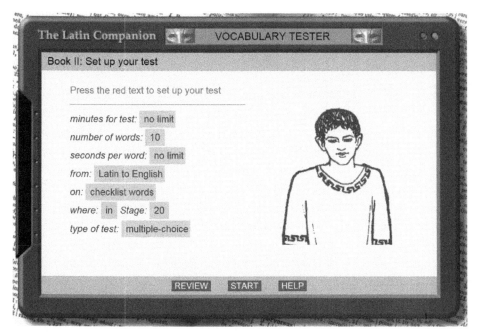

Figure 5 *Cambridge Latin Course* Vocabulary Tester interface (UK 4th Edition).

an effective way to *test* it. I have seen high-attaining students using the type-in the meaning version with great enthusiasm – a real sense of being up against the computer is highly motivating for them. But the multiple-choice version has great merits, especially for middle- and lower-attaining students. They are presented with three words from which to choose. If they make a wrong choice, they are shown which of the words is correct and must click on *that* word *before* the next word is revealed. Thus the student must perform an action to reinforce the correct answer. At the end of the text, the program lists all the words that the student got correct and those they did not. The teacher can keep a record of these words and encourage students to do the same and work on those alone. If a student chooses a large number of words to be tested on, the program remembers which of the words the student gets wrong and repeats them. Future developments in functionality include the possibility of teacher and students being forwarded information about the number of times that a student has used the program and the marks obtained. The vocabulary tester operates across all platforms, thus a student can test themselves anywhere they want.

Memrise (Memrise Ltd., 2015) is one of several vocabulary-testing apps designed for smartphones and tablets. Teachers and students can upload their own vocabulary lists, share vocabulary lists between one another, or use those in the *Memrise* 'family' – the latter are freely available. The *Memrise* app utilizes a number of features that are especially conducive to learning vocabulary: it uses a mixture of quiz formats and visual cues, retests vocabulary that the student didn't get correct, and automatically reminds students at regular interviews to test themselves. It also has the facility to provide feedback to the teacher (Walker, 2015). Teachers are increasingly using other generic testing apps, notably for recall and retrieval practice of vocabulary. Popular apps include Blooket and Kahoot! which provide a sense of competition among students; Quizlet and Socrative, which provide leader boards useful for comparisons of students' responses, and many others. Bungard (2020) explores the importance of visuals in helping students to learn vocabulary, using various apps. More research and experimentation needs to be carried out not so much now on using the apps to provide material, but on student participation rates, feedback and support for students to actually learn how to read phrases and sentences as well as recall individual items of vocabulary. There are interesting resources which provide students with digital texts and / or speech: these include the Latinitium website (https://latinitium.com/), which offers digital texts with spoken Latin and interlinear translations (see Pettersson & Rosengren, 2021 for details); and the Duolingo app for Latin (https://www.duolingo.com/course/la/en/Learn-Latin), about which I have written in Hunt (2022a, pp. 33–35).

Learning vocabulary through tests

Nation (2001) states that regular testing of vocabulary can encourage students to focus on vocabulary learning, but that the teacher needs to make sure that the students are not merely 'going through the motions to satisfy the teacher'. The act of students learning lists of vocabulary under threat of being tested does not necessarily equate to the sort of deep-seated learning the teacher desires. Regular testing is an incentive for students to take the learning of vocabulary seriously. The tests should be short and feedback should occur as soon as possible afterwards; there is an expectation that students should try hard to learn for the test in good time; students should be aware of learning strategies and possess appropriate resources. These strategies include:

- chunking words – smaller groups of words are easier to learn than a single long list of words;
- look, cover, write, check;
- concertina strips – the student translates words from Latin to English and from English to Latin on a strip of paper folded concertina-like. For example, the student translates a list of Latin words into English on the left-hand side of the strip before translating them back into English, then back into Latin again, and so on until they have covered the whole paper, front and back;
- making and using vocabulary flashcards (either physical or digital);
- asking friends or family members to test them on the words;

- writing the words out in different themes (such as military, the sea, love, the house);
- devising pictures as a reminder of hard-to-remember words; and
- inventing personal word associations, jingles and mnemonics.

Quizzes and games

When asked, a group of teacher-trainee mentors at the University of Cambridge Faculty of Education listed their top tips to encourage students to learn vocabulary. These included: making individual 'hit lists' of words the students can't remember; creating visual reminders; thinking of English cognates; thinking of word associations; using flashcards (digital and hard copy); student-made quizzes; mix-and-match activities on PowerPoint slides; labelling pictures; 'word of the week'; reciting silly verse, acronyms and mnemonics; creating 'stories' in which the Latin words are a feature (such as 'I walked down the road and before there was a *pugio* on the pavement. *eheu*! I said *mihi*,' while the students chip in with translations or write them on mini-whiteboards); using Latin bingo games; creating pictorial versions of prepositions; comparing words that are related – such as opposites, word-families, adjectives and adverbs; word-searches and crossword (crisscross) puzzles.

One of the easiest activities is simply to get students to 'play with words'. **Case Study 13** comes from one of my own classroom, where the students and I played around with words.

Case Study 13: Oakwood School

Encouraging reluctant learners to learn vocabulary – playing with words (Communication / Connections)

I'm was having problems with this class learning vocabulary. There are twenty-six Year 10 pupils of average to high attainment. The trouble is, half the class learn it and the other half don't. Thus vocabulary homework and tests only reveal the obvious: the ones who learn it know the words, and those who don't, don't. I can tell that without testing them.

I have given them the OCR Higher Tier Defined Vocabulary List. Rather than work through it word by word, I have started getting them to think about their own learning – so that those who want to learn vocabulary will know some strategies about how to set about it and perhaps find one which suits them. Thus we have so far collated all the words related to people and jobs, written them out, crossed off the ones we do know, and tried to learn the ones we don't – so far, so good. It's the process of choosing and selecting and actually doing something with words that helps the pupils to learn them. That worked just as well with the last homework I set, which was to collate all the words to do with war and violence. Or at least it worked for those who had done it – I could see the beautiful lists of words carefully written down (mostly by girls, I have to say). So instead I decided that rather than have a test – which would show me that half the pupils hadn't learnt the words at all – we would have a group learning activity – one that would make the words memorable because – I hoped – it would be fun!

Learning words out of context, on their own, from a list is unbearably dull and most definitely not the best way to learn them. It's much better if they learn words together – ideally in a sentence, better still being listened to or spoken. Not much chance of that in Latin, at home, even in Cambridge.

Next best thing is to group the words. In this case we were going to look at all the words to do with war and violence. But it could just as easily be words that express movement, or prepositions, or deponent verbs, or opposites, or abstract noun/verb combinations. The *Cambridge Latin Course* Books 3 and 4 (US Unit 4) is full of these sorts of little exercises, which are well worth doing because – even though the vocabulary is not in the examinations set list – the exercises themselves are good at making the pupils think about the concepts of abstract noun (for example) and the relationship between different parts of speech and different forms of the same word. And in the fullness of time, many of these words are very useful if the student studies Latin beyond GCSE.

Grouping the words is what we are doing here, then. But then I had a brainwave: I wanted to make learning words interesting. What story could I hang these words onto? Suddenly I realized that the story of Pandora's Box would be ideal. Out of the box flew all the evils of the world. The physical presence of the box and the excitement of the teacher revealing the evils (okay, I exaggerate) would engage the pupils – especially that awkward little word left at the bottom: *spes*.

So, start of lesson. Out comes an enormous box. Class falls silent with expectation. I lift the lid – cram it back on, 'Oh, such terrible evils!' Then I reluctantly lift the lid and hang a small notice on the front: *Pandora's*. The class immediately know the story and want to see what happens next.

Out come a series of large red cards, each with an evil printed on it: *vulnus, crudelis, dirus, interficio* and so on – all drawn from the defined vocabulary list. As each is brought out and I (hammily) intone the word, the pupils call back the meaning if they are able to do so. Eventually only *spes* remains, and I sadly point it out and put it back in the box. So those pupils who had learnt the words got a chance to show their knowledge. But what about those who hadn't?

Next activity was to catch those who had not learnt the words. I could, of course, just stand back and say, 'Hey! You haven't learnt the words! That's your problem!' But that will be problematic for two reasons: first, they'll do poorly in the exam and my performance pay is dependent on it; and second, they'll hold back everyone else and look miserable as sin as the course carries on. So I've got to do something.

Another set of cards: each one with a word in Latin on one side and the English meaning on the other. Each pupil takes one or two cards, showing only one side (it doesn't matter which word – Latin or English) to their friends, and then goes and tests as many people in the class as they can. When they get the word right – which is not too challenging – they move to the next person and take the new word with them. It's important that they exchange the cards so that they not only test but they also learn. There's quite a lot of noise, but they get some exercise! And noise is good: it shows they're doing something they enjoy. Meanwhile I set up the next activity.

I Blu-Tack® the first set of Pandora cards onto the whiteboard in random order. When they're all up, I call the class to order and they sit down. I collect their cards. Now we are going to think about the words we have just learnt. If we look at the same information in a different light, it helps us to assimilate it.

I ask the pupils to suggest which words belong together. Based on pupil suggestions and selection, we make a collection of the adjectives and of the verbs. I rearrange the words on the board as they suggest. We note that the verbs all end in -o apart from *morior* (more later). We then notice that there are three words for 'kill' – *neco*, *occido* and *interficio*. We play games with the word *occido*, which sounds like *Ocado*, the local supermarket delivery company (we have visions of the little van coming round and delivering not strawberries and ice-cream but little pots of poison). We notice that some words are related to each other and others are opposites. It is this word play – thinking about words – that reinforces the vocabulary and also the underlying concept of noun, verb and adjective and their interrelationship.

Finally, I want to lead into the next piece of work, which is going to be on the deponent verbs. I take *mors* and *morior* and display them. I point out that all the verbs we have encountered so far have ended in -o, but that the passive usually ends in -r. This is something we have been working on for the last few lessons. Now I want to show them that there are some words that look passive but are actually active – which is what we are going to be doing next lesson. Thus the new language feature builds on prior knowledge of the existing one.

That night I made my own Pandora's Box for classroom display: it's something to refer to each time, to get them to recall the whole classroom experience, which was more than just memorizing a set of words.

Learning vocabulary through derivatives

There is some debate about the value of using English derivatives as a way of recalling Latin vocabulary. There is evidence to suggest that Latin words that are closely cognate with an English word are much better recalled than those that are not. Thus words such as English *poet* for Latin *poeta* or *servant* for *servus* are generally effective, but others such as *agriculture* for *ager* or *juvenile* for *iuvenis* have their own problems – not least because students of middle- to low-attainment or whose mother tongue is not English do not tend to know these words in English in the first place and are thus easily confused. Furthermore, there are many false friends, such as *invite* from *invitus* (= unwilling) one has to be wary of. Yet students who have a wider vocabulary often delight in etymology: *procrastination* from *cras* and *accelerate* from *celer*. One of my Year 10 students delightedly noted the English derivative *ingredients* from *ingredientibus* (dative plural masculine of the present participle of *ingredior*) – something I had not spotted before. This is not to say that knowing English derivatives from Latin is in itself a bad thing: developing students' knowledge of vocabulary and their word-power is an important part of what teachers think the study of Latin achieves, as we have seen in Section 1. Nevertheless, the use of derivatives as a way of learning Latin vocabulary is not as clear-cut as it might be (Veysey, 2014).

Teaching literature in the original

Most Latin teachers would agree that the main reason for learning Latin is so that students can read Latin literature in the original. This hasn't always been the case. In the Victorian era, the study of classical languages had steered resolutely away from the content and the occasionally controversial issues that arose for contemplation and became instead an 'anodyne lesson in discipline' with a relentless focus on 'linguistic minutiae' (Stray, 1998b, pp. 44–45). In the UK in the 1920s to 1950s, for example, most Latin examinations consisted of translation into and out of Latin, with some grammar-spotting questions thrown in (Cambridge School Classics Project, 2014). The 1938 government-sponsored Spens Report into secondary education had complained that in the case of Latin, 'In no other subject has the end [that is, the study of literature] been placed at so great a distance, and the realisation of its value emerged so late' (The Spens Report, 1938, p. 176). Yet the warning signs that this state of affairs was contributing to the decline in interest in the subject were ignored. Typically, a student had to survive the four or five years of studying Latin grammar and translation into and out of English before they were introduced to original authors. If and when they were, it tended not to be assessed as *literature*, but as yet another opportunity for translation into English (Cambridge School Classics Project, 2014). Even by the 1960s, assessment of Latin literature, although practised more widely, was mostly optional and when students *did* take an examination in it, they found questions focused on their knowledge of the historical, social and political nature of the content (Cambridge School Classics Project, 2014). Many students therefore only ever learnt the Latin language as a kind of 'foundation for something that would never be built', as Pym (1962, p. 36) pointed out, which contributed to a steady decline in interest in its study. With this background, therefore, and in the face of the two crises in Classics mentioned in Chapter 1 – the abolition of Latin from the matriculation requirements of the Universities of Oxford and Cambridge and the re-organization of secondary schooling along comprehensive lines – a lively debate ensued in the pages of the classical journal *Didaskalos* about the need to update Latin courses to include literature properly taught and assessed. Bolgar set out the case for inclusion:

> The young see the record of experience there and seek after it in spite of the theories of their elders. They are right, and we could do worse than follow their lead. The time has now come for a serious study to switch from the textual field where a firm foundation has now been laid and to go beyond the now fashionable interest in aesthetic issues. We must recognise the fact that writing is one of the great human activities, on a par with earning a living and making war. It deserves study in all its aspects. The character of the emotions and ideas communicated, which depend upon the experience and values of the culture producing them, forms just as important a part of literary study as formal literary patterns, and is indeed more likely to interest our contemporaries.
>
> Bolgar, 1963, p. 22

Bolgar's call to action was still not universally welcomed, despite the approaching crisis. Some teachers claimed that students of Latin were not interested in anything other than the language pure and unadulterated, as typified in this exchange in the 1967 edition of the journal *Didaskalos* between two Classics teachers, the traditionalist Mark Mortimer and the more progressive John Roberts:

> Proposals to 'keep the Classics alive' (and teachers in business) by flogging pills of almost solid sugar to students who could get sweeter sugar elsewhere are, however, outside the scope of this piece; what concerns me is simply that the old pill should be available *unsugared* for diabetics, for that minority of students whose interest in the workings of language coincides with an equal *lack* of interest in Archaeology, History and evaluative Literary Criticism, and, more practically, with an antipathy to the writing of *essays* in those fields.
>
> Mortimer and Roberts, 1967

Mortimer's speaking up for the minority of such students – and for teachers like himself – was doomed to failure. Oxbridge switched off the life-support and teachers found themselves having to redefine what Latin was for. Amazingly it was not until 1988 and the introduction of the GCSE that all the examination boards recognized the value of Latin literature and made it a compulsory element, but in the meantime teachers had had plenty of time to realize that the opportunity to study Latin literature would attract a wider range of students than ever before. Latin for tests alone was gone; Latin as a study of some of the greatest stories told was a much more attractive proposition.

Teaching literature as *literature*

There is no set way that the teacher should teach students to comprehend Latin literature in the original, let alone respond to and comment on it. However, from the beginning the teacher should take care – even when students are learning to comprehend the earliest confected or made-up Latin stories – that they do not lose sight of the main purpose of reading a text, as Sharwood Smith (1977) noted:

> If experience has taught the pupil that a passage of Latin or Greek is mere material for a decoding exercise in which the message to be decoded is at best trivial, at worst meaningless, then he will acquire an attitude of mind and habit of procedure that will persist when he is invited to tackle Caesar, Virgil, Xenophon or Homer.
>
> Sharwood Smith, 1977, p. 36

The teacher must remember that getting through the story without the students understanding what it was they have read is a demotivating exercise, and may provoke boredom and poor behaviour. Students subject to such a routine are unlikely to be engaged.

In a paper about US college students, Carpenter (2000) argued that those who chose Latin to fulfil a 1–3 semester language requirement would never study very much (if any) original literature. He therefore suggested that teachers should redefine the role of Latin pedagogy as focusing on traditional grammar-analysis at this stage, because honing analytical skills would be of direct benefit to the students and to the needs of the US university system. I strongly disagree. All UK universities that offer Classics degrees (teaching Latin and Greek authors in the original) run one-year *ab initio* language courses for those students whose schools did not have Latin or Ancient Greek on the curriculum, with the expectation that the students will be able to comprehend original Latin authors (Lloyd Houlker, 2014). At school level typically, students reach the standard required to read original Latin authors, with assistance from the teacher, in two to three years, based on an hour or an hour and a half per week. Mary Beard showed in the popular TV series *Jamie's Dream Schools* how it was possible to get ten malcontent secondary school students to read and enjoy *Martial* in only a few days with no prior knowledge (Beard, 2012), and I have witnessed school students aged 17 at a local sixth-form college reaching A Level standard Latin authors such as *Virgil* and *Livy* from scratch in one year on a two-hour per week timetable. Carpenter (2000), who seems to suggest that because only a few students will be able to reach the standard we shouldn't try to help them, presents a solution which is likely to make the situation in the classroom worse rather than better. Even a little taste of literature may be a sufficient incentive:

> The reader obviously needs at least a reasonable reading competence in the medium for the literature to be meaningful to him. But, if he is convinced that a work has a message which he would like to hear, motivation may well enable him to acquire additional competence as he tries to reach the message.
>
> Hoskins, 1976, p. 251

The student who uses a reading approach course book derives ultimate pleasure and satisfaction from learning about the ancient world *and* the language that is used to express it. It is a challenge, but the reward of achieving both is worthwhile. Reading Latin literature has exactly the same challenge and the same reward. The teacher who uses a grammar-translation or Living Latin approach will probably experience more difficulty in transitioning to original texts if they leave it too late. Students will not only have had less experience in gaining reading fluency, but they may well lack some of the cultural knowledge to help them contextualize what they are reading.

In response to Carpenter (2000), Kitchell (2000) shares his different worries about the impact of students' linguistic and cultural inexperience on their motivation to study Latin literature, especially when they perceive that, compared with their fellow-students who are studying modern foreign languages, they do not seem to be able to read Latin sufficiently widely, quickly or fluently. He takes as a starting point Hirsch's (1988) populist theory of cultural literacy – the idea that, because of progressive education methods, many modern US students lack the background knowledge to enable them to recognize and understand culturally important references in literature and arts. Kitchell (2000) suggests that the reading of original Latin texts is, in this regard, especially problematic, with multiple references to events and ideas far removed from the students in time and space. Nearly twenty-five years earlier, Sharwood Smith (1977) had identified these challenges as both intellectual and cultural: intellectually challenging, because of the very nature of the Roman authors and their original intended audiences:

> The Roman authors wrote for highly sophisticated readers who had been educated in Greek literature and derived much of their enjoyment from the demands made on them by the allusive and elliptical techniques of their poets and the 'resonance' effected by creative imitation of Greek and Roman antecedents.
>
> Sharwood Smith, 1977, p. 53

And culturally challenging, because of the 'otherness' of the events about which they write:

> Not only were the members of the audience for whom the Roman poet wrote sophisticated, they were also contemporaries: he could naturally assume in them a familiarity not only with the prevailing literary conventions, but also with the happenings and the furniture of the world they shared. The present-day pupil does not see citizens of his town being carried round in *lecticae* or reeling home drunk by the light of flaming torches carried by slaves; nor can he glimpse *Soracte* from his front door; nor would he, if he escaped from a yachting disaster, hang up his clothes or any other *ex voto* in a nearby chapel; nor does he live under a dictator who is trying to restore the morals and piety of his fellow citizen by legislation, propaganda and example.
>
> Sharwood-Smith, 1977, pp. 53–54

To these challenges I would add that the Latin we read in school editions probably does not reflect the Latin that was spoken by ordinary Romans or was in common usage. It is highly polished and written for an intellectual audience, as Clackson (2015) reminds us. But I am of the view that these challenges are *precisely* the reason why students would want to study the Romans in their own words: the world that the Romans describe and the words they use to describe it are both sufficiently *similar* and at the same time sufficiently *different* to the daily life of a modern student. It is the constant cognitive dissonance caused by reading about people just like them, who experience many of the same sorts of feelings as they do, and then, suddenly, without warning, behave in ways that seem so alien and strange, which makes the challenge of understanding all the more worthwhile. We read about the Romans precisely because of this. Rather than deploring the fact that students do not pick up the cultural references, the teacher should take comfort from knowing that they are making a contribution to the students' wider cultural knowledge (Reedy, 1988). I am reminded of how one of my sixth-form students declared that the reason she had chosen to study Latin to the highest levels was because 'It's not like Stevenage' – her distinctly unlovely and unloved home town. Latin literature, therefore, does not just contain a message: it can also provide students with a sense of escapism and a chance to go beyond the normal experience of modern life. It is more than mere escape, however. Drsicoll and Frost (1999) suggest that learners of foreign languages develop not only an awareness of other cultures, but also the ability to make comparisons with their own. The language teacher should therefore 'ensure that learners are conscious of the criteria that they are using in their evaluation, and are able to turn their critical evaluation on to their own culture as well as that of others' (Driscoll and Frost, 1999, p. 143).

Latin teachers might like to consider Brockliss' assertion that reading Latin literature could be an even *better* education than learning a modern foreign language:

> The vast temporal and cultural range of Latin would seem to . . . offer learners an array of modes of expression and communicative contexts considerably broader than that afforded by the study of modern languages in only a contemporary context.
>
> Brockliss, 2013, p. 131

In summary, then, the study of Latin literature offers students the opportunity not only to get to find out about the thoughts, practices and deeds of the Romans but also to be able to make a personal response to the way in which they chose to represent it and to use it as a lens through which they might examine contemporary life.

Choice of author and text

The original texts the teacher chooses is vital. Although the comprehension process can be challenging for the student, it should be interesting and it should enable them to 'get under the skin' of the author in a way that reading Latin in translation does not. Above all, they should not think of the Latin text as being a particularly difficult linguistic puzzle, out of which arises something vaguely intelligible, like someone who – in Quinn's memorable image – 'goes about shelling peas – by ripping the text open, tearing out the intellectual nourishment it contains, and then throwing away the verbal husk' (Quinn, 1966, pp. 19–20). The words that the Romans used were important – as important as the meaning. They were not using a fiendishly difficult way to express common ideas. And it is a valuable lesson in itself for the students to find out that published translations are always inadequate, that they vary according to the whims, interests and intentions of the translator, and that they themselves have as much 'right' to making their own translation as any other. Some students find that idea frightening, others empowering.

Some problems caused by the lack of timetabling allocation

With a short timetable, getting the pupils up to speed for reading literature in the original is hard. At one or two lessons of 40–50 minutes per week in the UK, even schools that have four or more years to teach report difficulties getting their pupils adequately prepared for reading the set texts (OCR, 2014). That means that reading Latin in the original – which is meant to be a pleasurable activity, especially during the early years of learning Latin – tends to be carried out perfunctorily, at speed, and becomes rather more of an exercise in cramming and memorization as examinations loom, rather than affording a decent opportunity for true reader responses and critical engagement.

The ways in which students 'read' texts and teachers teach them for examinations are very different to the ways they approach unexamined ones. Often the only time many students experience Latin literature is when they are studying it to pass an examination. There is pressure both on the teacher and students for 'good' grades, leading the teacher to force 'approved' translations and interpretations on the students (Protherough, 1986).

Many pupils who learn Latin for two years, but who do not go on to national examinations, encounter no literature at all (in the original or translation). They learn the foundations for a building that is never seen.

Some possible solutions: making students aware of literature early

The teacher should introduce some simple Latin literature earlier in lessons to give pupils a 'taste' of what is to come (choosing carefully so as to encourage rather than discourage them). Short poems by *Martial* or *Catullus* are a good choice. *Latin for the New Millennium* bases all its reading material around original authors – abridged at first, then lightly adapted, then unadapted. The stories in the *Oxford Latin Course* derive from *Virgil* and *Livy*, which are designed to introduce students at the early stages to the achievements of the Romans as shown in their works of literature. The *Cambridge Latin Course* embeds some original abridged and lightly adapted literature in Book 5 (US Unit 4): some of them might be introduced earlier, heavily supported with vocabulary, at suitable stages in the story – such as in the *Dinner Party Scene* in Stage 7, or even in '*tonsor*' in Stage 3, where the poet recites a '*versus scurrilis*'.

The teacher ought to introduce Latin literature in translation wherever they can. It might be profitable to select some from the authors they know the students are going to be reading in the future. One of the most attractive features of Latin for younger students is the telling and retelling of mythological stories. At significant moments during the year, the teacher should select literature that has particular resonance. So, for example, on Valentine's Day, a bit of *Ovid ars amatoria*; at Christmas, the *Gospel of St. Luke*; for a student's birthday, anything that has resonance for that particular student.

Prose or verse texts?

It is obvious that much depends on the teacher's personal interest, the resources that are available to them, and their perceptions of what will appeal to their students. They might also consider which of the texts might provide a suitable foundation for study at a higher level if the opportunity arises.

Table 3 The advantages and disadvantages of prose and verse set texts.

Set text	Advantages	Disadvantages
Prose	The storyline is usually easy to follow	There is often complex syntax
	Characters are well-defined and appealing	The subject matter is sometimes not very motivating (e.g. war, rhetoric)
	The style is closer to what the pupils have experienced so far	Pupils need to experience something different – like verse
Verse	The poems capture pupils' imaginations	The storyline is sometimes allusive
	The number of characters is usually quite small	The word order is sometimes problematic
	The syntax is usually quite simple	Rendering the poetry into prose can 'deaden' the very liveliness of the poetry itself.

Anthology or narrative?

An anthology is a collection of works on a theme chosen by the examiners. In the UK, the national examination boards select which authors students must study. The examination specifications indicate which published resources are to be used at GCSE: the *Cambridge Latin Anthology* (Cambridge School Classics Project, 1996), the *OCR*

Table 4 The advantages and disadvantages of anthology and narrative set texts.

Set text	Advantages	Disadvantages
Anthology	Provides variety of text and genre – a good way to introduce pupils to a lot of different types of literature	It can be difficult for pupils to identify the links between the poems
	The shortness of the texts is sometimes motivating	Weaker pupils are disadvantaged by short poems, as they lack the internal resources that a longer poem affords
	It is easier to cross-reference between poems and look at different interpretations on similar themes	There are practical problems associated with keeping track of the short works
Narrative	Pupils can 'get in deep' with a longer work	The length of a narrative can appear daunting on the page
	There is less to worry about in terms of keeping track of a sequence of shorter works	Pupils do not read as much a variety of literature
	The internal narrative structure, plot and characterization motivate pupils to want to read, rather than just 'tick off' shorter works	It is possible to get 'bogged down' in a long text and become demotivated

Latin Anthology (McDonald and Widdess, 2009), or the *WJEC Latin Anthology* (Cambridge School Classics Project, 2015c). The relevant texts are usually offered by the Cambridge School Classics Project and by Hands Up Education / Suburani for free online. For narratives, set texts are often chosen from regular published versions of Virgil, Livy or Caesar. Details of which texts must be studied are published on the respective examination board's website and change in rotation periodically.

Teachers in the USA might be amazed at such centralized control of examinations by which every student taking Latin in the whole of the UK is assessed. They have more freedom to choose which authors they wish to read with their students. The standard course books such as *ecce Romani*, *Suburani* and the *Cambridge Latin Course*, as mentioned above, contain passages of abridged and lightly adapted Latin useful for the intermediate stages. US publisher *Bolchazy-Carducci* publishes a series of readers of selections from different authors designed for use in the classroom. Teachers even devise their own anthologies of student-friendly authors in bite-sized mouthfuls, such as that described by LaFleur (1984), which he and a group of other teachers drew up together for secondary schools – an excellent example of teachers designing assessment around topics which they themselves consider appropriate for their own students. Sadly this is something that has receded from sight in the UK owing to the domination of school curricula whose specifications are set centrally by external examination boards, and it is increasingly becoming prevalent in the USA where standardized testing is becoming common practice.

Workbooks

There appears to be a thriving cottage industry of workbook publishers. Each year there is great anticipation as to what the new set texts are going to be. They usually consist of Latin text with facilitating notes and vocabulary on one side of the page, with space for translation and other note-making on the other. Some of these workbooks also offer interlinear numbers to assist students to rearrange the Latin words into an English word order; yet others write in the vocabulary over each Latin word. These workbooks are often advertised privately through independent publishers and websites. Some teachers swear by workbooks. I find they slow down the process of reading to a snail's pace if they are used in the classroom. As preparation for the lesson to come, they can be useful, provided that students actually do carry out the tasks the workbooks set and complete their translations – a big ask in some cases. If the teacher does ask students to prepare the notes, they have to check that they have done so and correct mistakes in the lesson – time that could be spent, in my view, on reading and discussing the texts anyway.

Basic principles of teaching literature

Sharwood Smith (1977) describes two types of sixth-form literature lesson – both of them excellent, he says, in their own way – which represent the extremes of lesson planning, in which the development of students' understanding of literature is the aim. First, he describes the lesson which meanders, with the teacher pushing the discussion along, and the high-attaining, articulate students commenting on the text and each other's contributions, and which ends in no definite conclusion but with a sense that a thoughtful, expressive and illuminating conversation has taken place. Such a lesson is highly dependent on the subject knowledge of the teacher and the attentiveness and articulacy of the students involved. At the other extreme is the lesson in which,

> ... a number of items are to be established: tone, shape, diction and intention; effect of sound and rhythm, relationships between characters in the poem (interplay); contribution of metaphor, allegory, myth; the projection of the poet; the story, dramatic setting; ways of turning the poem into another media form such a film.
>
> Sharwood Smith, 1977, p. 59

The teacher of a lesson like this not only has to be fully cognisant of the subject matter of the text but also has to plan to teach the students the skills necessary to interpret it. Sharwood Smith avers that either of these two lessons could be excellent. But 1977 was a long time ago and appears to belong to a far gentler world. Schools and teachers today are held much more accountable for their students' grades and the earlier lesson would be unlikely today to convey to an outside observer that students were making measurable progress, particularly in relation to external assessment. I would certainly advise early-career teachers to veer closer to the latter rather than the earlier model and have very clear learning objectives in mind before they start.

Before the lesson

It is *essential* that the teacher prepare the text beforehand. This will consist of the following:

- Translating the whole text.
- Noting words and phrases that might cause the pupils difficulty and thinking of strategies to overcome this.
- Getting a sense of the theme of the passage, referring to notes and commentaries as appropriate.
- Reading the passage aloud so as to phrase the Latin appropriately, with meaning.
- Considering the use of images from the internet or books and other materials that will elucidate meaning.
- Considering ways in which the pupils might keep a record of the text.
- Deciding how to subdivide the text, if it is long, into manageable chunks. It should be possible to translate and discuss 15–20 lines per lesson (of about 45 minutes), provided that writing does not take up yet more time.

Case Study 14 illustrates the general sequence of teaching a poem (Horace, Odes III, 13 'fons Bandusiae'), focusing first on meaning and then on language and style. The ode is often taught to 18-year-old students in the UK at A Level. The recommendations are based on observations from a lesson in the classroom.

Case Study 14: Great Springs Free School

Year 13 class reading 'fons badusiae' (Horace, Odes III, 13) (Communication / Cultures / Connections / Comparisons / Communities)
During the lesson

1 Pace. The teacher should resist getting bogged down in grammar – it is of limited interest at this stage and there is the danger of losing track of the narrative or character development. If the teacher finds themselves getting too interested in the comparative adjective and ablative of comparison 'splendidior vitro', they have missed the point. Was Horace interested in the ablative of comparison at this point? It's just a way of conveying meaning. How shiny *was* Roman glass?

2 The key, main points, simply expressed. If the teacher cannot understand what the poem or passage is getting at, then the pupils won't either. What is the piece about? Sometimes it helps to have a research question at hand, which will be answered by looking closely at the passage. The teacher should think of the big question that the little bits of information are going to help answer. So they could start off with 'Why is this sacrifice

so important to Horace?', rather than 'Why does Horace say that the goat has a forehead swelling with horns?' This way the students will be able to slot the details into a bigger framework.

3 The power of suspense and surprise. The teacher should consider the power of revealing information at highly significant moments rather than at random or all at the outset. Sometimes it is worth posing a question, or leaving a cliff-hanger. If the teacher is very confident, especially in managing discussions, they can consider allowing the students to explore an issue that is partially or completely wrong, only to rein them in again, because that enables them to consider the literature in different and beneficial ways. So, for example, in *fons Bandusiae*, it might be worth letting the students consider the 'comic' idea of a poet apostrophizing a fountain –'so silly!' – only to get them to reverse their opinion when the teacher reveals the importance of a fountain in the dry dust of a Roman field in summer – and better still if a student makes the comment for themselves. As teacher, you can exhibit multiple views of the same piece, provided that the views shed light on the work as a whole and are not just random. In the end, the students will like to be assured which of the ways is more and less appropriate.

4 Read the poem aloud. There is plenty of evidence that Romans read aloud. Whether poetry or prose, there is a rhythm and aural component that was meant to be heard. More experienced pupils might be asked to read it aloud. Recordings of most set texts can be found on the Association for Latin Teaching website and the *Cambridge Latin Course* anthology page.

5 Comprehend the text. The teacher should try not to get too bogged down in the minutiae of grammar. The class wants to maintain the pace. Often a 'What's going on here?' approach (like an oral comprehension) is more effective at eliciting meaning than a 'Find the participle' approach. *Fons Bandusiae* is not merely a repository of interesting grammar features. So the teacher could ask, for example, 'What words reveal to us the quality of the water?' – and if that is too hard, then bit by bit: 'Horace says the water is "*splendidior vitro*" – what's he comparing the water to? And how does he compare it?' As soon as the teacher jumps into comparatives and ablatives of comparison – unless they can do it very quickly – as soon as they start to *test* the pupils' understanding of comparatives and ablatives, the lesson is five minutes down and the life-force will be sapping away.

6 The teacher and students together should make an 'official' translation of the text. This means putting it into normal, intelligible English. The teacher should remember they ought try to keep all nominatives as nominatives, singulars as singulars, and sort out actives and passives properly. Occasionally, that won't be possible, but it nearly always is. There is nothing to stop the teacher and students shortening the sentences either, as long as it continues to make sense and has not upset the flow of the original. The students should seek a translation that

best represents what the original says, but in a way that is intelligible. If it does not achieve that, then the lesson is not likely to succeed.

7 Whose translation? The examination boards have stated that they would prefer students not to have the same translation, claiming that this obviates the problem of all the students copying the same mistake made by a teacher. But there is more to it than that. In the classroom, the teacher should not try to close down students' interpretations to a 'teacher-approved' model but instead should prioritize the sort of divergent thinking that benefits critical understanding. The differences of interpretation that students have been encouraged to explore can be demonstrated through their own translations, and checked for accuracy by the teacher afterwards.

8 Can you give them a published translation beforehand? There are no rules. If the teacher thinks that giving the students a published translation is helpful, they should do so. Sometimes the published translation is close to but far enough removed from the real thing to act as a springboard for discussion (see, for example, Robson (2004) discussing the use of translations to help first-year undergraduates engage with original Greek texts, and Hunt (2013c) discussing teaching Year 13 Latin students using translations of the Horace text to prepare contextual knowledge in advance of classroom discussion of the Latin original). In some cases, the teacher may use multiple translations, which provide different perspectives of the same thing. The source book *Aestimanda* (Balme and Warman, 1965) provides a small but useful collection of such translations, which, even if they do not match the specific texts under discussion, can provide a model for the teacher to copy.

9 Images can be used to stimulate thoughts and ideas. An image of a real *fons* can easily be found on the internet: the teacher needs to consider at which point to show it to create the maximum impact. It can work extremely well as an initial stimulus (without telling the students what it actually is) before the ode is read – and as a place to gather students' ideas about what it might be and what it might be like to be near it, to drink from it, in the hot, dry summer months on a farm in Italy in the first century CE. Or the teacher could introduce the image at a later point   to bring out the contrast between the colours, temperatures and tastes of fresh water and animal blood.

10 Artefacts and creative activities. A favourite of mine is for students to create a label for a bottle of '*fons Bandusiae*' mineral water. Students write a label for delicious new water from Horace's farm. As a homework task, the teacher could get the pupils to make their own and stick it to a bottle.

11 Check understanding all the way through and especially at the end. The teacher should use big picture and small picture ideas – where the pupils look at a document from two perspectives: from the top down, overall view (the big picture); and from the underside, as it were, using the fragments that make up the whole (the small pictures). It is essential to check that the pupils understand what the piece is about.

Stylistic analysis

The teacher should resist getting the students to label the stylistic features from the off. They need to be able to recognize how a stylistic feature makes a piece of literature worth reading – not just be able to label it. The teacher should always move from concrete to abstract and encourage students to think about the features of the text in the following step-by-step order, until they have the confidence to do it for themselves.

- *What* does the author *say*?
- *How* do they say it – what vocabulary or syntax have they *chosen* to use?
- Do they put words *in a particular order*? Are there particular word *positions*?
- How does the vocabulary or the position of words *improve the reader's response to the story*?
- *What* do we call that feature?

You should want at all costs to avoid students saying that the Roman author uses alliteration in line 35 '*for effect*' or, only marginally better, '*for drama*'. Students seek confidence in being able to label. What they often lack, in fact, is the *English vocabulary* to explain what the author may be trying to achieve or how they feel an audience might respond to it.

The examiners are always at pains to point out that at GCSE pupils do not need to know the specialist terms to get full marks. Neither do they want students to say what is printed above. There is nothing wrong in getting students to use technical terms, but the teacher can get perhaps over-excited by supposed knowledge and mastery of obscure literary devices. In general, students will come across the following terms (not an exhaustive list) when learning English Literature:

- Onomatopoeia
- Alliteration
- Double negative
- Enjambment
- Rhythm
- Staccato
- Metaphor
- Simile.

The teacher may make judicious additions to the above list, depending on their perceptions of the needs and interests of their students. A list of what my teacher trainees considered essential is shown in Figure 6 – although there is plenty of evidence to suggest that such a display of verbal pyrotechnics can be off-putting to many students. I observed a lesson in which the early-career teacher and one student out of eight had a fruitful and happy time identifying parts of speech in Virgil's

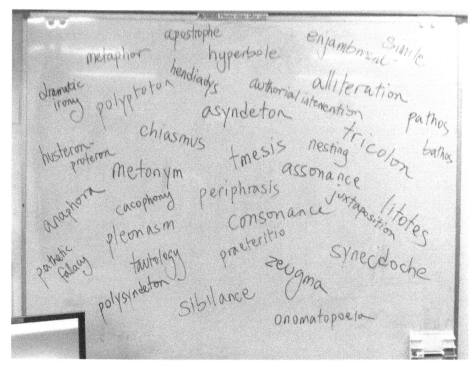

Figure 6 The joy of being a Classicist? Literary terminology contributed by teacher trainees.

Aeneid, while the remaining seven were completely ignored. Concerned by this, the teacher asked for advice:

Teacher:	The others just don't seem to get it!
Observer:	But what aren't they getting?
Teacher:	Well, they write everything down that [student X] and I talk about, but they never contribute and I'm worried they are bored.
Observer:	Maybe they are. Have you taught them what to do?
Teacher:	Yes. I've given them a list of all the technical terms, but they just don't seem to be able to see them except [student X] and me.

The answer lay in the fact that the teacher at no point asked the whole class *what was happening* in the story. They had assumed that as the class had translated the whole story first, they had a precise knowledge of every bit of the narrative. The teacher and the one student, therefore, went right to the other end of the thinking process, tried to spot examples of literary technique, and then retrospectively applied them to the events in the story. But, taking my advice, the teacher changed tactic and started by asking the whole class a more general question about what was going on in the story, whereupon everyone in the class was able to contribute something. With the ice broken, once a student was able to say something about the events in the story, the teacher could follow up: 'What do you think Aeneas was feeling at that moment? What word tells us that?' And then follow up again, depending on the particular response: 'That's a really interesting word – look at the spelling of it/sound of it/ appearance of it/position of it'; and then a further follow up: 'What other words suggest the same sort/contrasting idea?' This sort of oral framing or scaffolding device seemed to encourage reluctant students to find ways of talking about the choice and position of words because the idea of terminology without content seemed as alien to them as grammar without meaning.

I spotted a connected issue at a teachers' in-service training event for Latin teachers. I observed early-career teachers easily identifying stylistic devices all through a passage of Virgil's *Aeneid*. The teachers did not lack knowledge of Latin vocabulary or the terminology of literary criticism, but they did not seem to find it easy to think of more nuanced or 'spot-on' *English* words to express the *nature* of the events described in the Latin. They knew the meaning of the Latin vocabulary; they knew what was going on in the story; they knew the terminology – which they were very keen to use. What was missing was *the bit in the middle* – the English word or phrase that encapsulated the *intention* of the author (as far as it might be discerned): What did they mean to show by this action? What did they mean to suggest about the character of this person? What can we infer from this event? With little time to think, they were not able to suggest the idea that *Aeneas'* advance could be described as *inexorable* (they *could* say that he was *advancing*), that his hesitation before an altar *portended anxiety* (they *could* say he was *hesitating*), that the darkening sky suggested *looming menace* (they *could* say that the sky was *getting dark*). Caught on the spot, without time to prepare, they simply did not have ready access to the sort of sophisticated English vocabulary to critique the passage. So they stuck labels on everything they could find and hoped for the best. Their experience probably reflected the fact that of most of their students were also – through inexperience – in the process of developing the very same sort of English vocabulary they needed to describe character, motivation, tone, mood and setting. The teacher therefore needs to develop the students' knowledge of this *English vocabulary* as much as that of Latin.

Taking notes

The teacher needs to be sure that the students are taking the right sort of notes. It is easy for the teacher in the course of discussion to glance over and see that the students are writing something down and for them to assume that what the students are writing down is useful. But have they checked? The teacher should not fall into the trap of believing that the students' notes are all fine; and they should never assume or pretend that they are preparing students for the 'University Experience': if the teacher does not teach them how to take notes, the students will not get there.

A three-part strategy:

1 During the discussion, use the board to collate ideas and information, ensuring that students understand the key points and the correct technical vocabulary. This can be done as a brainstorm, spider diagram, or mind map. The point is that the students do not write anything at this stage – it is just a free flow of ideas.

2 The next stage is to make sense of what is on the board. The teacher (or, ideally, the students) might want to delete some of the more outré ideas, or those that they think are simply wrong. A good way of doing this is to ask the students how they would categorize the main points of the argument, or the content or whatever it is that is under discussion. So, for example, the class might want to categorize all the ways in which Horace uses colour imagery in *fons Bandusiae*, or the ways he describes the spring or the goat. It's up to the teacher and the students. At first, the teacher might need to model how to do this, before the students start to get the idea for themselves. False starts are allowed: the teacher wants to develop divergent rather than convergent thinking, which is much more beneficial for creativity and the learning process. It might be obvious to the teacher that a particular approach might be better than the one the students seem to be following, but it isn't yet obvious to them, and it is a great way to share expertise and knowledge around a class.

3 The final stage is to write up a proper note in the notebook. This might be simply copying what is on the board (the teacher might simply save this and print it off if they are using the interactive whiteboard), or the teacher might get the students to use the framework to answer a mini essay question.

Different kinds of writing about literature

- Informal writing: when using free writing, students keep writing about an idea or topic without stopping to worry about spelling, punctuation, grammar or the ordering of ideas. They may dictate their thoughts to another student or into a recorder. This preliminary activity builds students' confidence knowing that they have got something to say. Jotting down ideas as the class reads, drawing sketches and making lists are all ways to encourage students to break through the idea that they have to have something significant to say before making an utterance. Students can use journals to keep track of the narrative: they can write down ideas for themselves; share them with their peers; ask their peers to engage in a written conversation with their thoughts by periodically swapping journals and asking them to respond; assess themselves by making written comments about what they have or have not included at various points during the reading or at the end, revisiting the notes they made; make maps and diagrams to illustrate key moments in the narrative; create artwork, storyboards or comic books to represent particular elements in the story that appeal to the student.

- Multiple perspectives: '*Catullus on the couch*'. After quickly translating *Catullus VIII*, the students formed four groups. Each group rewrote the poem (as a letter, a dialogue) from the point of view of *Catullus* to his psychiatrist, *Lesbia* to another girlfriend, a drinking pal of *Catullus, Catullus*' doctor's notes. Pupils then shared their ideas (Cresswell, 2012). Students who had been reluctant previously to make a contribution found their voices when they could speak in 'someone else's voice'.

- Pupils re-interpret the story in a different idiom or genre, or from another person's perspective. Transferring information from one genre to another encourages a creative and selective approach.

- Rather than write for the teacher, students can be more creative and exploratory if they write for an imagined or real audience. The audience might consist of other students in the class, another member of staff, readers of the school newsletter, etc. I have seen students encouraged in a school to write articles and blogs for publication on the school or department website.

- Students rewrite the stories, using the same characters, but changing the outcome of events; they add in extra characters and respond to events as seen through their 'eyes'; they rewrite the texts in popular genre fiction, such as detective stories murder mysteries or fairy stories.

I advise teachers not to treat these activities as 'fun' or 'Friday afternoon' activities, or things 'you'd only do if you had to motivate the class'. Nor are they designed just to motivate and engage lower-attaining or bored students. They are standard learning tools used in English Literature classes. I rarely see them being used when reaching Latin.

Revision and review

Revision (called review in the US) is a different activity to teaching and learning: the teacher should not obsessively turn every literature lesson into creating a notebook to revise for the examinations – thereby turning assessment into the only kind of learning experience the students have. Knowledge gained by the students that may not explicitly be assessed by examination is highly beneficial to the students; the use of a workbook-dominated sequence of lessons – 'preparing for the test' – reinforces the idea, as Torrance (2007) found with post-secondary students, that only that which is assessed 'counts'. But there is more to it than a rose-tinted view that all learning, whether directly relevant or not, is a good thing: it is through classroom interactions that the students best construct knowledge and best recall that knowledge afterwards. There is also an issue of the environment in which the learning takes place: the teacher should avoid turning the literature lessons into a drudge, a solid march through the uplands of the text, solely in preparation for the examination. If the teacher is not enjoying teaching it, it is unlikely that the students are learning effectively.

In addition, if the teacher programmes in revision or review time and they make it active revision (that is, the teacher helping and guiding the students, rather than them going home to revise on their own), then the revision will be more effective the more often it is done. Thus, if the students look at the text for the first time, then revise it in small portions, then go back over it again in larger portions, and then finally go over it in the revision study leave, they will be far more well prepared than if the teacher teaches to the end of term and scrambles to revise the whole lot the day before the exam.

Assessment

We have already discussed the difference between summative and formative assessment and considered the importance of formative assessment as a standard classroom tool. Let us now turn to summative assessment.

There are, of course, many different forms of summative assessment. The UK national examination boards and the US National Latin Examination and Advanced Placement examinations have their own specifications regarding exactly what linguistic, socio-cultural and literary features (including the precise original texts) are to be tested at each stage and the means by which they ought to be tested. This is not the place to describe these, partly because they are subject to change, and partly because I want to address some practices that teachers can use in the classroom to suit their own students' needs rather than merely using the formats that the examinations demand. As the national examinations need to be standardized in order to be accessible to students who have learnt Latin by many different methods and in order to provide validity over a huge scale, a certain blandness of approach prevails, which can stifle other, perhaps, more appropriate assessment approaches that can be used in the classroom. Similarly, automated marking systems used by national examinations tend to prioritize multiple-choice questions over other techniques that might better reveal to both teacher and students how successful the learning is. All the major course books offer their own practice exercises and some have their own assessments either built-in or available separately. Details of these are given in Chapter 3. I offer the following advice to help teachers formulate their own assessment practices.

What is the test for?

Small, discrete tests are better than large ones. For example, four or five short sentences, each containing an example of a consecutive/result clause is as good a test as twenty short phrases testing knowledge of different prepositions. The assessment must be of a sort that can be used as a diagnostic of weakness of understanding of the specific thing that the test is designed for. Thus extraneous material – irregular vocabulary features and unusual items of vocabulary – should be avoided. The overall mark that is awarded should reflect the students' ability to understand the thing that is being tested and that alone.

Motivation is important. The test should be achievable by most of the students. The tests should be paced: whether with a sequence of short phrases or longer sentences or even with a continuous passage, some material should be easier and some material harder at intervals throughout. This aids motivation to complete the test and provides greater validity to overall mark.

What skills are to be tested?

In the past, the rote learning of charts and tables was seen as an end in itself. Thankfully, teachers follow more useful assessment practices, many of which rely on the testing of the comprehension of a continuous passage of Latin. In this case, testing should consist of the comprehension of Latin, not just of the student's memory. The passage should be long enough to have something worth saying, but short enough to be achievable, without rushing, in the time that is allocated. A final open-ended or personal response question is often a useful way to give students of all abilities an opportunity to sum up their feelings about the whole text and can be a useful extension task for the highest attaining students. The story should be worth reading in order to comprehend. There ought to be no nasty surprises. The exercises should reflect the vocabulary and socio-cultural situations with which the students encountered throughout the course of lessons they attended. In general, questions on a passage of Latin should be of three main types:

1 *Comprehension of the whole story.* Students retell the whole story in a sentence; they draw a picture to represent the story; they give the story a title; they answers questions such as why do you think some event happens or does not happen in the story? They suggest a different ending to the story; they choose a character from the story and explain their actions; they explain who they would like to be in the story.

2 *Comprehension of individual elements.* Students explain details of what happens in a story, where they occur, why they happen, and how; they choose a word in Latin which describes a particular character, event or scene; they select the most appropriate word – such as an adjective or adverb – to describe another (either from the passage itself, or from a list of synonyms, or from a multiple-choice list); they pick a word that contrasts with another.

3 *Comprehension of syntax.* Students must not merely identify the form of a word: they need to be able to explain its function within the sentence or phrase. Students might explain which person a noun or pronoun refers to; what a particular word suggests about the type of clause; which word (such as an adverb or adjective) describes another word and how can they tell. They can substitute one word or phrase for another; manipulate the formation of a word (such as singular to plural); explain the author's use of a subjunctive rather than indicative mood, or the use of one form over another; select a synonym for one word or phrase, perhaps from a given list; and rephrase, for example, *necesse est* with *debeo* (with a set of multiple choices, perhaps).

Testing vocabulary

We have already seen how students acquire and learn vocabulary. Testing vocabulary should always be done in context. Vocabulary that has been encountered several times during normal use of the course book takes precedence over vocabulary chosen at whim by the teacher or plucked randomly from an examination defined vocabulary list. The motivation for the test has to be made explicit – and the idea that students should learn vocabulary for a national examination some years or months ahead, while sufficiently motivating for some, it is not for most. Similarly, vocabulary chosen from a dictionary is often unsuitable, as there are often multiple meanings, reflecting the different authors' uses of the words over time and circumstances. However, being tested on vocabulary that will be useful in the short term for the purpose of reading the stories in the classroom has considerable saliency for the students. Matching words – Latin to English or English to Latin – is not the most effective way of testing students' understanding of vocabulary, as it merely pitches knowledge of lexis over form. Harrison (2010) showed that short sentences were a better test of her students' understanding of lexical items than individual words. She provided several short phrases to her students, with the words to be translated underlined as follows:

- *agricolam <u>iuvat</u>*, rather than *agricola* and *iuvo*;
- *<u>iacere debes</u>*, rather than *iaceo* and *debeo*; and
- *<u>fortunam</u> superant*, rather than *fortuna* and *supero*.

These phrases enabled her to judge students' understanding of the forms as well as the direct meanings of individual words – a common criticism of and by students who seem to be able to recall individual words but who seem to find difficulty relating their meaning in context. Other ways of testing vocabulary could consist of students drawing pictures or adding text to pictures; writing antonyms or synonyms for the words; writing down words that are related to a particular context or idea, such as words concerning the parts of a villa, the army, verbs of movement or perception.

Testing grammar

All good course books provide examples of the sorts of exercises that can be useful models for grammar tests. The most important thing to remember is that nothing should distract the students from focusing on the grammatical item being tested. Would failure on the test be a mark of poor vocabulary knowledge or failure to understand the new grammar feature? Thus, unusual or irregular vocabulary or forms should be avoided. Completion tests are useful: students fill a gap in a sentence by choosing among a given set of words. Tests that require the student to transform words or phrases – such as transforming masculine to feminine, singular to plural, active to passive – are more challenging but again can be completed by choosing from a set of alternatives.

Testing syntax

Students can be asked to select alternative versions of different sorts of clause, such as *oportet*/*debeo*/*neceese est*; gerundives of obligation; participle phrases with relative clauses; and contrast indirect speech with direct speech.

Reading tests

Reading tests are the staple of inter-school reading competitions but are very rarely considered appropriate as a form of test in lessons. Students might be asked (after preparation) to read aloud for *pronunciation* (double consonants, correct sounds of vowels and diphthongs); *intonation* (questions, statements, commands); and *phrasing and grouping* of words – 'Latinity'.

Dictation tests

The teacher reads Latin aloud while the students write down short phrases: *in mensis – in mensa*; *ab hostibus interfecta erat – a militibus interfectus est*, and so on. This trains the students' ear to follow and be alert to the spelling and the meaning of words.

In conclusion, Morris (1966) suggests that assessments used for the collation of marks for summative purposes – in an end-of-year examination, for example – must meet four criteria if they are to be useful:

- **Objectivity**: marking should be wholly objective: the students should know the criteria on which they are being assessed beforehand.
- **Reliability**: the assessment should be constructed in such a way that results are comparable across large numbers of students, perhaps taught by different teachers, and at different times.

- **Validity**: the test should assess what it is meant to. Written translation from Latin to English is only one of many ways of assessing students' understanding of Latin.
- **Appropriateness**: the test should be suited to the method of teaching and the type of course that has been used (after Morris, 1966, pp. 69–70).

The last of these criteria is especially significant. It relates specifically to the introduction of compulsory translation of English into Latin sentences or grammar-identification exercises at GCSE – assessment procedures which are not in line with the vast majority of teaching practices in the UK and which are not included in the most widely used course books, *ecce Romani*, the *Cambridge Latin Course* and *Suburani*, and have limited representation in the much less widely used *Oxford Latin Course*. It is a great surprise that these extensions to the national assessment criteria have been drawn up by the Department for Education without consulting teachers and without reference to existing teaching materials. For further details on the debate and methods, see Chapter 5 in Hunt (2022a).

3

Resources

It is a source of considerable pride to me that the number of students studying Latin in comprehensives is the highest ever. We are presiding over the greatest renaissance in Latin learning since Julius Caesar invaded.

Michael Gove, former UK Minister for Education; Hansard, 2011

Despite such a claim, support for Latin teaching in schools, compared with other subject areas, has been historically very limited, both financially and politically, and is subject to the interests of individual politicians and susceptible to withdrawal by head teachers at a moment's notice. It has been left, until very recently, to the subject associations, commercial book publishers, the examination boards, and a host of individuals – teachers and other interested parties – to maintain and develop Latin in schools today. This section, therefore, is intended to give readers some guidaance about where to go to and who to ask for advice. It is an overview of:

- the most widely used Latin course books;
- books on teaching practices and the state of Latin teaching today;
- journals, websites and blogs;
- subject associations and university outreach; and
- assessment and examinations materials.

Latin course books

The study of Latin in schools today has come to consist of an integrated study of the language, literature and civilization of Rome. Most widely used course books subscribe to this pattern, although they differ in the degree to which they put it into practice. While many of the individual course books have their own accompanying teacher's handbooks, there have been surprisingly few general handbooks for teachers of Latin and none in the past twenty years. A number of old-fashioned guides to teaching have been reprinted recently (see, for example, Sears, B., 1844 [2012]; Jones, 1906 [2012]; Bennett, 1911 [2012]; and Game, 1916 [2012]). Clearly of antiquarian interest, these books are unlikely to succeed as guides to effective practice today. They make fascinating reading, however, especially if one wants to see how Latin teaching has changed – mostly for the better in that it is now more accessible to students of all social and cognitive backgrounds. From the UK perspective, Morris' (1966) book *New Techniques in Latin Teaching* is interesting but very much of its time. From the US perspective, there are Distler's (1962) *Teach the Latin, I Pray You* and Davis' (1991) *Latin in American Schools*. Distler's work contains many useful and still-relevant pedagogical suggestions, but it inevitably reflects the age and circumstances of the times it was written. Davis' work does not pretend to be a teaching manual. It contains, *inter alia*, a set of guidelines on the linguistic features a school student might reasonably learn during their school career; it does not expand on how these topics might be taught.

Widely used Latin language course books

The course books described here are designed for school-age students learning Latin from the beginning. There are numerous course books designed for older students. I do not have the space to describe them all here.

Where possible, I have included details of In-Service Training (INSET) and Continuing Professional Development (CPD) events that the authors or publishers of the courses provide. Where possible, I have also included references to articles and websites that provide advice for teaching courses for which training is not regularly provided.

For each course book I have included a commentary on its style, presentation and use. I have tried to be as objective as possible. What is interesting is how different course books endeavour to achieve the same ends by such different methods: to enable students to be able to comprehend original Roman authors. How much they are able to do this is dependent, I suspect, more on the teacher's knowledge and ability and the students' diligence and application than on any particular feature of a given course book. The authors of course books try to make their courses 'teacher-proof', which results in very different approaches. For some, this means keeping the presentation simple, refined and absolutely focused on the essentials that are needed to learn how to comprehend Latin; for others, this means lengthy discourse and explanations of each and every grammatical and socio-cultural point.

Note that UK and US course books have traditionally ordered the cases of nouns as follows:

UK	USA
Nominative	Nominative
Vocative	Genitive
Accusative	Dative
Genitive	Accusative
Dative	Ablative
Ablative	Vocative

For students in secondary schools/high schools

Reading / inductive / communicative approach

Cambridge Latin Course, *UK fourth edition (Cambridge School Classics Project, 1998); UK fifth edition (Cambridge School Classics Project, 2022); US fifth edition (Cambridge School Classics Project, 2016), published by Cambridge University Press [www.cambridgescp.com]*

Number of course books: Five books (UK); four books (USA).

Teacher's handbooks: Yes – for each course book.

Ancillary printed materials: Independent learning books for students; *Cambridge Latin Grammar* book; *Cambridge Latin Anthology* (prose and verse texts from a range of authors, lightly adapted); worksheets that can be photocopied; Cambridge assessment tests and certificates; downloadable texts and workbooks for associated WJEC examination topics.

Digital resources: Online *Cambridge Latin Course* e-learning (includes all stories and exercises from the printed version); DVD resources for UK Books 1 and 2 (no longer supported by CSCP, but copies may still be available); an e-book is available for commonly-used platforms. In the US, access to the digital resources is via Elevate, a platform supported by the Cambridge University Press.

INSET/CPD: *Cambridge School Classics Project* (CSCP) organizes an annual conference in Cambridge and training events around the UK with external funding from the Department for Education and the Classical Association. CSCP also offers distance-learning courses for teachers and for students. See www.cambridgescp.com for details. The *North American Cambridge Classics Project* (NACCP) organizes regular training events around the USA and webinars.

Commentary: The *Cambridge Latin Course* is the best resourced of all the course books. There is little doubt among teachers, students and parents that it has been, as Morwood (2003, p. xvii) says, '[of] central importance to the survival of Latin [in the UK]'. The course is based around a continuous Latin story that takes the reader through historically plausible events starting in Pompeii in 79 CE and ending in the reign of Domitian in Rome. Book 5 (US Unit 4) also contains original verse and prose selections from Roman authors. The course is intended to teach students the skills to be able to read Latin in order to learn about life in the Roman world in the first century CE and to prepare them for reading more extensive original Latin authors. It consists of sections ('stages'), each of which presents new grammatical features gradually, with explanation, further consolidation and practice as the student progresses. Each stage follows the same pattern: an introductory photograph, model sentences, a series of Latin stories in confected or made-up Latin, grammar explanations and exercises, background material in English and a vocabulary list. There are no composition elements, such as English into Latin translation or free composition, but there are language manipulation exercises in every stage that ask the student to complete and/or translate Latin into English and English into Latin sentences. The whole course was originally designed to take around four years. Many schools in the UK find that they need to spend at minimum of four years on the course on an average timetable allocation of 1.5-2 hours per week.

Grammar is presented in a highly worked out linguistic scheme: rather than expecting students to process the language at a single word level, the course approaches language at phrase and sentence levels of increasing complexity. The course allows the teacher to judge when to introduce grammar – the teacher will know their class sufficiently well when to do this – but in any case, each stage has a clear explanation of the new grammatical features. The DVD has 'talking head' grammar explanations for the first two books. The first edition of the *Cambridge Latin Course* (1970) eschewed the traditional nomenclature for the cases, using instead 'Form A' and 'Form B' for the Nominative and Accusative, for example, but it has long since reverted to the standard terminology and is now in its full-colour fourth UK edition (1998). In response to criticism of the way in which female characters and enslaved people were represented in the Cambridge Latin Course, to reduce the amount of text and to accommodate a wider range of learners, CSCP has published a revised 5th edition of Book 1 for the US market in 2016 and UK teachers in 2022 received their own 5th edition of Book 1, which has been more extensively revised. A UK revised 5th edition for Books 2–3 is under development. For details of these revisions, see Joffe (2019) and Hunt (2022a) and elsewhere in this book.

The *Cambridge Latin Course* was designed for use with a much broader range of students than the previous traditional Latin course books. This it continues to do very well, being used by around 82% of schools in the UK (Cambridge School Classics Project, 2009) and perhaps a third of schools in the USA. Book 1 (US Unit 1) is well suited to teaching every student that teachers are likely to meet in the average secondary or high school.

The excellent selection of digital resources means that classroom activities can be remarkably varied. The online and DVD resources consist of digitized versions of the stories with a function to reveal, check and retest any vocabulary, drag and drop grammar exercises, video documentaries and drama reconstructions of the stories. Electronic quizzes and assessments are under development, which will report student responses to the teacher.

In the UK, CSCP worked closely with the WJEC examinations board to provide free downloadable materials such as set texts for examination at Level 1 certificates. It currently supports the GCSE examinations board Eduqas with digital resources for Latin GCSE literature.

Suburani (Hands Up Education, 2020), published by Hands Up Education Community Interest Company [https://hands-up-education.org/suburani.html]

Number of course books: Two course books, with a third under development.

Teacher's handbooks: Available online.

Ancillary printed materials: Two Latin short stories / novellas.

Digital resources: full, online resources, including online versions of the course book, practice exercises, quizzes and other activities, and links to external websites.

INSET/CPD: Hands Up Education provide regular training events in the UK and USA at various events throughout the year, including at the Institute of the American Classical League.

Commentary: *Suburani* is a continuous narrative, similar in style to the *Cambridge Latin Course* and the *Oxford Latin Course*, based on a continuous story set first in ancient Rome and then passing by way of Roman Britain, Spain and Portugal, set in the last years of the reign of Nero. The young and diverse range of characters is designed to represent more accurately that of the ancient world and to appeal to the modern student body. The book uses a mixture of graphic novel and more traditional narratives, interspersed with language notes, language exercises. The pace is, I feel, slightly faster than that of the *Cambridge Latin Course* and the grammar a little more explicit, although it follows a similar linguistic sequence. The books also include a great deal of information on the historical and socio-cultural background, including mythology. The subject matter is deliberately aimed at the present teenage market both in terms of production values and narrative content. For a description of the development of the characters, see Delaney et al. (2021). The digital resources are extensive. One important feature is that teachers can subscribe students to the digital course and track their progress: the exercises have a self-marking and reporting feature which teachers find helpful. The two books take students comfortably to the language requirements of the UK GCSE examination. The writers are currently developing a third book which will help students transition to original literature.

Oxford Latin Course (Balme and Morwood, 1996), published by Oxford University Press

Number of course books: Three course books.

Teacher's handbooks: Three teacher's handbooks.

Ancillary printed materials: Latin reader – a collection of short stories to translate into English.

Digital resources: Two CD ROMs.

INSET/CPD: None.

Commentary: The *Oxford Latin Course* is a continuous story based on the historical events surrounding the life of the Roman poet Horace in the first century BCE, including his early childhood, his education in Rome and 'discovery' by Maecenas, and his involvement in the Civil War. The course takes the opportunity to introduce students to some of the stories from Greek and Roman myths and Roman history. English to Latin sentences are offered as an option at the back of the book.

The presentation of material partly follows the pattern set by the *Cambridge Latin Course*. The book is popular among teachers of higher-achieving students and aims to take them through to GCSE and beyond. The mythological subject matter of the background material and the stories themselves can be appealing. Grammar is presented more up-front than in the *Cambridge Latin Course* and follows more traditional approaches.

Ecce Romani (Scottish Classics Group): first (1971) and second (1982) editions published by Oliver and Boyd; third (2005) and fourth (2009) editions published by Prentice-Hall. The first to third editions are generally still available in the UK. The fourth edition is designed for the US market.

Number of course books: The first edition has six books; the second and third editions have five each; the fourth edition has three.

Teacher's handbooks: Yes, for second and third editions.

Ancillary printed materials: Student's companion booklets for first and second editions; Roman studies handbook; languages activity booklets for third and fourth editions.

Digital resources: Some digital resources are under development. Useful websites include Pearson's http://www.phschool.com/atschool/ecce_romani/program_page.html and Gilbert Lawall's *ecce Romani Teacher's Corner* [http://people.umass.edu/glawall/ecceteach.html] where some resources are shared.

INSET/CPD: Some is available in the USA; there is usually a dedicated event at the annual Institute of the American Classical League.

Commentary: One of the earliest narrative textbooks for Latin, originally designed by the Scottish Classics Group as a two-year course. The course contains some Living Latin approaches and some prose composition but broadly comprises a mix of grammar-translation and reading approaches. The presentation of material in the chapters varies. In general, there is a continuous Latin story that takes the Cornelii family from the countryside farm to the centre of Rome to witness a party, entertainment in the Colosseum and Circus Maximus, a wedding and a death. There are tables of grammar to be learnt, practice exercises into and out of Latin, consolidation translation exercises, and background civilization material in English. *ecce Romani* has recently been reprinted in the UK. It is considerably less popular in the UK than in the USA where it has even more recently been reprinted and rearranged. Production values in this most recent US edition are high. An interesting feature is the inclusion of 'responde Latine' questions on the stories, in which students are asked questions in Latin to which they should reply in Latin. This approach is gaining interest more widely among teachers who favour a more communicative approach to teaching Latin.

Lingua Latin per se Illustrata [The Latin language, illustrated by itself] (Hans Oerberg, 1991), published by Hackett Publishing Company

Number of Course Books: Two main course books.

Teacher's handbooks: Yes.

Ancillary printed materials: Several additional readers, workbooks and grammar books.

Digital resources: No, but a strong social media presence among teachers.

INSET/CPD: Informal among teachers.

Commentary: The course book is entirely in Latin. Grammar and vocabulary are carefully introduced in a linguistic scheme which constantly relates new material to old. The book follows a Roman family and is a continuous narrative, with short exercises for checking comprehension at the end of each chapter. New vocabulary is introduced by means of images and by synonyms in Latin, as well as by the standard inductive approach of inference. While the start of the book seems especially simple, the course rapidly evolves into more complex grammar, all in the same process as before. The books include the beginners' Familia Romana, then Roma Aeterna and Colloquia Personarum. For experiences in using *Lingua Latina per se Illustrata*, see various chapters in Lloyd and Hunt (2021). The course has been much more in common use in US college education, but has become of interest in US high schools; its use in UK secondary schools is on a very small scale.

Via Latina [The Roman Way] (Aguilar & Tarrega, 2022), published by Cultura Clasica

A recently-published course book in the *Lingua Latina* mould. Illustrations are in full colour and there seem to be more exercises more frequently distributed among the readings than with *Lingua Latina*. This means, inevitably, that there is less to read, which may appeal to some or disappoint others. The narrative concerns the early history of Rome, based on the Roman historian Livy. For an interesting comparison of Lingua Latina and Via Latina, see Macdonald (2022).

Grammar-translation / deductive approach

So You Really Want To Learn Latin (various editions by Nick Oulton, Theo Zinn and Anne Wright), published by Galore Park (2006)

Number of course books: Three.

Teacher's handbooks: Answer books for each of the first three books.

Ancillary printed materials: Unseen practice book; Latin reader; crossword puzzle book; student workbook.

Digital resources: The author demonstrates the principles of the course [https://www.youtube.com/watch?v=E5Ozln5-o0U].

INSET/CPD: None.

Commentary: *So You Really Want To Learn Latin* was originally designed for students in UK private preparatory schools who will take the competitive entrance examinations for major independent /private secondary schools.

The course is swift and challenging from the start. Translation from English to Latin is expected. Each chapter is presented in the same way: an explanation of a grammatical feature is followed by practice exercises and a translation. Each activity is explained on one side of the page, with practice examples on the other. This rigid format is not always successful in dealing with the complexities of the syntax under discussion, as they do not always fit the page format. There is a brief English description of an aspect of Roman civilization or history at the end of the chapter. Presentation in two colours highlights grammatical features.

Latin to GCSE Part 1 *(Cullen and Taylor, 2016) and* ***Latin to GCSE Part 2*** *(Cullen and Taylor, 2018), published by Bloomsbury Academic*

Number of course books: Two.

Teacher's handbooks: None.

Ancillary printed materials: None.

Digital resources: None.

INSET/CPD: None, but the authors occasionally contribute to conferences and INSET which is organized by the Classical Association, for example.

Commentary: Latin to GCSE is a resolutely grammar-first course book with plenty of information about Latin grammar and comparisons with English. Each chapter follows the traditional path of a grammar explanation, list of vocabulary to learn, a table of morphology to learn, practice phrases or sentences, and a short passage for translation to test what has been learned. All of these in Latin – English. Interwoven are some exercises for translation into Latin, as optional extras. The no-nonsense appearance of the text is lightened by occasional information about the ancient world and the passages for translation from Latin draw inspiration from mythological and historical stories of the Roman period. Its quite a 'dry' book. Book 2 prepares students for the UK's Latin GCSE examination by offering a selection of GCSE-style passages for practice in translation and comprehension.

Essential GCSE Latin *(Taylor, 2014), published by Bloomsbury Academic*

Number of course books: One.

Teacher's handbooks: None.

Ancillary printed materials: None.

Digital resources: None at present.

INSET/CPD: None.

Commentary: *Essential GCSE Latin* is not a course book that teaches students Latin from the beginning. Instead, it is intended as a revision guide for students who are preparing for the GCSE examination in Latin. The book gives details of the major grammatical features needed for the present GCSE Latin examination, with practice exercises.

De Romanis. Book 1: dei et deae. (Radice et al., 2020) and **De Romanis. Book 2: homines** *(Radice et al., 2020), published by Bloomsbury Academic*

Number of course books: Two.

Teacher's handbooks: Available online.

Ancillary printed materials: Available online.

Digital resources: Online training and advice.

INSET/CPD: Delivered online, with some presentations at conferences / events in the UK.

Commentary: *De Romanis* takes students about halfway through to the language requirements for GCSE Latin (so subjunctives and subordination). It's a robust course, following the grammar-first principles described above for *Latin to GCSE*, but with the addition of extended background information and widespread use of colour in illustrations and design. Each chapter starts with Roman historical, literary or socio-cultural background material, and looks at ways in which this has been disseminated through the ages by means of the arts. The subject matter of the background material is then reflected in the stories in Latin which follow. There is a lot of material and the authors suggest that teachers need to be choosy about what will suit their students: there is no intention to use everything. Having said that, the breadth of material can be overwhelming and it is often difficult to see what might be essential material for use in a coherent sequence of lessons (for example, some of the morphological charts are given without explanation). At the end of the course of two books, one assumes that students then move on to *Latin to GCSE Book 2* to complete the GCSE language requirement (a third book is reported to be under development). The authors suggest, moreover, that those students who do not intend to continue with Latin will have received sufficient foundation in the classical world to be able to continue with a GCSE or A Level in Classical Civilization.

Imperium *(Morgan, 2014), self-published [available from Amazon and www. imperiumlatin.com]*

Number of course books: Three.

Teacher's handbooks: One.

Ancillary printed materials: Practice unseens (including Saucy Stories anthology and Virgil); grammar and syntax book.

Digital resources: e-book; online materials; an app; available on Kindle. Website http://www.imperiumlatin.com/index.html.

INSET/CPD: None.

Commentary: *Imperium* is a story-based course following the life and loves of the emperor Hadrian. The course presents Latin grammatical explanations ahead of a continuous text that has to be translated sentence by sentence into spaces on the page. It is therefore more akin to a course book combined with a workbook. *Imperium* includes cultural material in English and photographs relevant to the historical events described. *Imperium* also exists as a digital version, which is the same as the printed version but with the option of submitting answers electronically to the teacher.

Gwynne's Latin *(Gwynne, 2014), published by Ebury Press*

Number of course books: One.

Teacher's handbooks: None.

Ancillary printed materials: None.

Digital resources: None. Gwynne has his own website where he explains his course and demonstrates a lesson [http://gwynneteaching.com/gwynnes-latin/].

INSET/CPD: None.

Commentary: The book takes an ultra-traditional grammar-translation approach. Example sentences, nearly always given in English first, include side-swipes at other Latin courses and the supposed inadequacies of their teachers, such as 'The new-fangled teachers *did not realise* that grammar was such an important subject' (Gwynne, 2014, p. 136). The book prioritizes rote-learning of tables and translation of sentences from English into Latin. There is little consolidation or practice of continuous Latin in the book. The small format of the book, dense writing and lack of cultural context are significant drawbacks to classroom use.

Learn to Read Latin *(Keller and Russell, 2006), published by Yale University Press*

Number of course books: Two.

Teacher's handbooks: None.

Ancillary printed materials: Two student's workbooks.

Digital resources: None.

INSET/CPD: None.

Commentary: The course was designed for undergraduate use. The student needs to work with the grammar book and workbook together. Detailed explanations of Latin grammar are presented that students need to memorize. They then complete exercises in the workbook. Towards the end of Book One, the course introduces students to shorter and then longer unadapted extracts from original Roman authors, presented in chronological order.

Wheelock's Latin (Frederick Wheelock, in a new edition by Richard LaFleur, 2011), published by Collins Educational [www.wheelockslatin.com]

Number of course books: One.

Teacher's handbooks: One.

Ancillary printed materials: Student's workbook, reader; reading companion; flashcards.

Digital resources: Some online support [http://www.wheelockslatin.com/]; audio files; available on Kindle.

INSET/CPD: None, but popular in US training events.

Commentary: Wheelock has been around since the end of the Second World War and has recently undergone a makeover by Richard LaFleur. Now in its seventh edition, it uses the traditional grammar-translation approach, basing its practice exercises on extracts (barely adapted) from original Roman authors. Background context is provided for the texts themselves. In the UK, Wheelock is often used to teach in *ab initio* Latin classes at undergraduate level to those students who have joined a Classics degree course but who have not had the opportunity to study Latin at school. In the USA, the book has more widespread acceptance at high school level.

Mixed approach

Latin for the New Millennium (Tunberg and Minkova, 2008), published by Bolchazy-Carducci [http://www.bolchazy.com/Assets/Bolchazy/ClientPages/LNM.aspx]

Number of course books: Two.

Teacher's handbooks: Two.

Ancillary printed materials: Student's workbooks.

Digital resources: Some resources, based on www.quia quizzes.

INSET/CPD: None.

Commentary: Book One focuses on Classical Latin, Book Two on post-classical Latin. The course describes itself as a fusion of reading approach and grammar translation. Chapters contain reading passages, a commentary on grammatical features, consolidation and practice exercises, oral and aural activities, and an English essay on a cultural background topic. Texts are selected from original Roman authors wherever possible, so as to introduce students to the idea that they are reading original Latin from the beginning. There is no continuous character-led story, such as that encountered in standard reading approach courses. Instead, *Latin for the New Millennium* presents the idea of the story of the Latin language as a conveyor of literature, thought and ideas from the classical age to the renaissance. The course is designed to fit with the demands of the US National Latin Exam.

Latin via Ovid (Goldman and Nyenhuis, 1982), published by Wayne State University Press

Number of course books: One.

Teacher's handbook: None.

Ancillary printed materials: Student's workbook.

Digital materials: CD ROMs.

INSET/CPD: None.

Commentary: A combination of reading passages based on Ovid's *Metamorphoses* and traditional grammar charts and tables. Contains cultural background notes.

For students in primary schools/junior high schools

Minimus (Bell, 1999), published by Cambridge University Press

Number of course books: Two.

Teacher's handbooks: Yes.

Ancillary printed materials: *Minimus in Practice* resource book; short story Latin readers; teacher's book that can be photocopied; pencils, postcards and badges.

Digital resources: interactive quizzes, song-sheets and details of forthcoming events are available at: www.minimuslatin.co.uk. E-books are under development.

INSET/CPD: Training events take place regularly or can be provided in UK or US schools.

Commentary: *Minimus* features a cartoon-style storyline based around the adventures of a Romano-British family at the Roman fortress Vindolanda on Hadrian's Wall in the first century CE. The course puts great emphasis on how Latin can help younger pupils with English grammar and vocabulary. The Primary Latin Project can provide small grants to assist with the purchase of books.

Learning Latin Through Mythology (Hanlin and Lichtenstein, 1991), published by Cambridge University Press

Number of course books: One.

Teacher's handbooks: None.

Ancillary printed materials: None.

Digital resources: None.

INSET/CPD: None.

Commentary: The format is of a cartoon story introducing a mythological subject, followed by simple exercises and a mythological story in English.

Telling Tales with Ovid (Robinson, 2014), published by Souvenir Press

Number of course books: One.

Teacher's handbooks: Yes, downloadable from website.

Ancillary printed materials: None.

Digital resources: The IRIS website contains information for teachers using the book [http://irisproject.org.uk/index.php/resources/telling-tales-in-latin-teachers-guide2].

INSET/CPD: Undergraduate teachers in the IRIS Project receive training.

Commentary: The format is a short story in Latin based on a heavily adapted story from Ovid's *Metamorphosis*. Exercises follow. Like *Minimus*, the focus is on teaching English literacy through Latin. Although the stories are quite interesting, being Ovid they do not always quite make rational sense to a young student; meanwhile the Latin is sometimes rather forced to fit the original story, which leads to further cognitive difficulties. There are Latin grammatical errors in the book (for a list, see Spooner, 2014). The course contains the same vocabulary as that which is in the OCR Entry level examination.

Maximum Classics (Classics for All, 2022), published online by Classics for All

Number of course books: Digital resources only.

Teacher's handbooks: Yes, downloadable from website.

Ancillary printed materials: Downloadable from website.

Digital resources: The course is digital.

INSET/CPD: Classics for All provide free training in the use of the resource for UK state-maintained schools.

Commentary: *Maximum Classics* is designed to match the requirements of the English Key Stage 2 programmes of study for foreign languages and English. it comprises a set of slide-based resources which explore Latin/ English word roots, simple Latin vocabulary and grammar, and Roman civilization. Ancillary materials, such as worksheets and classroom activities are included on the website for download and printing.

Primary Latin Course (Hands Up Education, 2022), *published online by Hands Up Education Community Interest Company*

Number of course books: Digital resources only.

Teacher's handbooks: Yes, on website.

Ancillary printed materials: Online course.

Digital resources: The course is digital.

INSET/CPD: Occasionally provided in the UK by Hands Up Education.

Commentary: *The Primary Latin Course* is completely digital and simple to use. The course takes a highly visual narrative approach, following two young archaeologists as they explore the site of Herculaneum in the Bay of Naples. Latin is introduced through a cartoon picture strip as individual words, leading quickly into short phrases and sentences. It is vocabulary-driven. A 'click-and-tell' feature allows teachers and students to check the meanings of words by touching the screen; the words are also 'sounded' to help learning and recall.

Elementa. Teaching Literacy with Latin (The Paideia Institute), 2019), *published by The Paideia Institute of Humanistic Study.*

Number of course books: One.

Teacher's handbooks: One.

Ancillary Printed Materials: Available online.

Digital resources: Available online.

INSET/CPD: unknown.

Commentary: Elementa is a Latin for literacy programme which draws inspiration from classical mythology. It is essentially a derivations book, which makes comparisons between Latin word roots and Spanish and English. There is also some Graeco-Roman socio-cultural and political background. The programme is operated in the USA by the Paideia Institute.

Books about teaching Classics (including Latin)

A number of books have been published describing and evaluating the current position of Latin in schools and the practices of Latin teachers.

UK perspective

John Sharwood Smith's volume *On Teaching Classics* (1977) is the early model for books about the teaching of Classical subjects in schools. A wide-ranging book, it clearly is very much a product of its time – the 'day in the life of a Classics teacher' contained within the epilogue is a reminiscence from long ago. Nevertheless, Sharwood Smith's thoughtfulness and intellect and his beautiful prose still shine through and his arguments often still have much to commend them. There are chapters on the teaching of classical studies courses, the classical languages, and literature and ancient history. Sharwood Smith had been the driving force behind arguments for the development of more progressive course books and in order to proselytize his and others' views and offer a platform for proper debate about Classical subjects, he set up the subject association The Joint Association of Classical Teachers and the journal *Didaskalos* – the direct ancestor of the *Journal of Classics Teaching*.

Christopher Stray's *The Living Word: W. H. D. Rouse and the Crisis of Classics in Edwardian England* (1992) describes and evaluates the career and methods of the leading proponent of the Direct Method of Latin teaching (a precursor to the Living Latin approaches used today) in the early years of the twentieth century. More details about Rouse can be accessed on the Association for Latin Teaching website [www. arlt.org.uk]. The same author's *Classics Transformed: Schools, Universities, and Society in England, 1830–1960* (Stray, 1998a) contains a final chapter on the development of the 'new' Latin courses in response to changes needed in Latin teaching in UK schools in the 1960s.

Martin Forrest's magisterial *Modernising the Classics* (1996) describes the historical background to and development of the *Cambridge Latin Course* and his own materials for teaching the non-linguistic aspects of the ancient Greek and Roman worlds. It takes in events up to and including the introduction of the National Curriculum of 1988. Forrest also contributed the chapter *The Abolition of Compulsory Latin and its Consequences* (2003) in The Classical Association's centenary volume *The Classical Association: The First Century 1903–2003* and the effect it had on the formation of the subject association the Joint Association of Classical Teachers.

James Morwood's *The Teaching of Classics* (2003) provides a succinct overview of the state of Classics teaching in the primary, secondary, tertiary and museum sectors in the UK at the beginning of the twenty-first century. The first three chapters trace the historical developments of Classical subjects taught in schools from the 1960s to 2003: a sense of the subjects still being under siege only ten years ago pervades the atmosphere. Of particular interest for Latin teaching are the contributions by Barbara Bell on *Minimus*, Bob Bass on *Classics in Prep Schools*, Brenda Gay on *The Theoretical Underpinning of the Main Latin Courses*, Pat Story on the *Development of the Cambridge Latin Course*, and Maurice Balme and James Morwood on *The Oxford Latin Course*. Judith Affleck's contribution *Twilight Classics* calls for concerted action from the subject associations and government to work together to help Classics blossom in the darker corners of the educational system – a call which, at long last, seems to have been heard.

Bob Lister's *Changing Classics in Schools* (2007b) assesses the then current state of Classics in primary and secondary schools in the UK, with detailed statistical evidence of the subject's decline since the introduction of the National Curriculum in 1988. Lister goes on to describe the positive impact his own War With Troy resources (in the primary sector) and the development of digital resources for the *Cambridge Latin Course* (in the secondary sector) have had in the classroom. A major *caveat* throughout the book is that the development of resource materials – costly to make and long in development if they are to stand the test of time – is but one part of the challenge. The other consists of the provision of qualified teachers – a situation that is now only just partially being addressed in the UK and still subject to capricious change at the heart of government.

Arlene Holmes-Henderson, Steven Hunt and Mai Musié's multi-authored volume *Forward with Classics: Classical Languages in Schools and Communities* (2018) provides multiple case studies of how individuals, schools and other organizations have grown classical languages in their areas of expertise. In particular, readers will find the chapters on Latin in primary schools (Maguire, Bell and Wing-Davey) and in secondary schools (Darby, Robinson, Sanchez and Neto) most compelling.

Bartolo Natoli and Steven Hunt's multi-authored volume *Teaching Classics with Technology* (2019) contains useful examples of how digital technology is changing the face of Latin teaching in the classroom today. See in particular Hunt for teaching using projected text, the use of VLEs (Lewis, Searle) and technology of all sorts in a tour de force of classroom management (Hay).

Mair Lloyd and Steven Hunt's edited volume *Communicative Approaches for Ancient Languages* (2021) provides multiple case studies of Latin teachers' experiences with using more communicative approaches to teaching and learning Latin at the secondary school and college levels. In particular worth reading are the chapters by David Urbanski and Judith Affleck, who wrestle with the sometimes contrarian requirements of school practice and school assessment, and by Justin Slocu,m Bailey, Steven Hunt, Mair Lloyd and Clive Letchford who give vivid examples of teaching practices they have tried in their own classrooms.

Steven Hunt's *Teaching Latin: Contexts, Theories, Practices* (2022a) is the most up to date book on teaching Latin in print (bar this one). It takes some of the themes mentioned briefly in this book and expands on them, taking inspiration from approaches common to modern foreign languages teaching and applying them, not without scrutiny, to the Latin classroom.

Dexter Hoyos' *Latin: How to Read it Fluently. A Practical Manual* (2016) is an excellent booklet – not a text book in the usual manner, but a guide for teachers to use with whatever texts they are using with their classes to teach them how to read Latin texts as they were meant to be read – that is, from left to right as one might with most modern foreign languages. The principles are simple and straightforward and draw on examples from original Roman authors.

Ronnie Ancona's *A Concise Guide to Teaching Latin Literature* (2007), while written originally for the US Advanced Placement examination, is a useful and informative guide on a subject few have touched on and applicable to many other original texts.

US perspective

Richard LaFleur's volume *Latin for the 21st Century* (1998) contains much of value – and applicable outside the US too. Kenneth Kitchell's chapter *The Great Latin Debate: The Futility of Utility?* lays bare the arguments used over the last hundred years or so for the study of Latin. Glenn M. Knudsvig and Deborah Pennell Ross' chapter *The Linguistic Perspective* explores the rationale for the shift away from writing to reading Latin, while Martha Abbott's *Trends in Language Education: Latin in the Mainstream* advocates the importance of having Latin teachers learn from research into the teaching and learning of modern foreign languages and apply it to the teaching of ancient ones. A sequence of chapters follows with detailed description and evaluation of teaching models and practices in the elementary grades, at high school and at college levels. Edward V. George provides a number of case studies of teachers teaching Latin to students from Hispanic backgrounds; Althea C. Ashe describes her own experiences of teaching students with special educational needs.

John Gruber-Miller's edited volume *When Dead Tongues Speak: Teaching Beginning Latin and Greek* (2006c) contains a series of excellent chapters. His own *Communications, Contexts and Community: Integrating the Standards for Classical Languages in the Greek and Latin Classroom* is a good place to start; Andrea Deagon's chapter *Cognitive Style and Learning Strategies in Latin Instruction* is a thorough exposition of the importance the teacher should attach to thinking about their students' learning styles when planning lessons and choosing resources; Kathryn Argetsinger's *Peer Teaching and Cooperative Learning in the First Year of Latin* argues for teachers to move away from the silent, written 'lesson as test' traditional Latin-teaching methodology; Barbara Hill's *Latin for Students with Severe Foreign Language Learning Difficulties* adds more to the growing body of knowledge about teaching Latin to students with special educational needs. The further reading section is well worth perusing for its links to resources about language teaching and learning in general and to selected articles about the teaching and learning of ancient languages in particular.

Phyllis Culham and Lowell Edmunds' *Classics: A Discipline and Profession in Crisis* (1989) draws primarily on experiences from the college and university levels. However, Ed Phinney's chapter *The Classics in American Education* – a record of the collaboration between college professors and schools in supporting Classics in high schools in the 1980s – is worth reading to remind ourselves of the strength of impact the collaboration of the two sectors can have. It's a lesson worth repeating for each generation.

International perspective

Bob Lister's *Meeting the Challenge: International Perspectives on the Teaching of Classics* (2008) is an outstanding resource, containing chapters on the teaching of Latin (and Greek) from several international perspectives and experts in their fields. Of particular interest to Latin teachers and essential reading are the chapters by Deborah Pennell Ross on linear reading, Toon Van Houdlt on the strategic reading of Latin texts, Will Griffiths on the development of the e-learning resources for the *Cambridge Latin Course*, and Steven Hunt on ICT and teaching Latin literature.

John Bulwer's *Classics Teaching in Europe* (2006) outlines the state of Classics in fifteen European countries. Slightly out of date now, the book offers an interesting perspective on the value different nation-states put on the study of ancient languages and the efforts made by local subject associations to maintain and develop their study in schools and universities.

Journals and journal articles about Latin teaching and learning

UK

The **Journal of Classics Teaching** (JCT; formerly known as *Didaskalos, Hesperiam, The JACT Review* and *JACT Bulletin*) contains a wealth of articles that reflect the practice of the teaching of Classics in the UK and occasionally abroad over the last fifty years. Articles range from thought-pieces, through pedagogy, news and reports. JCT is a free open-access online journal in the Classical Association's stable of journals, hosted by Cambridge University Press. See https://www.cambridge.org/core/journals/journal-of-classics-teaching.

The **Council of University Classics Departments** (CUCD) very occasionally has articles that are of interest to teachers at secondary level in their annual bulletin. For further information, https://cucd.blogs.sas.ac.uk/bulletin/.

USA

Teaching Classical Languages is a free open-access online journal dedicated to exploring the teaching of Greek and Latin, sponsored by the Classical Association of the Middle West and South (CAMWS). Back issues to 2009 are available. Contact via http://tcl.camws.org/.

The Classical Journal contains a section entitled *Forum* which comprises articles, and sometimes notes, on various aspects of Graeco-Roman antiquity as they are presented in the classroom. For details, see http://cj.camws.org/. Back issues are available through JSTOR [http://www.jstor.org/].

The Classical Outlook is a journal for teachers in K-12 and college sectors. The journal contains articles of both a pedagogical and wider interest to teachers and students, as well as reviews and reports of events. The journal is available through the American Classical League [www.aclclassics.org/]. Back issues are available through JSTOR [http://www.jstor.org/].

Classical World periodically contains a section written by and for teachers of Classics. It can be found online at http://muse.jhu.edu/journals/clw/.

In addition to the chapters in books mentioned above that deal with teaching strategies, a number of journal articles are worth reading:

Peter Anderson and Mark Beckwith, 'Form-focused Teaching for the Intermediate Latin Student', *Teaching Classical Languages*, Fall 2010 (Anderson and Beckwith, 2010).
Jacqueline Carlon, 'The Implications of SLA Research for Latin Pedagogy: Modernizing Latin Instruction and Securing its Place in Curricula', *Teaching Classical Languages*, Spring 2013 (Carlon, 2013).
Jacqueline Carlon, 'Quomodo Dicitur? The Importance of Memory in Language Learning', *Teaching Classical Languages*, Spring 2016 (Carlon, 2016).
Rebecca Harrison, 'Exercises for Developing Prediction Skills in Reading Latin Sentences', *Teaching Classical Languages*, Fall 2010 (Harrison, 2010).
David Karsten, 'Teaching Comprehension', *Didaskalos*, 3 (3) (Karsten, 1971).
Ginny Lindzey, 'Teaching Skills for Reading Latin', *Journal of Classics Teaching*, 9 (Lindzey, 2006).
Donka Markus and Deborah Pennell Ross, 'Reading Proficiency in Latin Through Expectations and Visualization', *The Classical World*, 98 (1) (Markus and Pennell Ross, 2004).
Patrick McFadden, 'Advanced Latin Without Translations? Interactive Text-Marking as an Alternative Daily Preparation', *CPL Online*, 4.1 (McFadden, 2008)

General books on language teaching approaches

Diane Larsen-Freeman and Marti Anderson, *Techniques and Principles in Language Teaching* (Oxford: Oxford University Press, 2011).
Jack Richards and Theodore Rodgers, *Approaches and Methods in Language Teaching* (New York: Cambridge University Press, 2001).

Claire Kramsch, *Context and Culture in Language Teaching* (Oxford: Oxford University Press, 1993).

I. S. P. Nation, *Learning Vocabulary in Another Language* (Cambridge: Cambridge University Press, 2008).

Norbert Schmitt, *Vocabulary in Language Teaching* (Cambridge: Cambridge University Press, 2000).

Julian Bamford and Richard Day, *Extensive Reading Activities for Teaching Language* (Cambridge: Cambridge University Press, 2004).

Patsy Lightbown and Nina Spada, *How Languages are Learned* (Oxford: Oxford University Press, 2013).

Christine Nuttall, *Teaching Reading Skills in a Foreign Language* (London: Macmillan Education, 2005).

Organizations for Latin teachers

UK

The Cambridge School Classics Project [CSCP; www.cambridgescp.com] publishes the *Cambridge Latin Course* and ancillary materials and is the place to find the online e-learning resources, as well as links to other resources such as ancient Greek and Classical Civilization. CSCP also hosts the *War with Troy* project – an online resource based on storytelling through the *Iliad* of Homer. The teacher's area has details of teacher-training courses supported by the Department for Education, and the annual CSCP Conference held in Cambridge. A number of reports by CSCP have been made available in the past: interested parties should contact me for copies:

- A Survey of Access to Latin in UK Secondary Schools (Cambridge School Classics Project, 2008).
- A Statistical Report on Latin in UK Secondary Schools (Cambridge School Classics Project, 2009).
- Who is Latin for? Access to KS4 Latin qualifications (Cambridge School Classics Project, 2015a)

The website also contains links to the major sites and museums in the UK where there are significant holdings of classical artefacts.

The Classical Association [CA; www.classicalassociation.org/] is the largest organization devoted to Classics in the UK, publishing the journals *Greece and Rome*, *New Surveys in the Classics*, the *Classical Quarterly*, the *Classical Review* and the *Journal of Classics Teaching*. It organizes an annual conference, with panels and round-tables devoted to teaching and learning Classics. In January 2015, the Classical Association re-absorbed the Joint Association of Classical Teachers (JACT) and took over running the original JACT Summer Schools in a new organization called the JACT Summer Schools Trust (JSST). Details of these summer schools (for beginners or more experienced students of all ages) are at present to be found on the JACT website [www.jact.org] and are held annually as follows:

- Ancient Greek Summer School at Bryanston School;
- Ancient Greek and Latin Summer School at the University of Durham;
- Latin Summer School at Harrogate Ladies' College; and
- Classical Civilization and Ancient History Summer School at Mount St Mary's College.

The officers of JACT have formed a new group called the CA Teaching Board (CATB), which aims to take a proactive role in liaising with other bodies and promoting Classics more widely than JACT had been thitherto able to accomplish. The CATB has already commissioned a nationwide survey of classics teaching in secondary schools in 2021, for imminent release; it has established working groups for each of the four subject areas of Classics, and is being proactive in consultation with stakeholders about curriculum change, as JACT used to. The Classical Association has a network of local branches throughout the UK that organize local events, such as reading competitions between schools, lecture series and social occasions. Details of these may be found on the Classical Association website. The Classical Association also offers grants to members of the local branches to facilitate their meetings. In 2003, the Classical Association published its own commemorative volume *The Classical Association: The First Century 1903–2003* (Stray, 2003b). JACT published its own history *50 Years of the Joint Association of Classical Teachers* in 2013 (JACT, 2013).

The Association for Latin Teaching [ARLT; http://www.arlt.co.uk/] is an organization set up in 1911 by W. H. D. Rouse, the founder of the Direct Method of Latin teaching, for Latin teachers who shared his wish to 'reform' the then traditional approach (hence the 'r' in the title). The ARLT, made up of Classics teachers, organizes two events per year: an INSET Refresher Day and a Summer School, held at different places throughout the UK. Its website is a mine of information, including details of the Direct Method, and lists of schools in the UK where Latin and other classical subjects are taught. The ARLT published its own commemorative volume *ARLT 1911–2011: A Commemorative History of the Association for Latin Teaching* in 2011 (Soames and Hazel, 2011).

Classics for All [www.classicsforall.org.uk/] is a charity that raises financial support for state-maintained schools in both the primary and secondary sectors in the UK. School teachers are encouraged to make grant applications to the charity. Financial support is awarded for resources, training and networking events, which aim to link primary and secondary schools, and schools and universities together to build and develop stable and self-sustaining partnerships, especially in areas of deprivation and parts of the UK where there is poor provision of Classics subjects.

Personalized training is offered face to face in schools or through Zoom video conferencing, free of charge to teachers in state-maintained schools; an online summer school takes place each August.

Friends of Classics [http://www.friends-classics.demon.co.uk/] is a charity that promotes the learning of and love for Classics among teachers and the wider general public through its magazine *ad familiares*. It sometimes offers grants to schools to help develop Latin.

The Society for the Promotion of Roman Studies [www.romansociety.org/] offers grants to schools for the purchase of resources, such as books, and makes awards for museum internships and archaeological digs for young people in the UK.

The Primary Latin Project [https://www.primarylatinproject.org/] is the organization that supports the *Minimus* series of primary school Latin textbooks. It offers training, book grants and resources for schools to start teaching Latin at KS2.

The IRIS Project [http://irisproject.org.uk/] is an organization dedicated to bringing Classics, particularly Latin, into primary schools in the UK. With student volunteers going into schools, primary school students are introduced to the basics of the language and Roman culture and history. IRIS also operates a number of events throughout the year, some of which are based in the East Oxford Classics Centre, and others via outreach activities through UK universities. IRIS also publishes its own magazines: *Iota* for primary and *Iris* for secondary school students.

Oxford Outreach [www.classics.ox.ac.uk/Outreach.html] is part of the Classics Faculty of the University of Oxford – the largest Classics faculty in the world. Officers organize school visits and talks and coordinate events with colleges at Oxford and the Ashmolean Museum. They also arrange some training for teachers through IRIS and their own Saturday school in Latin for local students from state schools.

Classics in Communities [http://classicsincommunities.org/] aims to promote and encourage the teaching of Latin and Ancient Greek at primary and early secondary level in UK state schools. The project is founded on two key principles: information and support. It provides schools and teachers with information and guidance about teaching approaches and methods, material and digital classroom resources, and support available from Classics organizations.

Advocating Classics Education [http://aceclassics.org.uk/] is a UK-wide project to extend qualifications in Classical subjects across the secondary sector. ACE has a website to provide a permanent hub for discussion, sharing and dissemination of news, information, ideas and resources which further the project's mission.

USA

The North American Cambridge Classics Project [NACCP; www.cambridgelatin. org/] is CSCP's transatlantic sister organization. NACCP offers advice and resources for the US *Cambridge Latin Course* program. NACCP attends training events throughout the USA, including the American Classical League Institute and is pioneering webinars. Details of these can be found on the NACCP website.

The Society for Classical Studies [SCS; previously known as the American Philological Association; http://apaclassics.org/] is the main organization in the USA for the study of ancient Greek and Roman languages, literatures, and civilizations. Most members are drawn from among the ranks of college and university professors, but a sizeable number are teachers in secondary schools. The annual conference has something of value for teachers; the website and resources links are perhaps more useful. The SCS is currently engaging in a more proactive and outreaching programme of events, designed to showcase the breadth and value of the study of the Classics.

The American Classical League [ACL; www.aclclassics.org/] is the premier organization in the USA for teachers of Classics in schools. It organizes a conference – the ACL Institute – at various locations each year, which is well attended by teachers from all over the USA and further afield. A pre-Institute set of training events helps teachers fulfil their state CPD credentials. ACL's website is a treasure-trove of useful materials and links to many other sites, including:

- The National Committee for Latin and Greek [www.promotelatin.org/], which promotes the subjects at high level;
- Excellence Through Classics [http://www.etclassics.org/], which promotes Classics programs in schools and colleges;
- National Junior Classical League [http://www.njcl.org/], which promotes Classics in schools through conventions and national examinations (see below); and
- ACL Teacher Placement Service, which helps schools find Classics teachers.

There are many individual Classics organizations at local level throughout the USA, arranging conventions, social gatherings, lectures and events for local school students and their teachers. Some also offer news of jobs, grants, awards and certification routes. The most active among these include:

- Classical Association of the Middle West and South (CAMWS): https://camws.org/
- Classical Association of the Atlantic States (CAAS): http://caas-cw.org/wp/
- Classical Association of New England (CANE): http://caneweb.org/new/
- The New York Classical Club

Details of the many others can be found on the SCS and ACL websites.

Spoken Latin

A feature of the US is meetings and conventions where Latin is used as the medium for conversation and discussion. The most famous of these – held annually at the

University of Kentucky – is the **Conventiculum Latinum**, a workshop for spoken Latin. For details, see http://mcl.as.uky.edu/conventiculum-latinum. More details of other conventions can be found on the SCS website. The **Paideia Institute** [http://www.paideiainstitute.org/] also offers conventions at various locations around Europe and the USA for spoken Latin. **SALVI** (The North American Institute of Living Latin Studies) offers numerous events for speaking Latin immersively throughout the year. For details, see https://latin.org/wordpress/. For details of other courses and events in spoken ancient languages, see Avitus (2018).

Assessment

UK

National Assessment

The following national assessment bodies have responsibility for Latin examinations in the UK:

The Office of Qualifications and Examinations Regulation (Ofqual) regulates qualifications, examinations and assessments in England and vocational qualifications in Northern Ireland [www.gov.uk/government/organisations/ofqual].

Oxford and Cambridge and RSA (OCR) is a provider of examinations in Latin for state primary and secondary schools. Examinations are offered at Entry Level, GCSE and A Level [www.ocr.org.uk/].

Cambridge International Assessment (CIE) is a provider of examinations in Latin for secondary schools [www.cie.org.uk]. The International GCSE (IGCSE) is offered. From 2014, the IGCSE has been disallowed from the Department for Education's accountability measures as it does not align with the standards for the GCSE in England. Therefore, state-maintained schools (including Academies and Free Schools) are not recommended to use it.

Welsh Joint Examinations Committee (WJEC) is a provider of examinations in Latin for secondary schools, offering Level 1 and Level 2 Certificates in Latin language, Civilization and Literature [www.wjec.co.uk/]. The Level 2 Certificates have been withdrawn.

EDUQAS is the approved provider of GCSE examinations for England, set by WJEC. It offers Latin GCSE (https://www.eduqas.co.uk/)

Typical examination materials comprise:

- *Entry Level*: Some or all of: vocabulary questions; simple translation from unseen Latin into English; comprehension questions in English on a passage of unseen Latin, answered in English; an essay on an aspect of Roman life, in English.

- *Level 1 Certificate*: Some or all of: simple translation from unseen Latin into English; comprehension questions in English on a passage of unseen Latin, answered in English; questions and/or an essay on an aspect of Roman life, in English; questions and/or an essay on a passage or passages of original and/or translated Roman literature, in English.
- *GCSE/Level 2 Certificate*: Some or all of: translation from unseen Latin into English; translation of short English sentences into Latin or simple grammar analysis; comprehension questions in English on a passage of unseen Latin, answered in English; questions and/or an essay on an aspect of Roman life, in English; questions and/or an essay on a passage or passages of original Roman literature, in English; word derivation questions. The Level 2 Certificate in Latin has now been withdrawn.
- *A Level/Pre-U*: Some or all of: translation from unseen Latin into English; comprehension questions in English on a passage of unseen Latin, answered in English; questions and/or an essay on an aspect of Roman life, in English; questions and/or an essay on a passage or passages of original Roman literature, in English; translation of English sentences or passages into Latin or grammar identification exercises. The Pre-U qualification in Latin has now been withdrawn.

For a full description of all UK classics examinations , see *School Qualifications in Classical Subjects in the UK: a brief overview* (Hunt, 2020b).

Other certificates and awards

There are a number of other certificates to show student progress, but are not nationally accredited by Ofqual and therefore have no points tariff for the purposes of school comparison in the league tables. These include the *Graded Test Certificates* for the *Cambridge Latin Course* assessments at the end of each of Books 1–4, and *Minimus* certificates for the course books of that name. More details can be found on the relevant websites.

USA

In the absence of a national examination, the subject associations have devised a series of national exams to incentivize students to continue learning Latin and to measure achievement. These examinations include the National Latin Exam, the National Mythology Exam, the Exploratory Latin Exam, the National Classical Etymology Exam, the National Roman Civilisation Exam and the National Latin Vocabulary Exam. These examinations can be taken at different levels and in schools during certain time periods. The ALIRA Latin exam is an online exam which uses adaptive computer assessment to measure students' proficiency in the comprehension of Latin language texts of the type used in instructional settings (see, Hunt, 2022a, p. 196–7). Full details can be found on the ACL website [www.aclclassics.org/].

Details of the Advanced Placement Examinations can be found at https://apstudent. collegeboard.org/apcourse/ap-latin. Students are expected to be able to read, understand, translate and analyse Latin poetry and prose through careful preparation and translation of Latin readings, including Virgil and Caesar in the original Latin.

International

The International Baccalaureate examination [www.ibo.org/] also offers a Latin language and literature component.

Teacher training

UK

The centralized nature of the UK education system means that teacher training in Classics is relatively easy to undertake, although numbers of places funded by the Department for Education are regulated by the National College of Teaching and Learning (NCTL) and are insufficient to meet demand. The website www. stevenhuntclassics.com gives details of the courses available for Classics teachers and the application process. In essence, the qualification that allows someone to teach in a UK state school is *Qualified Teacher Status* (QTS), which can be gained through one of the following routes: the Higher Education Institution-led *Postgraduate Certificate in Education* routes (PGCEs); *School-Centred programmes* (SCITTs). The PGCE is itself a further academic teaching qualification, recognized as a teaching qualification abroad, where QTS on its own is not. Other teacher training routes, such as *Troops to Teachers* and *Teach First* do not at present provide training for Classics or Latin.

Higher Education Institution-led routes

At the time of writing (April 2015), the University of Cambridge and King's College London both offer a PGCE in *Latin with Classics* (with QTS). These well-established teacher training institutions have a wealth of experience and a nationwide network of training schools and alumni. The University of Sussex began offering PGCEs in *Classics with History* and *Latin with History* (with QTS) in 2014. Teacher trainees on these courses are allocated training bursaries and grants from the NCTL to assist with the cost of fees and maintenance while training. The University of Durham has started a PGCE in Classics in 2022.

The private University of Buckingham offers a PGCE in Classics (with QTS). Trainees on this course must already be employed in an independent (private) school and do not attract bursaries or maintenance from the Department for Education to assist with fees.

School-Centred Initial Teacher Training (SCITT)

At the time of writing (February 2015), only three SCITTs regularly train Classics teachers: King Edward's Consortium, based in a school group in Birmingham in the West Midlands, Liverpool College, based in the North-West of England, and Harris Academies, based in Essex. Because of the small number of schools within the consortium, it is only able to offer two placements each year. Trainees are awarded QTS and can attract bursaries and maintenance from the Department for Education.

School Direct

The principle behind School Direct teacher training is that the teacher is selected by the school where the training will take place, and that the school will liaise with a local HEI provider to validate QTS and (sometimes) a PGCE. *School Direct (salaried)* means that the teacher, employed as an unqualified teacher by the school as a nearly full-time member of staff, attends HEI training at weekend conferences or on day-release. Applicants for SD (salaried) must have been in employment (not necessarily as a teacher) for three years prior to employment as the trainee. *School Direct (fee-paying)* means that the teacher, initially working alongside the other staff in the school, much as a PGCE teacher trainee would, eventually takes classes by themselves. These teachers are not paid, but can apply for the bursaries and maintenance grants that trainees on the PGCE and SCITTs can apply for. Neither route seems to provide many opportunities for training teachers of Classics in state-maintained schools, because they expect there to be a number of qualified mentors available in the schools from whom the trainee may learn the craft of teaching Classics. Most state schools do not have such large departments or the relevant expertise or time allocation to perform these functions. Moreover, the number of HEIs that have the experience to validate the training of Classics teachers remains tiny and geographically concentrated in London and the South East. It is unlikely, therefore, that we will see much expansion of this route beyond the four or five there are nationally at present.

Application to all teacher training routes (except for the University of Buckingham, to whom application must be made direct through the school in which the trainee is working) is through the Department for Education's dedicated teacher training website.

There is uncertainty about teacher training routes overall. The former Coalition Government's view was that as much teacher training as possible should take place in schools, with minimal contact with the university faculties of education, which supposedly cast a malign influence over the practice of teaching by instilling in trainees too much theory and insufficient practice in the classroom. It is a curiosity of the situation then that many of the replacement School Direct places require validation for QTS by the very same university faculties that are so despised by the political rhetoric; indeed, trainees on many of the School Direct (fee-paying) programmes find themselves sitting alongside their PGCE companions and following the exact same courses, as happens on the teacher training courses at King's College London and at the University of Sussex, for example. The difference is that the HEI providers are not able to predict how many trainees will come through the School Direct route, while the number of PGCE places is centrally controlled and destined to be reduced. This uncertainty looked like it would make the HEI-led PGCE courses 'vulnerable' to closure (*Times Educational Supplement*, 2012); the Department for Education had already noted that between 2013–14 and 2014–15 recruitment nationally for all courses fell from 95% to 93% of allocated places (Department for Education, 2014b). The former Coalition government already had an answer: in the same way that teachers in independent/private schools did not need to employ teachers with teaching qualifications, state-maintained schools with academy status and free schools could choose whomever they please. Former Minister of Education, Michael Gove, at a news conference, reported in the *Times Educational Supplement* in 2010, encouraged such thinking:

> 'Innovation, diversity and flexibility are at the heart of the free schools policy,' he said. 'We want the dynamism that characterizes the best independent schools to help drive up standards in the state sector.
>
> 'In that spirit, we will not be setting requirements in relation to qualifications. Instead, we will expect business cases to demonstrate how governing bodies intend to guarantee the highest quality of teaching and leadership in their schools.
>
> 'Ensuring that each free school's unique educational vision is translated into the classroom will require brilliant people with a diverse range of experience.'
>
> *Times Educational Supplement*, 2010

Gove's suggestion that such a reform would enable free schools and academies to have the same opportunities as independent/private schools to choose unqualified teachers if they wished because of the 'dynamic' experience that such an arrangement provides is at worst insulting to teachers who have undertaken training and at best misguided about its supposed benefits. If Gove also wanted to provide more of an opportunity for teachers – qualified or not – to be able freely to move between sectors, the evidence has not provided the truth for his ambitions. Andrew Adonis, former Labour Minister for Education, pointed out that the number of trained teachers entering the state sector from the independent/private sector has always been negligible. Instead, the movement has been very much in the other direction: 'By far the single largest source of new teachers in private schools is experienced teachers in state schools … There is net annual recruitment of 1,400 experienced teachers from state schools into private schools' (Adonis, 2012, p. 152).

Gove's belief in his own rhetoric, of course, knew no bounds. Supported by books like *Progressively Worse: The Burden of Bad Ideas in British Schools*, written by his admirer Robert Peal (2014) in order to deprecate the teacher training that purportedly had run down education in the UK, and the commentaries of journalist cum free school founders like Toby Young, Gove failed to see the absurdities of the contradictions in his own policies (such as simultaneously removing the need for qualifications to work in certain types of state-maintained schools, while demanding even higher entry requirements for the teacher training courses which were left). Nor did he use the levers of government to make the significant changes that would be necessary to achieve his aims through existing structures. Rhetoric has always been cheaper. Furthermore, ideas about levelling the playing field between the state and the independent/private sector, insofar as teacher training was concerned, has been undermined by the head teachers of a number of leading independent/private schools themselves who have set up their own HEI-led PGCE teacher training course with the University of Buckingham [www.hmcteachertraining.org.uk/]. Such schools value teacher qualifications after all. With Gove's downfall in July 2014 there is at the time of writing (February 2015) something of a policy lacuna. Current plans for the future of teacher training in the state sector are currently unstable. The Carter Review of Initial Teacher Training (Carter, 2015), initiated by Gove himself, was carefully emollient to all forms of initial teacher training and reported that a mix of providers ought to provide a better solution to the needs of the country than a swing in any particular direction to or from HEI-led or school-led training: partnerships between schools and HEIs were once-again recommended. Nicky Morgan, the successor to Gove as the Conservative Minister for Education, made no comments so far on changes to Gove's policy. Her colleague David Laws, the Liberal Democrat Minister for Schools, however, declared in a widely reported speech to the *CentreForum* policy group in London that all teachers in the state-maintained sector should be qualified (Laws, 2014) – an opinion shared by Tristram Hunt, the Labour Opposition Minister for Education, who gave a similar speech in Nottingham to the *North of England Education Conference* (Hunt, T, 2014). Meanwhile, there was nothing reported about their opinions on the initial teacher training routes themselves. There have been several Education Ministers since, who have all continued to ignore the shortage of teacher trainees in their midst. Having split teacher training into a myriad small components, the Department for Education has now set itself the target of deciding which providers shall meet its requirements set for accreditation from 2024 – a process far removed from the urgency of a staff recruitment and retention crisis. Successful providers will have to align their own curricula with the Department's own vision for teacher training, based around the Core Content Framework. The outcome of this process is, at the time of writing, unclear; however, providers, many of which are universities with huge experience, feel they are being sidelined and edged out in favour of a small number of preferred organizations which are happy to toe the Government's line (Schools Week, 2022).

I mention the present situation in some detail as it is an area that is of great significance for the health of the teaching of Latin – as it is, of course, for the teaching of any other subject. A teacher who knows what they are doing – and why they are doing it – is the most important determinant of the success of the students' learning in the class that no amount of any other type of resource can account for.

INSET / CPD events. A number of university Classics departments provide subject knowledge enhancement courses in the ancient languages and civilization that may be useful for teachers:

- The University of Liverpool [www.liv.ac.uk/]: subject support days for Ancient History teachers.
- The University of Birmingham [www.birmingham.ac.uk/]: subject support days for Classics teachers.
- King's College London [www.kcl.ac.uk] or University College London [www.ucl.ac.uk]: London Summer School in Classics.
- The University of Reading [www.reading.ac.uk/]: Summer School in Latin.
- The University of Lampeter [www.uwtsd.ac.uk/]: Summer School in Greek and Latin.
- The University of Cork [www.ucc.ie/en/classics/]: Summer School in Greek and Latin.
- The University of Swansea [www.swansea.ac.uk/]: Summer School in Ancient Languages.

USA

I am not sufficiently qualified to go into detail about the routes for teacher training in general or for Latin teachers in particular. I point readers in the direction of the following information.

Teacher certification requirements for individual states are explained in the Society for Classical Studies excellent report on *State Certification Requirements in Latin* (2017), which can be found online [https://classicalstudies.org/education/guide-state-certification-requirements-december-2017].

The *Standards for Latin Teacher Preparation* (American Classical League, 2010), based on advice from (among others) the American Council on the Teaching of Foreign Languages, should be seen as essential guidance for those gaining accreditation. The 2010 document is currently being revised and will likely be published in 2024.

Teachers of Latin should adhere as far as possibe to the *Standards for Classical Language Learning* (American Classical League, 2017), mentioned in Section 1 of this book.

Writers have explored how the *Standards for Classical Language Learning* might be put into practice in the classroom (see the Special Issue of Teaching Classical Languages, (Volume 9.1) published in 2018 for full discussion: https://tcl.camws.org/sites/default/files/TCL9.1.pdf) The process of gaining teacher certification through graduate programmes or alternative routes is complex and qualified teacher supply, just as much in the UK, does not meet demand. The joint ACL / SCS publication Standards for Latin Teacher Preparation is, of course, essential reading (American Classical League / American Philological Association, 2010) . But the supply of teachers in the US continues to bedevil expansion (Ancona & Durkin, 2015; Kitchell, 2019). These pieces perhaps bear some comparison with some of the present ways in which the Department for Education in the UK is trying to make up the shortfall through reducing the requirement for any qualifications at all to become teachers in state-maintained English schools and through establishing training routes which are school-based apprenticeship models rather than those through established postgraduate courses at university.

Communication and persuasion

What messages do we need to send out? Kitchell (2008, p. 162) pointed out that the field of Classics was once 'bolstered by roles and societal conditions which no longer exist'. Latin teachers have to fight for recognition in what they do as no other subject teachers must. While the present government has shown support for Classics in general, and Latin in particular, it has not taken enough notice of what teachers and students actually achieve in the classroom and has not always made the right decisions to enable more of them to do so. It is likely that the latest round of examination reform, for example, may close off many of the routes that have recently opened up by which accessibility to the study of Latin has improved over the last few years (Cambridge School Classics Project, 2015). Kitchell (2008) advocates coordinating efforts at both national and local level and draws on his own experiences in bringing together the university Classics departments, subject associations and schools to present a concerted and thought-through argument. This is something that has to be ongoing if it is to have the desired effect: politicians and administrators tend to move on, and so Latin teaching needs to be reaffirmed each time. It also has to be proactive rather than reactive: individuals within government, examination boards, journalists and academics all need to be kept informed and on-message. An interview with the then Opposition Minister for Education, now Mayor of London, Boris Johnson in the *Journal of Classics Teaching* (Johnson, 2007) shows how out of touch one of the UK's proudest proponents of Classics can be about what most students actually learn about in Latin in schools today. Harrison's (2009) description of the lengths to which the AQA examination board might go to avoid its obligations when it tried to withdraw a national examination in Ancient History is a reminder of the breakdown between groups that can occur if one side avoids consulting the other.

The situation is changing. Evidence is being collected and disseminated. In the same way as the success of the US Foreign Languages in the Elementary Schools Latin language programs of the 1980s were widely disseminated by Mavrogenes (Polsky, 1998) and LaFleur's (1981) research showed the positive impact on SAT scores that learning Latin seemed to have, we need to gather the sort of evidence which convinces politicians and administrators to keep on with Latin. Small research projects in the UK in Swansea and Norfolk, focused on improving literacy and student aspiration, are frequently cited by politicians as reason enough for the study of Latin. The other evidence worth collating consists of simple quantitative and qualitative evidence. Enrolments for Latin at school level are easy to find: the number of students taking examinations is publicly available. The impact of changes of government policy should be possible to be inferred over time. In the UK, such evidence was used to help politicians and the Department for Education to develop policy decisions about teacher training, KS2 languages and the restructuring of national examinations at both GCSE and A Level with better regard to the outcomes that everyone desires. Meanwhile, the 'softer' pieces of evidence can be used to feed into the media to create the right sort of environment in which Latin and the other classical subjects may flourish. There are now regular meetings between the subject associations, the examination boards, school teachers and universities. As a delegate for the last few years at the American Classical League Institute, I have been struck how much that organization works tirelessly to support Latin across the country, with a dedicated team of university and school teachers developing resources, promotional literature and other information. Not everything is perfect: there is still a shortage of certificated Latin teachers. But the message is clear that a relatively well-funded organization with dedicated personnel drawn from across the spectrum of schools and universities can drive change rather than wait for directives from above, which might never come, or which, when they do, might not be quite what are needed or desired. In the UK, the formation of the Classical Association Teaching Board out of the remains of the Joint Association of Classical Teachers looks the best bet for similar action.

Perhaps statistics about enrolments and arguments for the retention, support and development of Latin can be shared across Anglophone countries. Recent news from Australia, where the national government is encouraging state schools to teach Latin, might also benefit from such information – as indeed might countries elsewhere in the world where Latin is at risk. Latin needs a coherent narrative to suit the demands of a technocratic society and a road-map to hand out to show interested parties how to get it into schools. I hope this little book achieves something of both of these.

Epilogue

The Department for Education has been recently – and unusually – helpful in offering not just rhetorical support for Latin in state schools but also financial support for training teachers to teach it. I am still wary, however, for the future of Latin. Much of the running seems still to have been made by an overtly right-wing political agenda that equates the learning of Latin as a demarcator of status, privilege and exclusivity (Beard, 2013a). For politicians such as Michael Gove, Boris Johnson and Nick Gibb, and political commentators like Toby Young and Harry Mount, Latin is the means by which a student accesses particular, research-intensive universities, the professions and a good job – as if this is almost the only purpose of Latin. There is no evidence to suggest that there is some quality peculiarly resident in the subject that can be pinned down to cause such achievement; nor do I expect any to be found. Are we meant to take seriously Gove (2011) and Young's (2014) rhetorical fantasies that learning Latin was the sole thing that made Mark Zuckerburg, founder of the social media website *Facebook*, a multi-billionaire? Meanwhile, some university academics offer distinctly unhelpful views. A recent move to make the translation of English sentences into Latin an element of the Latin GCSE has been publicly supported by Davie (2012) and Butterfield et al. (2013), academics working in the two most selective Classics departments in the UK, without recourse to asking teachers in state-maintained schools whether such a thing is feasible, let alone desirable. In his turn, without consulting state school teachers, and despite entreaties from the other representatives from the same universities and from the subject associations themselves, Gove ordered Ofqual to instruct the examination boards to re-introduce English into Latin as part of his plans to make all GCSE examinations more 'rigorous' (Hunt, 2014c). An unpublished research report by the *Cambridge School Classics Project* (2015) commissioned by the Department for Education itself suggested that a quarter of state schools would find this an intolerable burden on their timetables and on their students – just at the moment that the subject had become more available in the UK than for the last quarter of a century, and just at the moment that the government was investing in more teacher training of specialist and non-specialist Latin teachers for those same schools.

Lister (2015a) also points out the challenges that still face teachers of Latin today: while resources and teaching practices have changed for the better and have made

Latin more accessible to students of every background than before, there are still loud and very public voices, such as Jones (2013) and Mount (2013), distinctly off-message, who use their privileged positions to carrying the debate away from where it matters: ignoring the experience of the subject community and teachers in schools themselves. Lister also expresses a double anxiety: that the subject associations lack the capacity to be much more than reactive, and that they have in the past been insufficiently communicative with their members to be representative of their experiences and needs (Lister, 2015b). I have a little more confidence. The subject organizations for Latin teaching, the examinations boards, charities like Classics for All and the universities – through the necessity of outreach into their communities – have started to work together, to better understand one another and to better shape thinking. Better links are being made with the Department for Education – now more amenable with Gove gone. The time is right not to follow, but to take the lead. The journal *Didaskalos* was originally set up in the 1960s with the intention of providing a platform for reasoned debate about the status and purpose of the classical subjects. Contributors argued their points with passion born from the experience of teaching in the classroom and in the university. Such debate dwindled as new courses and new approaches to teaching were developed. The Association for the Reform of Latin Teaching, founded in 1911, renamed itself the Association for Latin Teaching in 1976, implying that the fight for reform was over (Soames and Hazel, 2011). Serious public discussion about whether Latin examinations were fit for purpose arose fitfully, with Lister (2004) and Morwood (2005) arguing against one another over ten years ago: Was GCSE too easy or too difficult? Who was the examination for? How much time did it need to cover? Did it discriminate against students in any particular school sector? A proposal by Weeds (2005) for the subject organizations to devise their own Four-Unit portfolio award, based on the vocational model of ICT invented by the state-maintained Telford School, would have been truly radical and, sadly, now disallowed under present Ofqual regulations. But the idea of utilizing the framework of forms of examination other than the GCSE has been used by the WJEC Level 1 and Level 2 Certificates in Latin language, civilization and literature. Examples of more subject-led developments to examinations can be found: the *Intermediate Certificate in Classical Greek* was developed by teachers and academics who perceived the GCSE in Classical Greek to be too demanding for students on the sort of short timetable allocation available in most schools (Le Hur, 2021). Could a similar certificate be developed for Latin? The International Baccalaureate examination was developed with teachers' input to reflect contemporary teaching preferences, including a form of free composition (Trafford, 2022).

In the USA, a certain amount of discontent with the Advanced Placement Latin examinations (reported in social media *passim*) has led to teachers seeking alternative certification for their students. There has been some experimentation in the USA with digital assessment, with the ALIRA assessment programme for Latin reading comprehension. The UK assessment boards are already investigating digital means of assessment – it remains to be seen what this might look like, and whether it should simply digitize current assessment models, or be sufficiently flexible to accommodate teachers' preferred pedagogies rather than fossilize them forever. It is to be hoped that the pre-eminent Anglophone journals about the teaching of Classics – the *Journal of Classics Teaching* in the UK and *Teaching Classical Languages* and *The Classical Outlook* in the USA – will be able to play their parts in contributing to the debates. I look forward to the Classical Association in the UK setting the running on curriculum development in much the same way as the American Classical League does across the Atlantic. It has already commissioned a national survey of teachers of classics in 2021, with a report imminent. Meanwhile, it is gratifying to see an increase in the number and quality of teacher panels at the academic conferences around the world – at the invitation of the subject associations themselves.

My proposal is a simple one: for the subject community to define what is reasonable for an ordinary student in a non-selective state-maintained school, adequately-funded, taught by a trained specialist or trained non-specialist teacher, for three to four years (depending on timetable allocation) to be expected to achieve at GCSE. Non-state-maintained schools who might say that they find this insufficiently challenging are allowed to use their own examination system, from which state-maintained schools are effectively barred by the accountability system of national league tables: the state-maintained schools must create a qualification that more fully accords with their students' experiences in the classroom. There should be a number of linguistic and non-linguistic pathways to choose from, to suit the student and the teacher's interests and the resources they have to hand. There should be a value and point in each stage of the student's learning, even if they did not go on to study at GCSE itself. GCSE should be an end in itself – worthwhile doing and doable by everyone who wants to – as well as a preparation for further study. These points for discussion are exactly the same ones that were put forward fifty-three years ago by Brink (1962), when Latin teetered on the edge of the abyss A welcome intervention from the Department for Education is, of course, the sponsorship of the Centre for Latin Excellence. The injection of £4 million into forty state-maintained schools across the UK at last speaks to the very real difficulties schools have faced without financial support. We look forward to seeing the results over the four year lifespan of the project. Meanwhile, the subject associations and universities together need to write and keep to a coherent narrative about what the teaching and learning of Latin in schools entails, and must keep opinion formers in the media and elsewhere aware of it, and of such matters as the number and types of schools where Latin (and the other Classical subjects) are taught, the numbers of students and so on. Finally, of course, governments need to be reminded that they cannot merely wish it into existence or provide the opportunity for it to develop as it were from thin air. The subject associations, teachers and universities need to make the case for the continued political and financial support of Latin in state-maintained schools with regular, hard, concrete evidence where success occurs and challenges are identified, and make suggestions about how these might be overcome. I have every belief that they will do so.

Bibliography

Abbott, M. (1998). Trends in Language Education: Latin in the Mainstream, in R. A. LaFleur (ed.), *Latin for the 21st Century: From Concept to Classroom* (pp. 36–43). Glenview, IL: Scott Foresman-Addison Wesley.

Adams, E., Capewell, S., Downes, C., Hunt, S. and Ryan, C. (2014). Apps in Classics Teaching and Learning. *Journal of Classics Teaching*, 29, 37–9.

Adonis, A. (2012). *Education, Education, Education*. London: Biteback Publishing.

Affleck, J. (2003). Twilight Classics, in J. Morwood (ed.), *The Teaching of Classics* (pp. 159–69). Cambridge: Cambridge University Press.

Aguilar, M. L. and Tarrega, J. (2022). Via Latina. *De Lingua et Vita Romanorum*. Granada; Cultura Classica.

Alexander, R. (2004). *Towards Dialogic Teaching: Rethinking Classroom Talk*. Cambridge: Dialogos.

Amenabar, A. (Director) (2009). *Agora* [Motion Picture].

American Classical League (2010). *Standards for Latin Teacher Preparation*. Philadelphia, PA: American Classical League and American Philological Association.

American Classical League / American Philological Association (2010). Standards for Latin Teacher Preparation. Retrieved from *American Classical League* [https://www.aclclassics.org/Portals/0/Site%20Documents/Publications/LatTeachPrep2010Stand.pdf].

American Classical League (2017). Standards for Classical Languages Learning. Retrieved from [https://www.aclclassics.org/Publications/Other-Reports-and-Information].

Amos, E. (2020). A case study investigation of student perceptions of women as seen in the Cambridge *Latin Course in a selective girls grammar school. Journal of Classics Teaching*, 21 (42), pp. 5–13.

Ancona, R. (1982). Latin and a Dyslexic Student: An Experience in Teaching. *Classical World*, 76, 33–6.

Ancona, R. (2007). *A Concise Guide to Teaching Latin Literature*. Norman: University of Oklahoma Press.

Ancona, R. (2009). Latin Teacher Certification: Training Future Secondary School Teachers. *Classical World*, 102, 311–15.

Ancona, R. (2010). College Professors and the New Standards for Latin Teacher Preparation, *Teaching Classical Languages*, Spring, 157–61 [http://tcl.camws.org/sites/default/files/TCL_I_ii_Spring_2010.pdf].

Ancona, R. (2011). *State Certification Requirements in Latin*. Philadelphia, PA: American Philological Association.

Ancona, R. (2014, December 15). *State Certification Requirements in Latin*. Retrieved from Society for Classical Studies [http://apaclassics.org/education/state-certification-requirements-latin].

Ancona, R. (2022). Introducing a Bit of Active Latin into Your Current Advanced Latin Classroom: Usus loquendi et audiendi de Terentio Catulloque, *New England Classical Journal:*, 49, 1, pp. 55–65.

Ancona, R. and Dugdale, E. (2012). Teaching About Classics Pedagogy in the 21st Century. *Classical World*, 106 (1), 103–29.

Ancona, R. and Durkin, K. (2015). There is a Shortage of Certified Latin Teachers: Please Spread the Word! *Amphora* 12.1, 6–7.

Anderson, P. (Director) (2014). *Pompeii* [Motion Picture].

Anderson, P. and Beckwith, M. (2010). Form-focused Teaching for the Intermediate Latin Student. *Teaching Classical Languages*, Fall, 31–52 [http://tcl.camws.org/sites/default/files/TCL_2.1_31-52_Anderson_Beckwith_0.pdf].

Arcenas, S. (2019). Teaching Ancient Geography with Digital Tools, in Natoli, B. and Hunt, S. (eds), *Teaching Classics with Technology* (pp. 165–80). London: Bloomsbury Academic.

Argetsinger, K. (2006). Peer Teaching and Cooperative Learning in the First Year of Latin, in J. Gruber-Miller (ed.), *When Dead Tongues Speak: Teaching Beginning Greek and Latin* (pp. 68–85). New York: Oxford University Press.

Ash, R. (2019). Untextbooking for the CI Latin class: Why and how to begin. *Journal of Classics Teaching*, 20 (39), pp. 65–70.

Ashe, A. (1998). Latin for Special Needs Students: Meeting the Challenge of Students with Learning Difficulties, in R. LaFleur (ed.), *Latin for the 21st Century: From Concept to Classroom* (pp. 237–50). Glenview, IL: Scott Foresman-Addison Wesley.

Asher, J. (2012). *Learning Another Language Through Actions*. Los Gatos, CA: Sky Oak Productions.

Assessment Reform Group (2002). *Assessment for Learning: 10 Principles* [http://www.aaia.org.uk/content/uploads/2010/06/Assessment-for-Learning-10-principles.pdf].

Atkinson, T. (2012). Making Social Media Work. *Journal of Classics Teaching*, 26, 24.

Avitus, A. (2018). Spoken Latin: Learning, Teaching, Lecturing and Research. *Journal of Classics Teaching*, 19 (37), pp. 46–52.

Baker, K. (1989). The National Curriculum and Classics. *Joint Association of Classical Teachers Review*, 2 (5), 3–4.

Baker, L. (2013). Classics Teacher Training – Scotland. *Journal of Classics Teaching*, 28, 72.

Bakhtin, M. (1984). *The Dialogic Imagination*. Austin, TX: University of Texas Press.

Ball, R. and Ellsworth, J. (1996). The Emperor's New Clothes: Hyperreality and the Study of Latin. *Modern Languages Journal*, 80 (1), 77–84.

Balme, M. and Morwood, J. (1996). *Oxford Latin Course*. Oxford: Oxford University Press.

Balme, M. and Morwood, J. (2003). The Oxford Latin Course, in J. Morwood (ed.), *The Teaching of Classics* (pp. 92–4). Cambridge: Cambridge University Press.

Balme, M. and Warman, M. (1965). *Aestimanda: Practical Criticism of Latin and Greek Poetry and Prose*. Oxford: Oxford University Press.

Bamford, J. and Day, R. (2004). *Extensive Reading Activities for Teaching Language.* Cambridge: Cambridge University Press.

Bartelds, D. (2022). Lemma navigation by excellent secondary school students of Ancient Greek. *Journal of Classics Teaching*, 23 (46), pp. 126–37.

Bass, B. (2003). Classics in Prep Schools, in J. Morwood (ed.), *The Teaching of Classics* (pp. 67–72). Cambridge: Cambridge University Press.

Bastille (2013, June 20). *Pompeii.* British Museum, London, UK.

Baty, C. (1962). Classics in the Schools: A Survey of the Position and Prospects, in T. Melluish (ed.), *Re-Appraisal: Some New Thoughts on the Teaching of Classics* (pp. 10–14). Oxford: Clarendon Press.

BBC (2008). The Fires of Pompeii. *Doctor Who.* London: BBC.

BBC (2011, October 20). *The One Show.* London: BBC.

BBC (2014, December 3). *BBC News.* Retrieved from BBC News/Education [http://m. bbc.co.uk/news/education-30216408].

Beard, M. (2012). Jamie's Dream School. *Journal of Classics Teaching*, 25, 18.

Beard, M. (2013a, June 15). *A Don's Life.* Retrieved from *The Times Literary Supplement* [http://timesonline.typepad.com/dons_life/2013/06/does-latin-have-a-future.html].

Beard, M. (2013b, July 16). Interview on the Leonard Lopate Show WNYC. (L. Lopate, interviewer).

Beard, M. and Henderson, J. (2000). *Classics: A Very Short Introduction.* Oxford: Oxford University Press.

Bell, B. (1999). *Minimus.* Cambridge: Cambridge University Press.

Bell, B. (2003). *Minimus,* in J. Morwood (ed.), *The Teaching of Classics* (pp. 61–6). Cambridge: Cambridge University Press.

Bell, B. (2015). Report of the Primary Latin Project February 2015. *Journal of Classics Teaching*, 31, 41–2.

Bell, D. (2015, January 9). Science Education: Trusting the Frontline. Presented to the *Association of Science Education Annual Conference*, Reading, Berkshire, UK.

Bell, S. (2008, July 1). *Borisnukes.* Retrieved from Bellworks [http://www.belltoons.co.uk/ bellworks/index.php/if/2008/6277-1-7-08_BORISNUKES].

Beneker, J. (2006). Variations on a Theme: An Experiment in Latin Prose Composition. *CPL Online*, 3.1 (Fall), 1–13 [https://camws.org/cpl/cplonline/files/Benekercplonline. pdf].

Benn, M. (2011). *School Wars: The Battle for Britain's Education.* London: Verso.

Bennett, C. (1911 [2012]). *The Teaching of Latin and Greek in the Secondary School.* London: Forgotten Books.

Black, P. and Wiliam, D. (2014). *Inside the Black Box: Raising Standards Through Classroom Assessment.* London: Learning Sciences.

Bolchazy-Carducci Publishers, Inc. (2014, December 31). *Latin for the New Millennium.* Retrieved from Bolchazy-Carducci Publishers, Inc. [http://www.bolchazy.com/ Assets/Bolchazy/ClientPages/LNM.aspx].

Bolgar, R. R. (1963). A Theory of Classical Education 1. *Didaskalos*, 1 (1), 5–26.

Bookwalter, G. (2015, March 12). Latin Endangered in Lake Forrest, but Thrives Elsewhere, Experts Say. *Chicago Tribune.*

Bracke, E. (2013). Literacy Through Latin in South Wales: MFL Approaches to Primary Latin Teaching. *Journal of Classics Teaching*, 28, 43–6.

Brink, C. (1962). Small Latin and the Classics, in T. Melluish (ed.), *Re-Appraisal: Some New Thoughts on the Teaching of Classics* (pp. 6–9). Oxford: Clarendon Press.

Brockliss, W. (2013). Latin and Power: Warnings and Opportunities from the Long History of the Language. *Teaching Classical Languages*, Spring, 123–40 [http://tcl.camws.org/sites/default/files/Brockliss_0.pdf].

Bulwer, J. (2006). *Classics Teaching in Europe*. London: Bloomsbury.

Bungard, C. (2020). Visualizing Vocabulary: Student-Driven Visual Vocabularies. *Teaching Classical Languages*, 11.1, pp. 51–88.

Butterfield, D., Andersen, S., Radice, K. and O'Sullivan, D. (2013). *Latin for Language Lovers: Ancient Langauges, the New Curriculm and GCSE*. London: Politeia.

Cambridge School Classics Project (1998). *Cambridge Latin Course* (4th edn). Cambridge: Cambridge University Press.

Cambridge School Classics Project (1996). *Cambridge Latin Anthology*. Cambridge: Cambridge University Press.

Cambridge School Classics Project (2008). *A Survey of Access to Latin in UK Secondary Schools*. Cambridge: Cambridge School Classics Project.

Cambridge School Classics Project (2009). *A Statistical Report on Latin in UK Secondary Schools*. Cambridge: Cambridge School Classics Project.

Cambridge School Classics Project (2014). *Changing Demands in Latin and Ancient Greek Examinations 1918 to 2012*. Unpublished Report for the Deprtament for Education. Cambridge: Cambridge School Classics Project.

Cambridge School Classics Project (2015a). *Who is Latin For? Access to KS4 Latin Qualifications*. Cambridge: Cambridge School Classics Project.

Cambridge School Classics Project (2015b, April 19). *Starting Latin*. Retrieved from Cambridge School Classics Project [http://cambridgescp.com/Upage.php?p=sl^top^home].

Cambridge School Classics Project (2015c, May 1). *WJEC Qualifications*. Retrieved from WJEC [http://wjec.co.uk/qualifications/qualification-resources.html?subject=Latin&level=Level12Certificate].

Cambridge School Classics Project (2016). *Cambridge Latin Course* (US 5th edn). Cambridge University Press.

Cambridge School Classics Project (2022). *Cambridge Latin Course* (UK 5th edn). Cambridge University Press.

Cambridge University Press (CUP) (2015, April 25). Personal communication.

Capital Classics (2014, November 28). *Capital Classics*. Retrieved from Capital Classics [http://www.capitalclassics.org.uk/].

Capps, J., Murphy, J. and Overman, H. (Directors) (2013). *Atlantis* [Motion Picture].

Carlon, J. (2013). The Implications of SLA Research for Latin Pedagogy: Modernizing Latin Instruction and Securing its Place in Curricula. *Teaching Classical Languages*, Spring, 106–122 [http://tcl.camws.org/sites/default/files/Carlon_0.pdf].

Carlon, J. (2016). Quomodo dicitur? The Importance of Memory in Language Learning. *Teaching Classical Languages*, 7. 2, pp. 109–35.

Carpenter, D. (2000). Reassessing the Goal of Latin Pedagogy. *The Classical Journal*, 95 (4), 391–5.

Carter, A. (2015). *Carter Review of Initial Teacher Training (ITT)*. London: Department for Education.

Carter, D. (2011). Hans Oerberg and his Contribution to Latin Pedagogy. *Journal of Classics Teaching*, 22, 21–2.

Centre for Latin Excellence (2022). Retrieved from [https://latinexcellence.org/the-centre].

Churchill, L. J. (2006). Is There a Woman in This Textbook? Feminist Pedagogy and Elementary Latin, in J. Gruber-Miller (ed.), *When Dead Tongues Speak: Teaching Beginning Greek and Latin* (pp. 86–109). New York: Oxford University Press.

Clackson, J. (2015). *Language and Society in the Greek and Roman Worlds*. Cambridge: Cambridge University Press.

Clark, E. (2013). An Assessment of the Effectiveness of TPRS as a Means of Teaching Latin Vocabulary and Grammar. *Journal of Classics Teaching*, 28, 34–42.

Classics for All (2021). Impact Report 2010–21. Retrievd from Classics for All [https://classicsforall.org.uk/sites/default/files/uploads/impact%20report/CfA-Impact-Report_20102021_Digital_0.pdf].

Classics for All (2022). *Maximum Classics*. Retrieved from Classics for All [https://classicsforall.org.uk/].

Cleary, C. (2022). A Case Study Investigation of Year 8 Students' Experiences with Online Learning Through the Padlet App in a State-Maintained Girls' Grammar School. *Journal of Classics Teaching*, 23 (46), pp. 165–75

Cleveland, A. and Cerulli, L. (2021). A Style Guide for Gender Inclusivity in the Latin Language. Retrieved from [https://www.lupercallegit.org/post/a-style-guide-for-gender-inclusivity-in-the-latin-language].

Coe, B. and Hunt, S. (2022). Adaptive teaching for GCSE and A level classical literature. *Journal of Classics Teaching*, 23 (46), pp. 109–11.

Coffee, N. (2012). Active Latin: Quo Tendimus? *Classical World*, 105 (2), 255–69.

Coker, A. (2012). The Liverpool Classics Graduate Teaching Fellow Partnership: An Initial Report. *Journal of Classics Teaching*, 26, 22–4.

Conway, D. (2021). Style Variations in Latin Novellas: an Analysis of Three Authors' Works. *The Classical Outlook*, 96, 3, pp. 114–19.

Corson, D. (1982). The Graeco-Latinate Lexical Bar. *Hesperiam*, 5, 49–59.

Counsell, C. (2003). The Forgotten Games Kit: Putting Historical Thinking First in Long-, Medium- and Short-Term Planning, in T. Haydn and C. Counsell (eds), *History, ICT and Learning in the Secondary School* (pp. 52–108). London: Routledge.

Counsell, C. and Haydn, T. (2003). History, ICT and Learning, in T. Hadyn and C. Counsell (eds), *History, ICT and Learning in the Secondary School* (pp. 248–59). London: Routledge.

Cox, J. (2007). Electronic Aids in the Classroom. *Journal of Classics Teaching*, 7, 16–18.

Craft, J. (2019). Bridging the Gap between Students and Antiquity: Language Acquisition Videos with Minecraft and CI / TPRS, in Natoli, B. and Hunt, S. *Teaching Classics with Technology* (pp. 181–92). London: Bloomsbury Academic.

Cresswell, L. (2012). Personal Responses to Catullus at GCSE. *Journal of Classics Teaching*, 26, 11–13.

Culham, P. and Edmunds, L. (1989). *Classics: A Discipline and Profession in Crisis*. Lanham, MD: University Press of America.

Cullen, H. and Taylor, J. (2016). *Latin to GCSE. Part 1*. London: Bloomsbury Academic.

Cullen, H. and Taylor, J. (2018). *Latin to GCSE. Part 2*. London: Bloomsbury Academic.

Davie, J. (2012). *In Pursuit of Exellence: A Paper on the Teaching of the Classics*. London: Parliament Street.

Davis, S. (1991). *Latin in American Schools*. Atlanta, GA: Scholars Press, for the American Philological Association.

Davisson, M. (2004). Prose Composition in Intermediate Latin: An Alternative Approach. *CPL Online*, 1.1 (Fall), 1–6 [https://camws.org/cpl/cplonline/files/DavissoncplFORUMonline.pdf].

Deagon, A. (2006). Cognitive Style and Learning Strategies in Latin Instruction, in J. Gruber-Miller (ed.), *When Dead Tongues Speak: Teaching Beginning Greek and Latin* (pp. 27–49). New York: Oxford University Press.

DeKnight, S. and Tapert, R. (Directors) (2010). *Spartacus* [Motion Picture].

Delaney, C., Smith, H., Tims, L., Smith, T., and Griffiths, W. (2021). Keeping the ancient world relevant for modern students with Suburani. *Journal of Classics Teaching*, 22 (43), 64–7.

Department for Education (2013, September). *History Programmes of Study: Key Stages 1 and 2. National Curriculum in England*. Retrieved from Gov.UK [https://www.gov.uk/government/uploads/system/uploads/attachment_data/file/239035/PRIMARY_national_curriculum_-_History.pdf].

Department for Education (2014a, January 8). *Freedom of Information Request: Number of Secondary Academies in England*. Retrieved from Department for Education [https://www.gov.uk/government/publications/number-of-secondary-academies-in-england/number-of-secondary-academies-in-england].

Department for Education (2014b). *Initial Teacher Training Census for the Academic Year 2014 to 2015*. London: Department for Education.

Department of Education and Science (1984). *Classics in Independent Schools*. London: HMSO.

Department of Education and Science (1988). *Classics from 5–16: Curriculum Matters 12*. London: HMSO.

Department for Education (2022). *Initial Teacher Training: Core Content Framework*. Retrieved from [https://www.gov.uk/government/publications/initial-teacher-training-itt-core-content-framework].

Department for Education (2022). Open academies, free schools, studio schools, UTCs and academy projects in development. Retrieved from [https://www.gov.uk/government/publications/open-academies-and-academy-projects-in-development].

Dickey, E. (2015). An Immersion Class in Ancient Education. *Journal of Classics Teaching*, 31, 38–40.

Distler, P. (1962). *Teach the Latin, I Pray You*. Chicago, IL: Loyola University Press.

Downes, C. (2013). Using QR Codes in the Classroom. *Journal of Classics Teaching*, 28, 17–18.

Downes, C., McDonnell, C. and Hunt, S. (2012). All Can, Most Can, Some Can: Some Practical Ideas for Using Differentiation Strategies in the Classics Classroom. *Journal of Classics Teaching*, 26, 25–9.

Driscoll, P. and Frost, D. (1999). *The Teaching of Modern Foreign Languages in the Primary School*. London: Routledge.

duBois, P. (2001). *Trojan Horses: Saving the Classics from Conservatives*. New York: New York University Press.

Dugdale, E. (2011). Lingua Latina, Lingua Mea: Creative Composition in Beginning Latin. *Teaching Classical Languages*, Fall, 1–23 [http://tcl.camws.org/sites/default/files/Dugdale_0.pdf].

DuPree, M. (2011). Severus Snape and the Standard Book of Spells, in N. R. Reagin (ed.), *Harry Potter and History* (pp. 39–53). Hoboken, NJ: Wiley.

Dyson, J. (2003). *Enjoyably Difficult: An Evaluation of the Responses of Gifted and Talented Students in a Socially-Deprived Urban Area of London, United Kingdom, to Involvement in the Cambridge Online Latin Project*. London: Barking and Dagenham Community Inspection and Advisory Service.

Eales, J. (2015) What Some Students Found Difficult about Indirect Statement in Prose Competition. *Journal of Classics Teaching*, 31, 19–31.

Eaton, J. (2013). Using VLEs to Enhance Teaching and Learning in Classics. *Journal of Classics Teaching*, 28, 10–12.

Evans, M. (2009). Digital Technology and Language Learning, in M. Evans (ed.), *Foreign-Language Learning with Digital Technology* (pp. 7–31). London: Continuum.

Forrest, M. (1996). *Modernising the Classics: A Study in Curriculum Development*. Exeter: University of Exeter Press.

Forrest, M. (2003). The Abolition of Compulsory Latin and its Consequences, in C. Stray (ed.), *The Classical Association: The First Century 1903–2003* (pp. 42–66). Oxford: Oxford University Press.

Friends of Classics (2010). *Classics in Schools: The Research Report*. London: Friends of Classics.

Gaga, Lady (Performer) (2013, October 26). *The X Factor*, London, UK.

Gall, A. (2020). A study in the use of embedded readings to improve the accessibility and understanding of Latin literature at A Level. *Journal of Classics Teaching*, 21 (41), pp. 12–18.

Game, J. (1916 [2012]). *Teaching High School Latin: A Handbook*. London: Forgotten Books.

Ganschow, L. and Sparks, R. (1987). The Foreign Language Requirement. *Learning Disabilities Focus*, 2, 116–23.

Gardner, H. (1983). *Frames of Mind. The Theory of Multiple Intelligences*. New York: Basic Books.

Gay, B. (2003). The Theoretical Underpinning of the Main Latin Courses, in J. Morwood (ed.), *The Teaching of Classics* (p. 73–84). Cambridge: Cambridge University Press.

George, E.V. (1998). Latin and Spanish: Roman Culture and Hispanic America, in R. LaFleur (ed.), *Latin for the 21st Century: From Concept to Classroom* (pp. 227–37). Glenview, IL: Scott Foresman-Addison Wesley.

Gibb, N. (2010). Speech to Politeia. *Latin for Language Learners. Opening Opportunity for Primary Pupils.* London: Politeia.

Goddard, C. (2013). What Does the Media Think of Us? *Journal of Classics Teaching*, 28, 54–5.

Goldman, N. and Nyenhuis, J. (1982). *Latin via Ovid*. Detroit, MI: Wayne State University Press.

Goodhew, D. (2003). Using ICT in Classics, in J. Morwood (ed.), *The Teaching of Classics*. Cambridge: Cambridge University Press.

Gove, M. (2011, November). Speech at Twyford School, London.

Gove, M. (2014, February). Speech at the London Academy of Excellence, London.

Griffiths, W. (2008). Increasing Access to Latin in Schools, in B. Lister (ed.), *Meeting the Challenge: International Perspectives on the Teaching of Latin* (pp. 71–90). Cambridge: Cambridge University Press.

Griffiths, W. (2010). Latin Levels Among Non-Specialist Latin Teachers. *Journal of Classics Teaching*, 20, 3–4.

Gruber-Miller, J. (2006b). Teaching Writing in Beginning Latin and Greek, in J. Gruber-Miller (ed.), *When Dead Tongues Speak: Teaching Beginning Greek and Latin* (pp. 190–220). New York: Oxford Univesity Press.

Gruber-Miller, J. (ed.) (2006c). *When Dead Tongues Speak: Teaching Beginning Greek and Latin*. New York: Oxford Univesity Press.

Gwynne, N. (2014). *Gwynne's Latin*. London: Ebury Press.

Hands Up Education (2020). *Suburani*. Haverhill: Hands Up Education Community Interest Company.

Hands Up Education (2022). *Primary Latin Course*. Retrieved from Hands Up Education Community Interest Company [https://hands-up-education.org/primarylatin.html].

Hanlin, J. and Lichtenstein, B. (1991). *Learning Latin Through Mythology*. Cambridge: Cambridge University Press.

Hansard (2011). *Education Questions at the House of Commons, July 11*. London: Hansard.

Harrison, R. (2010). Exercises for Developing Prediction Skills in Reading Latin Sentences. *Teaching Classical Languages*, Fall, 1–30 [http://tcl.camws.org/sites/default/files/TCL_2.1_1-30_Harrison.pdf].

Harrison, T. (2009). The Campaign for the Ancient History A Level in Great Britain, in A. Chaniotis, A. Kuhn and C. Kuhn (eds), *Applied Classics: Comparisons, Constructs, Controversies* (pp. 167–82). Stuttgart: Franz Steiner Verlag.

Heller, B., Milius, J. and MacDonald, W. (Directors) (2005). *Rome* [Motion Picture].

Hill, B. (2006). Latin for Students with Severe Foreign Language Learning Difficulties, in J. Gruber-Miller (ed.), *When Dead Tongues Speak: Teaching Beginning Greek and Latin* (pp. 50–67). New York: Oxford University Press.

Hill, B., Downey, D., Sheppard, M. and Williamson, V. (1995). Accommodating the Needs of Students with Severe Language Learning Difficulties in Modified Language

Learning Courses, in G. Crouse (ed.), *Broadening the Frontiers of Foreign Language Education* (pp. 45–56). Lincolnwood, IL: National Textbook.

Hirsch, E. D. (1988). *Cultural Literacy: What Every American Needs to Know*. New York: Random House.

Holmes-Henderson, A., Hunt, S. and Musié, M. (eds) (2018). *Forward with Classics. Classical Languages in Schools and Communities*. London: Bloomsbury Academic.

Hoskins, A. J. (1976). The Accessibility of Classical Literature. *Didaskalos*, 5 (2), 250–61.

Hoyos, D. (2016). Latin. How to Read it Fluently. *Practical Manual*. CANE Press.

Hubbard, T. (2003). Special Needs in Classics, in J. Morwood (ed.), *The Teaching of Classics* (pp. 51–60). Cambridge: Cambridge University Press.

Hunt, C. (2022). The internet brings spoken Latin back into classrooms. *Blog: Found in Antiquity*: https://foundinantiquity.com/2022/01/05/the-internet-brings-spoken-latin-back-into-classrooms/

Hunt, F. (2018). Teaching and Learning Latin in the Key Stage 3 Classroom: Using the Cambridge Latin Course Explorer Tool. *Journal of Classics Teaching*, 19 (38), pp. 42–9.

Hunt, S. (2008). Information and Communication Technology and the Teaching of Latin Literature, in B. Lister (ed.), *Meeting the Challenge* (pp. 107–20). Cambridge: Cambridge University Press.

Hunt, S. (2011). Training Classics Teachers. *Journal of Classics Teaching*, 24, 2–3.

Hunt, S. (2012). Government Inconsistency Over Teacher Training in Classics. *Joint Association of Classical Teachers Bulletin*, 2 (1), 1–2.

Hunt, S. (2013a). Pompeii Exhibition: Linking the Exhibition with Teaching Practice. *Journal of Classics Teaching*, 27, 44–52.

Hunt, S. (2013b). How Does the Reading Approach Work? Pupils Translate. Presentation to the *American Classical League Pre-Institute Conference*, Memphis, TN.

Hunt, S. (2013c). The Development of Teaching and Learning Through the Use of ICT in the Latin Classroom. *Journal of Classics Teaching*, 28, 24–8.

Hunt, S. (2013d). The Roman Society News Report. *Journal of Classics Teaching*, 28, 73–4.

Hunt, S. (2014a). What Does the Media Think of Us? Part 2. *Journal of Classics Teaching*, 29, 19–20.

Hunt, S. (2014b). Digital Instructional Technology in the Classroom: Plaything or Catalyst for Pedagogical Development? *Journal of Classics Teaching*, 29, 42–7.

Hunt, S. (2014c, December 2). Personal communication, Department for Education.

Hunt, S. (2016). Teaching Sensitive Topics in the Secondary Classics Classroom. *Journal of Classics Teaching*, 17 (34), pp. 31–43.

Hunt, S. (2019). On Stage and Screen. 'Big Book' Latin and Dialogic Teaching, in Natoli, B. and Hunt, S. (eds), *Teaching Classics with Technology* (pp. 193–206). London: Bloomsbury Academic.

Hunt, S. (2020a). School Qualifications in Classical Subjects in the UK: a brief overview. CUCD, 49. Retrieved from CUCD [https://cucd.blogs.sas.ac.uk/files/2020/01/HUNT-School-qualifications-in-classical-subjects-in-the-UK-3.pdf].

Hunt, S. (2020b). Sight Unseen: Visible and Invisible Teachers in Online Teaching. *Teaching Classical Languages*, 11.2, pp. 33–66.

Hunt, S. (2022a). *Teaching Latin: Contexts, theories, practices*. London: Bloomsbury Academic.

Hunt, S. (2022b). Mind the Classics Gap. Current position of classical studies in English schools from Key Stage 2 to Key Stage 3. Challenges and solutions. *CUCD Bulletin*, 51. Retrieved from CUCD [https://cucd.blogs.sas.ac.uk/files/2022/09/Mind-the-Classics-Gap.pdf].

Hunt, S. (2022c). Novellas and Free Voluntary Reading: An overview and some starting points for further research into practice. *Journal of Classics Teaching*, 23 (46), pp. 176–83.

Hunt, S. (2022d). Editorial. *Journal of Classics Teaching*, 23 (46), pp. 105–8.

Hunt, S. (2022e). The Latin Excellence Programme (England, 2021). The Story So Far. *The Classical Outlook*, 97, 2, pp. 66–73.

Hunt, T. (2014, January 15). Speech to the North of England Education Conference, Nottingham.

Hyde, M. (2013, March 28). *My Little Katie Gives Rein to Her Inner Centaur*. Retrieved from The Guardian Lost In Showbizz Blog [http://www.theguardian.com/media/lostinshowbiz/2013/mar/28/my-little-katie-price-centaur].

Johnson, B. (2007, March 6). An Interview with Boris Johnson (S. Carr, interviewer).

Johnson, B. (2008, June 5). *London Evening Standard* (unknown interviewer).

Joffe, B. (2019). Teaching the Venalicius Story in the Age of #MeToo: a Reconsideration. *The Classical Outlook*, 94 (3), 125–38.

Joint Assocation of Classical Teachers (JACT) (2013). *50 Years of the Joint Assocation of Classical Teachers*. London: JACT.

Joint Council for Qualifications and Assessment (JCQA) (1988). *Inter-Awarding Body Statistics, Winter 1987/8 and Summer 1988*. London: Edexcel.

Joint Council for Qualifications and Assessment (JCQA) (1997). *Inter-Award Body Statistics Winter 1996/7 and Summer 1997*. London: Edexcel.

Joint Council for Qualifications (JCQ) (2013). *GCSE and Entry Level Certificate Results Summer 2013*. London: JCQ.

Jones, P. (2013, June 22). It's Vital that Children Translate English to Latin at GCSE. *The Spectator*.

Jones, P. (2014, December 5). Personal communication (S. Hunt, interviewer)

Jones, W. (1906 [2012]). *The Teaching of Latin*. London: Forgotten Books.

Jones, K. (2019). *Retrieval Practice. Research and Resources for Every Classroom*. Woodbridge: John Catt.

Karsten, D. (1971). Teaching Comprehension. *Didaskalos*, 3 (3), 492–506.

Keller, A. and Russell, S. (2006). *Learn to Read Latin*. New Haven, CT: Yale University Press.

Kennedy, R. F. (2022). Teaching Race in Greco-Roman Antiquity: Some Considerations and Resources. *The Classical Outlook*, 97, 1, pp. 2–9.

Khan-Evans, A. and Hunt, S. (2010). (R)evolution in Classics. *Journal of Classics Teaching*, 20, 4–6.

Kilby, M. (2014). Key Stage 4 Latin Initiative, 2014–15. *Journal of Classics Teaching*, 30, 52–3.

Kitchell, K. (1998). The Great Latin Debate: The Futility of Utility?, in R. LaFleur (ed.), *Latin for the 21st Century: From Concept to Classroom*. Glenview, IL: Scott Foresman-Addison Wesley.

Kitchell, K. (2000). Latin III's Dirty Little Secret: Why Johnny Can't Read. *New England Classical Journal*, 27, 206–26.

Kitchell, K. (2006). Hands Across the Water. *Journal of Classics Teaching*, 9, 9–11.

Kitchell, K. (2008). Promotion of the Classics in the United States: New Initiatives for a New Millennium, in B. Lister (ed.), *Meeting the Challenge: International Perspectives on the Teaching of Latin* (pp. 150–64). Cambridge: Cambridge University Press.

Kitchell, K. (2019). Latin Teacher Training: Does It Have a Future Tense? Retrieved from *American Classical League* [https://www.aclclassics.org/Portals/0/Site%20 Documents/Publications/Kitchell%20%20Teacher%20Training%20with%20 appendix.pdf].

Knudsvig, G. M. and Pennell Ross, D. (1998). The Linguistic Perspective, in R. LaFleur (ed.), *Latin for the 21st Century: From Concept to Classroom*. Glenview, IL: Scott Foresman-Addison Wesley.

Kramsch, C. (1993). *Context and Culture in Language Teaching*. Oxford: Oxford University Press.

Krashen, S. (1981). *Second Language Acquisition and Second Language Learning*. Oxford: Pergamon Press.

LaFleur, R. (1980). The CAMWS Committee for the Promotion of Latin: The First Year and the Future. *The Classical Journal*, 76, 48–66.

LaFleur, R. (1981). Latin Students Score High on SAT and Achievement Tests. *The Classical Journal*, 77, 254.

LaFleur, R. (1984). Latin Poetry for the Beginning Student. *The Classical Journal*, 80 (2), 151–6.

LaFleur, R. (ed.) (1998). *Latin for the 21st Century: From Concept to Classroom*. Glenview, IL: Scott Foresman-Addison Wesley.

LaFleur, R. (2011). *Wheelock's Latin*. New York: Collins Educational.

Lamb, M. G. (2020). Access and Opportunity: Technology Tools for Transitioning Online. *Teaching Classical Languages*, 11.2, pp. 109–14.

Lampert, M. (2001). *Teaching Problems and the Problems of Teaching*. New Haven, CT: Yale University Press.

Larsen-Freeman, D. and Anderson, M. (2011). *Techniques and Principles in Language Teaching* (3rd edn). Oxford: Oxford University Press.

Laserson, T. (2005). To What Extent can Electronic Resources Enhance the Study of Latin? An Evaluation, with Particular Reference to the Learner's Perspective. Unpublished Thesis for the Masters in Education, Cambridge University.

Latousek, R. (1998). Computamus: We Compute!, in R. LaFleur (ed.), *Latin for the 21st Century: From Concept to Classroom* (pp. 263–75). Glenview, IL: Scott Foresman-Addison Wesley.

Lawall, G. (1978). The College Classics Department as a Catalyst for New Latin Programs in the Public School. *Classical World*, 71 (5), 329–32.

Lawrence, C. (2015, April 25). Retrieved from The Roman Mysteries [http://www.romanmysteries.com/].

Laws, D. (2014, November 27). Education: Lessons from this Parliament and Directions for the Next. *Speech to CentreForum*, London.

Le Hur, C. (2022). A New Classical Greek Qualification. *Journal of Classics Teaching*, 23 (45), pp. 79–80.

Lewis, E. (2019). VLEs, Latin literature, and Student Voice, in Natoli, B. and Hunt, S. (eds), *Teaching Classics with Technology* (pp. 53–66). London: Bloomsbury Academic.

Lightbown, P. and Spada, N. (2013). *How Languages are Learned.* Oxford: Oxford University Press, 2013.

Lindzey, G. (2002). Validating Spanish in the Latin Classroom. *Cloelia*, Spring.

Lindzey, G. (2006). Teaching Skills for Reading Latin. *Journal of Classics Teaching*, 9, 11–14.

Lister, B. (2004). GCSE – Time for Reform. *Journal of Classics Teaching*, 3, 19–20.

Lister, B. (2007a). Integrating ICT into the Classics Classroom. *Journal of Classics Teaching*, 11, 4–7.

Lister, B. (2007b). *Changing Classics in Schools.* Cambridge: Cambridge University Press.

Lister, B. (ed.) (2008). *Meeting the Challenge: International Perspectives on the Teaching of Latin.* Cambridge: Cambridge University Press.

Lister, B. (2015a). Exclusively for Everyone, in E. Archibald, W. Brockliss and J. Gnoza (eds), *Learning Latin and Greek from Antiquity to the Present* (pp. 184–97). Cambridge: Cambridge University Press.

Lister, B. (2015b). In memoriam JACT, 1963–2015. *Greece and Rome*, 62, 2, 206–17.

Lloyd Houlker, M. (2014, February 4). Finding the Gap: Some Contrasts Between Ancient and Modern Language Learning. *eLatin and iGreek Teaching and Learning Symposium*, London.

Lord, K. (2006). Imagining Nelson Mandela in Ancient Rome: A New Approach to Intermediate Latin Prose Composition. *CPL Online*, 3.1, 1–17.

Lloyd, M. and Hunt, S. (eds) (2021). *Communicative Approaches for Ancient Languages.* London: Bloomsbury Academic.

Lovatt, H. (2011). Siting on the Fence or Breaking Through the Hedge? Risk-Taking, Incentives and Institutional Barriers to Outreach Work Among Academics and Students, in G. Baker and A. Fisher (eds), *Arts and Humanities Academics in Schools: Mapping the Pedagogical Interface* (pp. 28–42). London: Continuum.

Macdonald, S. (2011). Krashen and Second Language Acquisition (SLA) Theory – A Re-Evaluation of How to Teach Classical Languages. *Journal of Classics Teaching*, 22, 2–5.

Maguire, J. and Hunt, S. (2014). The North Norfolk Latin Cluster Group: Two Case Studies. *Journal of Classics Teaching*, 30, 41–4.

Manzoor, S. (2013, July 25). When in E17, Do As the Romans Do. *The Times*.

Markus, D. and Pennell Ross, D. (2004). Reading Proficiency in Latin Through Expectations and Visualization. *Classical World*, 98 (1), 79–93.

Marshall, N. (Director) (2010). *Centurion* [Motion Picture].

Masciantonio, R. (1970). *How the Romans Lived and Spoke: A Humanistic Approach to Latin for Children in the Fifth Grade. Teacher's Guide.* Philadelphia, PA: Instructional Services, The School District of Philadelphia.

Masciantonio, R. (1984). A Means for Expanding the Teaching of Latin at the School Level. *The Classical World*, 77 (3), 167–70.

Mataya, N. (2022). Teaching Classics with Texts from Non-Ethnic Romans. *Teaching Classical Languages*, 12, 2, pp. 81–9.

McDonald, P. and Widdess, M. (2009). *GCSE Latin Anthology for OCR Students' Book*. Oxford: Oxford University Press.

Macdonald, S. (2022). Via Latin; a review. Retrieved from *The Patrologist* [https://thepatrologist.com/2022/06/14/via-latina-a-review/].

McEvoy, S. (2012, July 12). Interview at Varndean College, East Sussex (S. Hunt, interviewer).

McFadden, P. (2008). Advanced Latin Without Translatons? Interactive Text-Marking as an Alternative Daily Preparation. *CPL Online*, 4.1, 1–15 [https://camws.org/cpl/cplonline/files/McFaddencplonline.pdf].

McGlathery, D. (2022). Changing perspectives: Making a Paradigm Shift in Course Content – Introduction. *The Classical Outlook*, 97, 1, p. 1.

McPherson, L. (2017). An Appropriate Stepping Stone? A case study into student and teacher perceptions of the value of the WJEC Level 1 Certificate in Latin. *Journal of Classics Teaching*, 18 (35), pp. 1–12.

Mead, G. (2014). Video-Conferencing Latin. *Journal of Classics Teaching*, 2, 4.

Melluish, T. (1962a). Latin Inquiry, in T. Melluish (ed.), *Re-Appraisal: Some New Thoughts on the Teaching of Classics* (pp. 42–7). Oxford: Clarendon Press.

Melluish, T. (1962b). Re-Appraisal, in T. Melluish (ed.), *Re-Appraisal: Some New Thoughts on the Teaching of Classics*. Oxford: Clarendon Press.

Millar, F. (2015, January 13). Election Big Idea Should be: Trust Teachers. *The Guardian*, p. 39.

Minkova, M. and Tunberg, T. (2008). *Latin for the New Millennium*. Mundeleion, IL: Bolchazy Carducci Publishers.

Morgan, J. (2005). *CIRCE: A Classics and ICT Resource Course for Europe*. Brussels: Het Gemeenschapsonderwijs.

Morgan, J. (2014). *Imperium*. Unknown: Amazon.

Morgan, J. (2015, January 17). *J-PROGS*. Retrieved from J-PROGS [http://www.j-progs.com/centaur.html].

Morrice, A. (2021). Using 'ORBIS' software to explore ancient geography: an action research project. *Journal of Trainee Teacher Education Research*. Retrieved from [https://jotter.educ.cam.ac.uk/volume12/643-668morricea/index.html].

Morris, S. (1966). *Viae Novae: New Techniques in Latin Teaching*. London: Hulton Educational Publications.

Mortimer, M. and Roberts, J. (1967). The Narrow-Minded Linguist. *Didaskalos*, 2 (3), 100–14.

Morwood, J. (2003). *The Teaching of Classics*. Cambridge: Cambridge University Press.

Morwood, J. (2005). GCSE – Time for Reform 2. *Journal of Classics Teaching*, 4, 10.

Moss, J. (2013). Computer-Assisted Learning in Second-Year Latin. *Teaching Classical Languages*, 84 (2, Spring), 86–105 [http://tcl.camws.org/sites/default/files/TCL%20Spring%202013_0.pdf].

Mount, H. (2010, December 1). *Latin Returns – te, Michael Gove, discituri salutamus*. Retrieved from *The Telegraph* [http://blogs.telegraph.co.uk/culture/harrymount/100049427/latin-returns-te-michael-gove-discituri-salutamus/].

Mount, H. (2013, September 17). The Tragic Dumbing Down of Latin in our Schools. *The Daily Telegraph*.

Nappa, C. (2022). Vergil's Aeneid and 21st-Century Immigration. *Teaching Classical Languages*, 12, 2, pp. 90–117.

Nation, I. S. (2001). *Learning Vocabulary in Another Language*. Cambridge: Cambridge University Press.

Nation, I. S. P. (2008). *Learning Vocabulary in Another Language*. Cambridge: Cambridge University Press.

Natoli, B. (2014). Flipping the Latin Classroom: Balancing Educational Practice with the Theory of Learning. *Journal of Classics Teaching*, 30, 37–40.

Natoli, B. and Hunt, S. (eds) (2019). *Teaching Classics with Technology*. London: Bloomsbury Academic.

Neto, N. (2019). Developing a Classics Department from Scratch, in Holmes-Henderson, A., Hunt, S. and Musié, M. (eds), *Forward with Classics: Classical Languages in Schools and Communities* (pp. 166–170). London: Bloomsbury Academic.

Nevin, S. (2015). Animations of Ancient Vase Scenes in the Classics Classroom. *Journal of Classics Teaching*, 31, 32–7.

New York Daily News (2013, April 22). Earning an 'A': Brooklyn Latin Tops in US News and World Report's High School Ranking. *New York Daily News*.

Nuttall, N. (2005). *Teaching Reading Skills in a Foreign Language*. London: Macmillan Education.

Oak National (2022). Retrieved from [https://teachers.thenational.academy/subjects/latin].

OCR (2014, October). Personal communication.

OCR (2022). Examinations statistics for classical subjects. Unpublished.

Oerberg, H. (2011). *Lingua Latina per se illustrata*. Newburyport, MA: Focus Publishing.

Ofqual (2015a, March). *GCSE Subject Criteria for Classical Subjects*. London: Ofqual.

Ofqual (2015b, April 19). *GCSE Reform*. Retrieved from School and College Qualifications and Curriculum [https://www.gov.uk/government/policies/reforming-qualifications-and-the-curriculum-to-better-prepare-pupils-for-life-after-school/supporting-pages/gcse-reform].

Olimpi, A. (2019). Legere discitur legendo: Extensive reading in the Latin classroom. *Journal of Classics Teaching*, 20 (39), pp. 83–9.

Olive, P. and Murray-Pollock, X. (2018). Developing Classics Teaching in London – Capital Classics: a case study, in Holmes-Henderson, A., Hunt, S. and Musié, M. (eds) *Forward with Classics: Classical Languages in Schools and Communities* (pp. 154–9). London: Bloomsbury Academic.

Oulton, N. and Zinn, T. (2006). *So You Really Want to Learn Latin?* Tenterden, UK: Galore Park.

Pagain, V. E. (2022). Gentle Touches to the Tiller: Gradual Paradigm Shifts in the Latin Classroom. *The Classical Outlook*, 97, 1, pp. 16–19.

Parker, A. (2013). Teacher, Pupil and Parental Perceptions Surrounding the Study of Latin for Pupils Diagnosed with Dyslexia. *Journal of Classics Teaching*, 27, 6–15.

Paterson, C. (2012). Ancient Texts and Modern Tools: Cicero and Interactive Whiteboards. *Journal of Classics Teaching*, 25, 14–16.

Patrick, M. (2019). Free Voluntary Reading and Comprehensible Input. *Journal of Classics Teaching*, 20 (39), pp. 78–82.

Patrick, R. (2011). TPRS and Latin in the Classroom: Experiences of a US Latin Teacher. *Journal of Classics Teaching*, 22, 10–11.

Patrick, R. (2019). Comprehensible Input and Krashen's theory. *Journal of Classics Teaching*, 20 (39), pp. 37–44.

Paul, D. (2013). Film in the Classics Classroom: Sixth Form Pupils' Choices of Video-Clips to Illustrate Themes from Homer's *Odyssey*. *Journal of Classics Teaching*, 27, 28–33.

Paul, J. (2009). 'I Fear it's Potentially Like Pompeii': Disaster, Mass Media and the Ancient City, in D. Lowe and K. Shahaburdin (eds), *Classics for All: Reworking Antiquity in Mass Culture* (pp. 91–108). Newcastle upon Tyne: Cambridge Scholars Publishing.

Paul, J. (2013). Cinematic Representations of Antiquity in the Classroom. *Journal of Classics Teaching*, 27, 26–8.

Peal, R. (2014). *Progressively Worse: The Burden of Bad Ideas in British Schools*. London: Civitas.

Pearcy, L. T. (2005). *The Grammar of Our Civility: Classical Education in America*. Waco, TX: Baylor University Press.

Pelling, C. (2014, February 9). Giving the Gift of Ancient Tongues. *The Sunday Times: Education*.

Pennell Ross, D. (2008). Latin Pedagogy at the University of Michigan, USA: Linear Reading Using a Linguistic Perspective, in B. Lister (ed.), *Meeting the Challenge: International Perspectives on the Teaching of Latin* (pp. 44–53). Cambridge: Cambridge University Press.

Phinney, E. (1989). The Classics in American Education, in P. Culham and L. Edmunds (eds), *Classics: A Discipline and Profession in Crisis?* (pp. 77–87). Lanham, MD: University Press of America.

Piantaggini, L. (2021). Teaching Latin with Novellas to Students who do not Know Latin and do not Care Much about the Romans. *The Classical Outlook*, 96, 3, pp. 102–8.

Pike, M. (2014, October 10). *DT in the Latin Classroom*. Retrieved from Cinis et Favilla [http://cinisetfavilla.blogspot.co.uk/2014/10/dt-in-latin-classroom.html].

Pike, M. (2015). Gamification in Latin. *Journal of Classics Teaching*, 31, 1–7.

Polsky, M. (1998). Latin in the Elementary Schools, in R. LaFleur (ed.), *Latin for the 21st Century: From Concept to Classroom* (pp. 59–69). Glenview, IL: Scott Foresman-Addison Wesley.

Protherough, R. (1986). *Teaching Literature for Examinations*. Milton Keynes: Open University Press.

Pym, D. (1962). The Fig Tree, in T. Melluish (ed.), *Re-Appraisal: Some New Thoughts on the Teaching of Classics* (pp. 35–41). Oxford: Clarendon Press.

Quinn, K. (1966). The Critical Study of Literature. *Didaskalos*, 2 (1), 15–25.

Radice, K. Cheetham, A., Kirk, S. and Lord, G. (2020). *De Romanis. Book 1: dei et deae*. London: Bloomsbury Academic.

Radice, K. Cheetham, A., Kirk, S. and Lord, G. (2020). *De Romanis. Book 2: homines*. London: Bloomsbury Academic.

Ramahlo, M. (2019). On starting to teach using CI. *Journal of Classics Teaching*, 20 (39), pp. 45–50.

Ramsby, T. (2022). The Utility and Representational Opportunity of Latin Novellas, *New England Classical Journal*, 49, 1, pp. 102–11.

Reedy, J. (1988). Cultural Literacy and the Classics. *The Classical Journal*, 84 (1), 41–6.

Reinard, A. (2009). Social Networking in Latin Class. *Teaching Classical Languages*, Fall, 4–29 [http://tcl.camws.org/sites/default/files/TCL_I_i_4-29_Reinhard.pdf].

Rendall, H. (1998). *Stimulating Grammatical Awareness: A Fresh Look at Language Acquisition*. London: CILT.

Rexine, J. E. (1966). Teacher Training and the Classics. *Classical World*, 59 (8), 257–60.

Richards, J. and Rodgers, T. (2001). *Approaches and Methods in Language Teaching*. New York: Cambridge University Press.

Riener, C. and Willingham, D. (2010). The Myth of Learning Styles. *Change: The Magazine of Higher Learning*, 42, 5, 32–5.

Robinson, L. (2014). *Telling Tales with Ovid*. London: Souvenir Press.

Robson, J. (2004). 'Night was Departing ...': Using Translations in Post-Beginners' Language Teaching, in D. Fitzpatrick (ed.), *Different Lights, Different Hands: Working with Translations in Classics and Ancient History at University* (pp. 85–100). Milton Keynes: Open University Press.

Rosenshine, B. (2012). Principles of Instruction: Research-based strategies that all teachers should know. *American Educator*, pp. 12–20

Ryan, C. (2010). Running a Key Stage 4 Latin INSET Day at Oxford. *Journal of Classics Teaching*, 10, 13–14.

Ryan, C. (2011). Chains and Controversia: Non-Judgmentally Exploring the Richness of the Past with Primary School Children, in G. Baker and A. Fisher (eds), *Arts and Humanities Academics in Schools: Mapping the Pedagogical Interface* (pp. 130–41). London: Continuum.

Sanchez, O. (2014). Differentiation: Exploring Ways of Introducing Sources to a Mixed-Attainment Ancient History GCSE Class. *Journal of Classics Teaching*, 29, 26–9.

Sapsford, F., Travis, R. and Ballestrini, K. (2013). Acting, Speaking and Thinking Like a Roman: Learning Latin with Operation Lapis. *Journal of Classics Teaching*, 28, 13–16.

Schmitt, N. (2003). *Vocabulary in Language Teaching*. Cambridge: Cambridge University Press.

Schools Week (2022). DfE hopes snubbed teacher trainers will help plug 'cold spots'. Retrieved from [https://schoolsweek.co.uk/dfe-hopes-snubbed-teacher-trainers-will-help-plug-cold-spots/].

Schwamm, J. (2019). Auream Quisquis Mediocritatem Diligit: the Joyful Learning Community Model for Learning Latin Online, in Natoli, B. and Hunt, S. (eds), *Teaching Classics with Technology* (pp. 19–28). London: Bloomsbury Academic.

Scott, R. (Director) (2000). *Gladiator* [Motion Picture].

Sears, B. (1844 [2012]). *The Ciceronian; Or, the Prussian Method of Teaching the Elements of the Latin Language*. London: Forgotten Books.

Sears, L., and Ballestrini, K. (2019). Adapting antiquity: Using tiered texts to increase Latin reading proficiency. *Journal of Classics Teaching*, 20 (39), pp. 71–7.

Sellers, R. (2012). Latin Teachers in Film. *Classical World*, 105 (2), 237–54.

Sharwood Smith, J. (1977). *On Teaching Classics*. London: Routledge & Kegan Paul.

Shelton, C. (2021). Latin Novellas in the College Classroom. *The Classical Outlook*, 96, 3, pp. 93–101.

Smith, A. (2012). The Use of Collaborative e-Learning Technology for GCSE Latin. *Journal of Classics Teaching*, 26, 3–8.

Soames, L. and Hazel, J. (2011). *ARLT 1911–2011: A Commemorative History of the Association for Latin Teaching*. Unknown: ARLT.

Spooner, A. (2014). Review: Telling Tales in Latin. *Journal of Classics Teaching*, 29, 104.

Stephenson, D. (2014). WJEC Level 2 Latin: A Teacher's Viewpoint. *Journal of Classics Teaching*, 29, 53–5.

Story, P. (2003). The Development of the Cambridge Latin Course, in J. Morwood (ed.), *The Teaching of Classics* (pp. 85–91). Cambridge: Cambridge University Press.

Stray, C. (1992). *The Living Word: W. H. D. Rouse and the Crisis of Classics in Edwardian England*. Bristol: Bristol Classical Press.

Stray, C. (1998a). *Classics Transformed: Schools, Universities, and Society in England, 1830–1960*. Oxford: Clarendon Press.

Stray, C. (1998b). Schoolboys and Gentlemen: Classical Pedagogy and Authority in the English Public School, in Y. L. Too and N. Livingstone (eds), *Pedagogy and Power: Rhetorics of Classical Learning* (pp. 29–46). Cambridge: Cambridge University Press.

Stray, C. (2003a). Classics in the Curriculum up to the 1960s, in J. Morwood (ed.), *The Teaching of Classics* (pp. 1–5). Cambridge: Cambridge University Press.

Stray, C. (2003b). *The Classical Association: The First Century 1903–2003*. Oxford: Oxford University Press.

Stray, C. (2011). Success and Failure: W. H. D. Rouse and Direct-Method Classics Teaching in Edwardian England. *Journal of Classics Teaching*, 22, 5–7.

Taylor, J. (2014) *Essential GCSE Latin*. London: Bloomsbury Academic.

The Paideia Institute (2019). Elementa. *Teaching Literacy with Latin*. New York; The Paideia Institute for Humanistic Study.

The Spens Report (1938). *Secondary Education, with Special Reference to Grammar Schools and Technical High Schools*. London: HMSO.

The Washington Post (2014, August 8). *Spoken Latin: A Modern Remedy for the Nation's Age-old Reading Problems?* Retrieved from *The Washington Post* [http://www.washingtonpost.com/lifestyle/magazine/spoken-latin-a-modern-remedy-for-the-nations-age-old-reading-problems/2014/07/31/20269f54-0792-11e4-a0dd-f2b22a257353_story.html?wprss=rss_local].

Thompson, W. B. (1962). Reading the Classics – Aloud, in T. Melluish (ed.), *Re-Appraisal: Some New Thoughts on the Teaching of Classics* (pp. 19–23). Oxford: Clarendon Press.

Times Educational Supplement (2010, December 7). *Unqualified Staff can Teach in Free Schools, says Gove.* Retrieved from TES Connect [https://www.tes.co.uk/article.aspx?storycode=6064221].

Times Educational Supplement (2012, November 23). *Fears for Universities in Training Overhaul.* Retrieved from TES Connect [https://www.tes.co.uk/article.aspx?storycode=6301733].

Times Educational Supplement (2015, January 1). *'No Evidence' Academies and Free Schools Raise Standards, say MPs.* Retrieved from TES Connect [https://news.tes.co.uk/b/news/2015/01/26/39-no-evidence-39-academies-and-free-schools-raise-standards-report-says.aspx].

Titcombe, D. (2022). Cheating or learning? An investigation into Year 8 students' perceptions of the Cambridge Latin Course Explorer Tool and its role in both classroom teaching and online learning. *Journal of Classics Teaching*, 23 (46), pp. 147–54.

Toda, K. (2014, August 7). *TPR (Total Physical Response) for the First Week of Latin 1.* Retrieved from Todally Comprehensible Latin [http://todallycomprehensiblelatin.blogspot.co.uk/2014/08/tpr-total-physical-response-for-first.html].

Torrance, H. (2007). Assessment as Learning? How the Use of Explicit Learning Objectives, Assessment Criteria and Feedback in Post-Secondary Education and Training can Come to Dominate Learning. *Assessment in Education: Principles, Policy and Practice*, 14 (3), 281–94.

Trafford, S. (2022). Reflections on the new International Baccalaureate Diploma Classical Languages Syllabus. *Journal of Classics Teaching*, forthcoming.

Travis, R. (2019). Using Annotations in Google Docs to Foster Authentic Classics Learning, in Natoli, B. and Hunt, S. (eds), *Teaching Classics with Technology* (pp. 207–16). London: Bloomsbury Academic.

Trego, K. (2014). Composition, Competition, & Community: A Preliminary Study of the Use of Latin Composition in a Cooperative Learning Environment. *Teaching Classical Languages*, 5 (2, Spring), 70–85 [http://tcl.camws.org/sites/default/files/TCL%20Spring%202014.pdf].

Tristram, D. (2003). Classics in the Curriculum from the 1960s to the 1990s, in J. Morwood (ed.), *The Teaching of Classics* (pp. 6–19). Cambridge: Cambridge University Press.

Tunberg, T. (2011). De Instituto Studis Latinis Provehendis, Quod Annum Iam Decimum In Academia Kentukiana Floret. *Journal of Classics Teaching*, 22, 16–18.

Twigg, S. (2013, March 1). Gove is Fighting a War Which Ended Years Ago. *Times Educational Supplement Magazine*.

Upchurch, O. (2014). How do Students Perceive Women in Roman Society as a Result of Studying the Cambridge Latin Course? A Case Study of a Year 9 Class at an Urban Comprehensive School. *Journal of Classics Teaching*, 29, 30–6.

Urquhart, C. (2013, April 10). Pompeii is Hottest Ticket for British Tourists Fired Up by New Shows on Ancient Disaster. *The Observer*, p. 13.

Van Houdt, T. (2008). The Strategic Reading of Latin (and Greek) Texts: A Research-Based Approach, in B. Lister (ed.), *Meeting the Challenge: International*

Perspectives on the Teaching of Latin (pp. 54–70). Cambridge: Cambridge University Press.

VanTassel-Baska, J. (2010). A Case for the Teaching of Latin to the Verbally Talented. *Roeper Review*, 9 (3), 159–61.

Vanderpool, E. (2021). Novellas as a Bridge to Authentic Latin Literature. *The Classical Outlook*, 96, 3, pp. 108–13.

Veysey, J. (2014). An Investigation into Teachers' and Pupils' Perceptions of the Value of Teaching and Learning Latin Derivations at GCSE. *Journal of Classics Teaching*, 30, 13–21.

Vygotsky, L. (1978). *Mind in Society*. Cambridge, MA: Harvard University Press.

Walden, V. (2019). Distance Learning and Technology: Teaching Latin, Greek and Classical Civilization at a Distance, in Natoli, B. and Hunt, S. (eds), *Teaching Classics with Technology* (pp. 29–38). London: Bloomsbury Academic.

Walker, L. (2015). The impact of using Memrise on student perceptions of learning Latin vocabulary and on long-term memory of words. *Journal of Classics Teaching*, 16 (32), pp. 14–20.

Watson, J. (2011). Classics, Citizenship and Cambridge Latin Course Stage 11. *Journal of Classics Teaching*, 24, 4–5.

Weeds, J. (2005). Classics in the 21st Century: Some Modest Proposals (with Apologies to Mr. Jonathan Swift). *Journal of Classics Teaching*, 4, 8–9.

Westwood, P. (2018). *Inclusive and Adaptive Teaching: Meeting the challenge of diversity in the classroom*. Abingdon: Routledge.

Wikipedia (2015, April 27). *The Bullingdon Club*. Retrieved from Wikipedia [http://en.wikipedia.org/wiki/Bullingdon_Club#Cultural_references].

Wilby, P. (2015, January 6). From the Maker of Lara Croft: A Teenager's Dream of a Free School. *The Guardian*, p. 40.

Wiliam, D. (2014). Foreword, in D. Christodoulou, *Seven Myths About Education* (pp. xi–xii). London: Routledge.

Williams, T. (2004). Classics Education, in T. Bryce and W. Humes (eds), *Scottish Education: Post-Devolution* (pp. 501–6). Edinburgh: Edinburgh University Press.

Wills, J. (1998). Speaking Latin in Schools and Colleges. *Classical World*, 92, 27–34.

Witzke, S. (2022). Reading from Outside: Revealing and Teaching Violence and oppression in our Texts. *The Classical Outlook*, 97, 1, pp. 10–15.

Wolf, A. (2011). *Review of Vocational Education: The Wolf Report*. London: Department for Education.

Woolcock, N. (2015, February 23). *Latin Under Threat in State Schools*. Retrieved from The Times Education [http://www.thetimes.co.uk/tto/education/article4362216.ece?CMP=Spklr-149783653-Editorial-TWITTER-TimesEducation-20150222&linkId=12500996].

Young, H. (1990). *One of Us*. London: Pan.

Young, T. (2011, February 3). *Forget Mandarin: Latin is the Key to Success*. Retrieved from *The Spectator* [http://blogs.spectator.co.uk/coffeehouse/2011/02/forget-mandarin-latin-is-the-key-to-success/].

Young, T. (2012, July 18). *The Daily Telegraph*.

Young, T. (2014, January 18). Want to Create the Next Mark Zuckerberg? Teach Latin! *The Spectator*.

Zhang, S, Xu, H. and Zhang, X. (2021). The Effects of Dictionary Use on Second Language Vocabulary Acquisition: A met-Analysis. *International Journal of Lexicography*, 34, 1, pp. 1–38.

Index